Kate Hogg studied at the London College of Fashion. After two years working on cosmetic and fashion trade magazines, she joined *Vogue* to work on the beauty and health pages, followed by three years in the fashion department. She now lives in Wales with her husband and three children and writes on fashion, interiors and gardens.

VOGUE

EVEN MORE DASH THAN CASH

GUILD PUBLISHING LONDON

KATE HOGG

For Willow

This edition published 1989 by
Guild Publishing by arrangement
with Century Hutchinson Ltd

First published with the title *More Dash Than Cash* in 1982
Reprinted 1983 (twice), 1984
Published as a Hutchinson Paperback 1983
This revised edition published 1989
© Kate Hogg and The Condé Nast Publications Ltd 1982 and 1989

All rights reserved

Designed by Paul Bowden and Heather Johns

Set in Monophoto Photina by Vision Typesetting, Manchester
Printed in England by Butler & Tanner, Frome

CN4459

CONTENTS

INTRODUCTION 8

AN INDIVIDUAL STYLE 11

WARDROBE TACTICS 25

THE CLASSICS 49

OUTSIDE INSPIRATIONS 69

THE ALTERNATIVES 87

READING FASHION 113

INSIDE STYLE 131

FASHION CHARACTERS 163

ACKNOWLEDGEMENTS 189

LIST OF PHOTOGRAPHERS 190

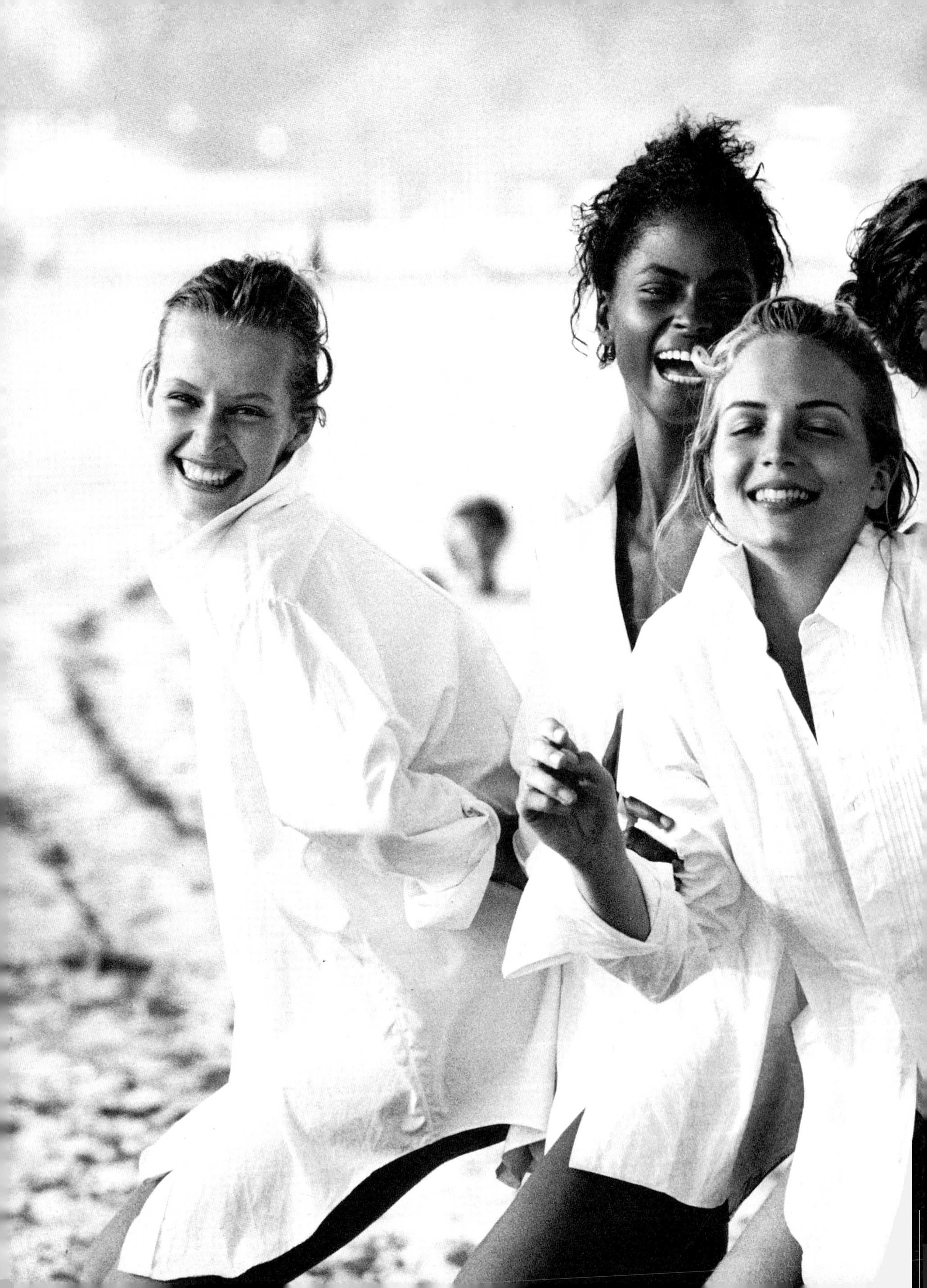

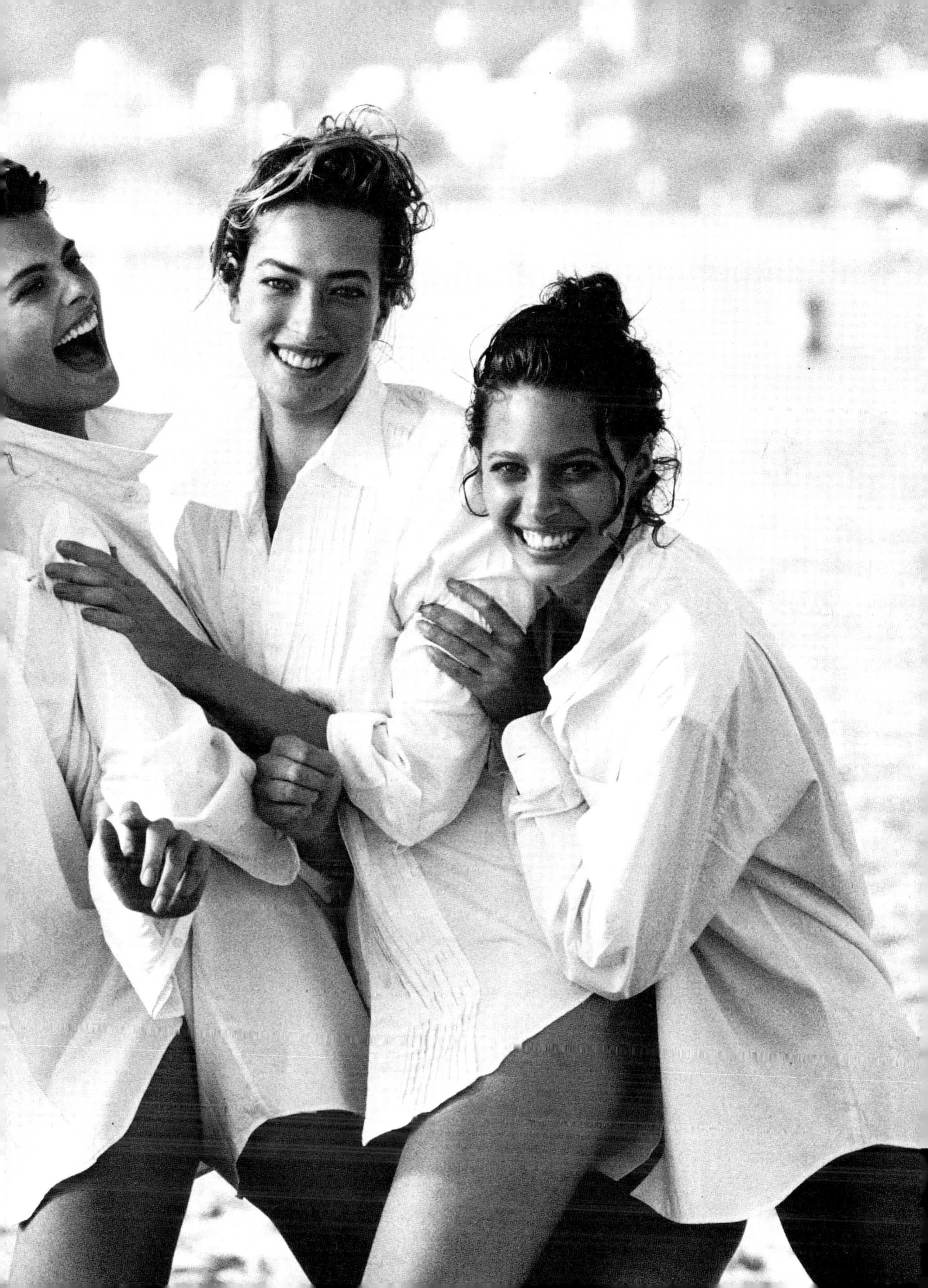

INTRODUCTION

This book is intended as a guide and inspiration to contemporary fashion which is an ever increasing issue of personal choice. Having rejected the inflexible dictates of the past two decades, women in the late eighties are free to choose the kind of clothes that appeal to them and suit their individual way of life. Designers at all levels respond to the current demands for versatile options of silhouette, proportions, hemlines and colour, and produce a wide spectrum of often conflicting images that are all equally 'in fashion'. It falls to the individual to decide on her own style. The diversity of choice is liberating, but also bewildering. So much freedom can confuse the final appearance. Fashion devotees are carried away by unflattering innovations; others retreat in confusion, playing safe with predictable basics.

A small budget can no longer take the blame for looking scruffy or dull. The nationwide accessibility of well-made mass market clothes – from high fashion to classic – brings personal style within everyone's financial reach. This has been accelerated by rival high street empires, by the improvement in mail order design and quality and the acknowledged consensus that women everywhere want to enjoy their clothes and spend more time and money on their appearance.

In a competitive, career-minded climate, looks do count and looking good is a great asset. Not that clothes should ever dominate your character, but they should be used to advantage. What you wear creates an image that is an extension of your personality. Of course, the person inside the clothes counts far more, but people may not discover your character, humour, intellect or warmth if they are not drawn by your appearance in the first place.

The original more-dash-than-cash concept of scooping up bargains – army surplus, ethnic, jumble or whatever – has been updated. Now affordable ready-to-wear is everywhere. There are various options:

innovative chain stores which rapidly interpret the strongest looks from the ready-to-wear collections; investing in fewer, more expensive but classic pieces; or waiting for the sale of a coveted designer, which in the end can mean the same outlay. The accessibility of instant fashion makes it even more important to be original. Shopping has been simplified by design conscious stores and mail order companies who offer a complete coordinated wardrobe each season. But the packaged look needs to be kept in perspective. Clothes and accessories should never become an identikit uniform to slot into.

While contemporary fashion is undoubtedly about being an individual, it is still impossible to escape from the perennial rules of style. The revived mood for dressing up has underlined the need for well-planned accessories – the shoes, jewellery, bags, hats, gloves – that complete the picture. Stock clichés that advise a well-balanced, colour-coordinated wardrobe, that stress the value of quality classics are all still relevant and worth acknowledging – hence their inclusion in this book. Whatever level you aspire to on the fashion ladder, quality is still a key criterion. It is essential to be realistic and choose the best you can afford within your price range. Instead of aspiring to cheap suede or leather, wear less expensive, high quality tweed. Choose fine cotton in preference to skimpy silk, bold costume jewellery rather than meagre gold plate.

Above all, clothes should be something to have fun with, not be tyrannized by. Fashion is notoriously fickle and the yardstick of what is considered beautiful or chic shifts from one season to the next. What does remain constant is the criteria for looking good – the confidence to be yourself and establish a personal style that makes you stand out. It does take time and energy, but a positive attitude is more vital than a large bank balance.

Much of the fashion featured in this book is concerned with the everyday basics that belong in most wardrobes. It is not a directory of new styles to rush out and buy. A fresh approach to what you already own can be as constructive as an extravagant shopping spree. Imagination, a sense of challenge and self-motivation are the essential accompaniments. Although this book concentrates on current fashion, the photographs, drawn from a span of over ten years, prove how timeless the best of fashion can be.

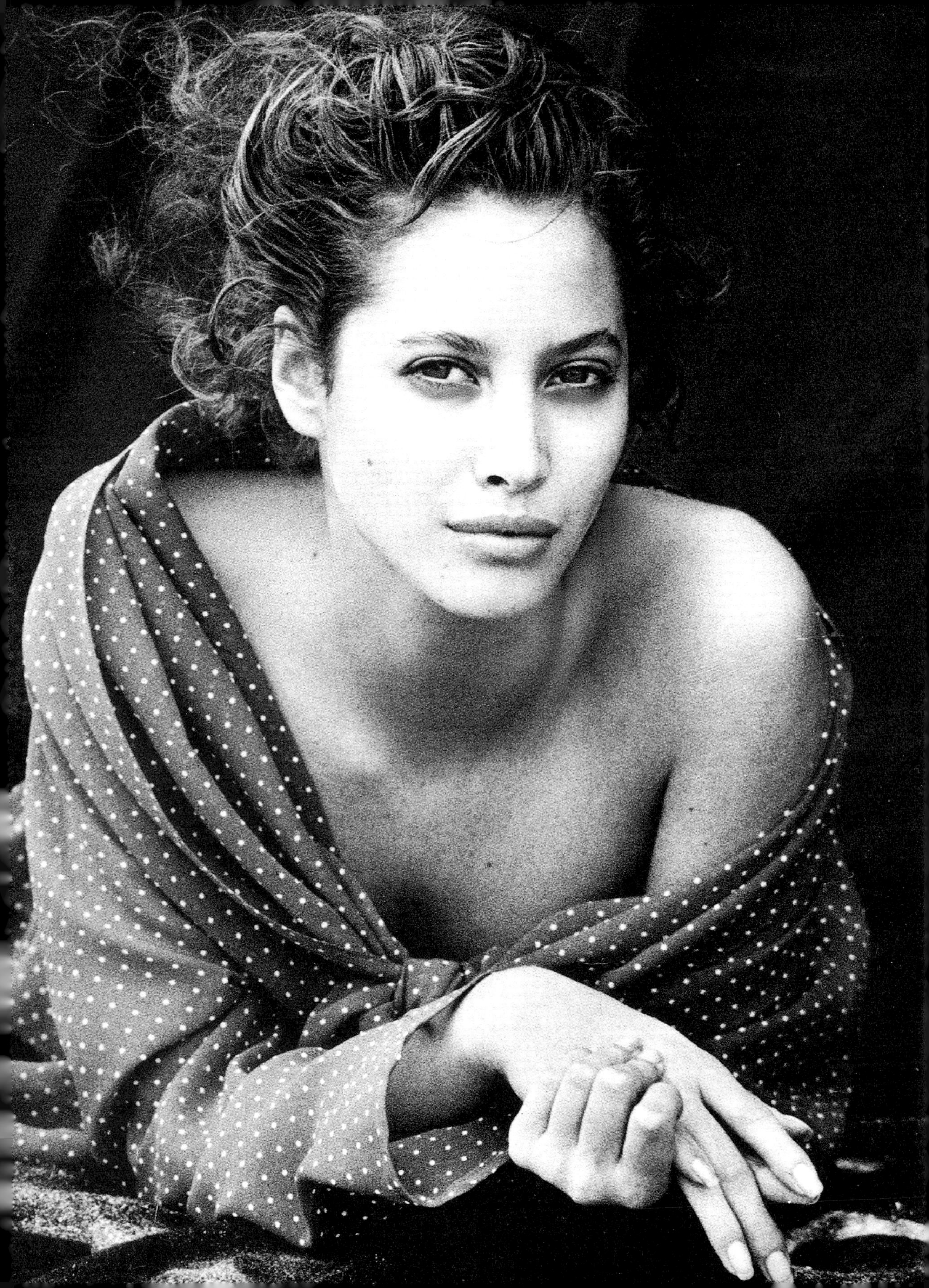

AN INDIVIDUAL STYLE

There is more to style than being fashionable. Unlike fashion, style does not change. It is a timeless, constant quality that elevates an individual from the crowd. Style cannot be bought. It has to come from within, as a part of your character and attitude. Everybody has some sort of style, just as everybody has some sense of humour. Although easily recognizable, it is an abstract quality that cannot be measured as clearly as a talent for art or music. Some people are born with instinctive good style. Others can develop their own with practice, self-discipline and honesty. The key to individual style is to be genuine, true to yourself.

Good style springs from a confident, positive attitude. It breeds self-assurance that has a striking influence on the appearance – affecting what is worn and how it is worn. Stylish people are never overawed by their clothes. Whether dressed in jeans or evening dress, they keep a special identity that projects them as an individual, not a clothes hanger. They stand out in a crowded room, not with outrageous fashion, in fact others often feel uncomfortably overdressed, but with an uncalculated ease. You often remember their conversation more distinctly than what they wore – proof that style leaves a more lasting impression than elaborate clothes. As Coco Chanel believed: 'If a woman is poorly dressed you notice the clothes. If she is impeccably dressed, you notice the woman.'

Self-assurance is the foundation for originality. Stylish people are not afraid to be innovators. The temptation is to copy, but unlike fashion trends, style is less easy to follow. Like interior decoration, there is more to an attractive room than its colour and furniture. The owner's personality, their lifestyle and period of house all contribute to the atmosphere. Each one complements the other.

As with fashion, transplanting a look from one house to another gives a conflicting result. The starting point is to come to terms with yourself.

Style is a constant, timeless quality

Realize you are only going to feel and look happy in clothes that suit your personality and way of life. However much you love them on other people, clothes that camouflage or contradict your true self turn fashion into a battle of wills. *You* must wear the clothes, never let them wear you. The essential point is to feel comfortable enough to forget about what you have on. Feeling self-conscious destroys any hope of style.

Good style cannot be learnt from a rule book, but it helps to scrutinize people who do stand out – living or legendary – determining what makes them special. They are not necessarily great beauties, more in possession of a certain *je ne sais quoi*. The best guideline is to follow your own instincts. But having recognized the direction of your look, there is nothing wrong with watching others for inspiration providing you realize that no two people can or should want to look identical. It is pointless to copy, but you can interpret ideas to suit yourself. Style is a matter of *how* you wear as much as what you wear.

One hallmark of good style is consistency. It does not mean being predictable, but it gives a personal stamp to your appearance – showing you have the confidence to be discriminating and select fashion that reinforces your style. Consistency to your own look also keeps fashion in perspective, never letting it become an overwhelming issue.

The diversity of fashion can confuse individual style. Without firm guidelines of what to wear the easiest solution can be to muddle along looking mediocre, much the same as everyone else. It feels safer. Remember the humiliation at school when everyone wore regulation jerseys and you stuck out with a (probably far prettier) home-made one? Like uniform, middle-of-the-road clothes provide a safe anonymity which is a dangerous niche to slide into. It is more comfortable to go with the crowd than risk the embarrassment of looking different and being stared at. But it is essential to step out of the standard mould to be an individual. People only stare because they recognize, and wish they had, the nerve and ingenuity to be more original. When you feel confident and proud of your appearance you can safely assume that most second glances and turning heads can be taken as compliments.

So how do you set about being a fashion individual? The ovewhelming variety of clothes that confronts you in a shop can be daunting, but it need never be limiting. There is no excuse for eveyone to look the same, even in a small town. Common sense is the first guideline. Choose clothes that fit your lifestye and give you the best value for money – in terms of how often you can wear them, and how well they work with the rest of your wardrobe. This may sound simplistic, but there is a lot of truth in the idea that the clothes you love and long to own should, within reason, be the ones that suit you best. Buying something because you think it is a good investment spoils the fun. It treats fashion as a commodity like sugar and salt or stocks and shares. Everything you own should make you feel good, not just sensible.

Common sense should be used on a more practical level. It is pointless to invest in clothes which you can't afford the time or money to maintain. Don't buy the kind of clothes that need regular dry-cleaning if your budget does not stretch that far. It is shortsighted to opt for a smart, groomed image if you do not have the energy to carry it through. Establish a style of fashion that works around you, not one that rules your life, and you will find a thread of unity running through your wardrobe. The plaintive 'I've got nothing to wear' cry should fade into the past.

The idea that you need plenty of money to look distinctive is an outdated concept. There are advantages in a small budget. It forces you to be disciplined, to think hard about how much you really need every article you buy. A large wardrobe can be more of a hindrance than a help; the wider the choice, the harder it is to establish a consistent style. Wearing different clothes every day is not a sign of being well dressed.

Time is more important than a large budget. What counts is how you wear clothes; not just whether you drape a shawl over your shoulders but the condition of everything you put on. The seemingly insignificant details become finishing touches that make all the difference between a striking and an undistinguished impression. It does involve effort, but it is an approach that soon becomes second nature. Find time to look after your clothes; however inexpensive they may be, they deserve proper treatment. Whether you live in jeans and tee shirts, jumble-sale finds or tailored separates, the same standards apply. Wearing casual clothes is no reason to be scuffy. Treat everything you own as if it cost five times its price. A basic rule is to follow cleaning or laundering instructions on every single garment. The quickest way to spoil clothes is to throw them in a washing machine at the wrong temperature or to ignore the 'dry clean only' labels.

Ironing can be a bore but it is vital. Nothing ruins an appearance so much as crumpled, unpressed clothes. If you measure the time it takes to iron a shirt against the crisp impact it creates, the effort is worthwhile. Have an ironing board set up permanently, ideally, where you dress, so that everything can be pressed before it goes on. Some clothes, especially crease-prone cotton and linen, need ironing every time you wear them, not just after each wash. Ironing time can be cut down if clothes are stored properly; skirts and trousers kept on clip-top hangers, not folded on wire coat hangers. If you have the space, hanging shirts reduces the creases. Knitwear should always be folded flat, as hanging encourages it to sag out of shape. Coats, jackets and dresses look much better if they are kept on wooden or padded hangers, instead of wire ones. Don't adopt the

Even when you do spend hours deciding what to wear, create the impression of an effortless, unrehearsed appearance

Accessory impact: one luxurious muffler can make all the difference to everyday basics

attitude that second best is good enough today and you will do something about it tomorrow. If you care about your appearance, you owe it to yourself to look good all the time, however tired you may feel. Fate has a nasty habit of making you bump into somebody important when you have dirty hair, tights with holes, a sweater darned in clashing wool, a jacket with buttons missing and scuffed shoes.

It is difficult to lay down rules about how much to spend on clothes and how to spread a budget. Now that fashion is such a personal choice, there are no set values of what is a good or sensible buy. When fashion was predictable it was easier to work out a spending scale. You needed a sensible coat, useful day dresses, an evening gown, and enough set aside for hats, gloves, shoes and underwear. But now the priorities are whatever you want them to be. It is essential to be open-minded and to rethink the price scale when necessary. Shake off drummed-in notions that certain garments like a coat, an evening dress, a jacket, justify a high price, while it is extravagant to spend the same amount or more on shoes, knitwear, belts and other accessories. When you mix different price levels your success depends on unexpected combinations. It is more original to add a marvellous belt to a cheap dress, than to spoil the effect of an expensive dress with a plastic belt. It is not immoral if the belt costs more than the dress – no one else will know the financial breakdown of your outfit. A great accessory is still sadly underrated. it can stamp ordinary clothes with individuality.

View clothes from a fresh angle, unprejudiced by what you expect to pay and see. Switch things round to avoid looking predictable. Wear your oldest jeans with a beautiful suede belt and satin wrap blouse; a tee shirt with a silk skirt; a plain crew-neck sweater with a luxurious cashmere scarf worth twice the price. Transform a chain-store cardigan with gilt buttons. You are never happy to be ordinary, everything has to be a little different – not pretentious but original and seemingly effortless. Even if you do spend three hours deciding what to wear, the trick is to create an impression that your appearance is quite unrehearsed – that everything happened quite by chance when you threw a few old things together.

The most versatile clothes are those that are the simplest and least detailed. It is impossible to stamp a style on anything already too gimmicky or exaggerated. Fashion is no longer something you have to keep up with. It is not that fashion stands still, just that there are many more options to choose. There are no rigid divisions between fashions, nothing to stop you wearing a skirt from two winters ago with a new jacket if it looks and feels right.

The fashion cycle is like an enormous, slow-moving wheel with several smaller, fast-moving wheels turning in the same direction, but at

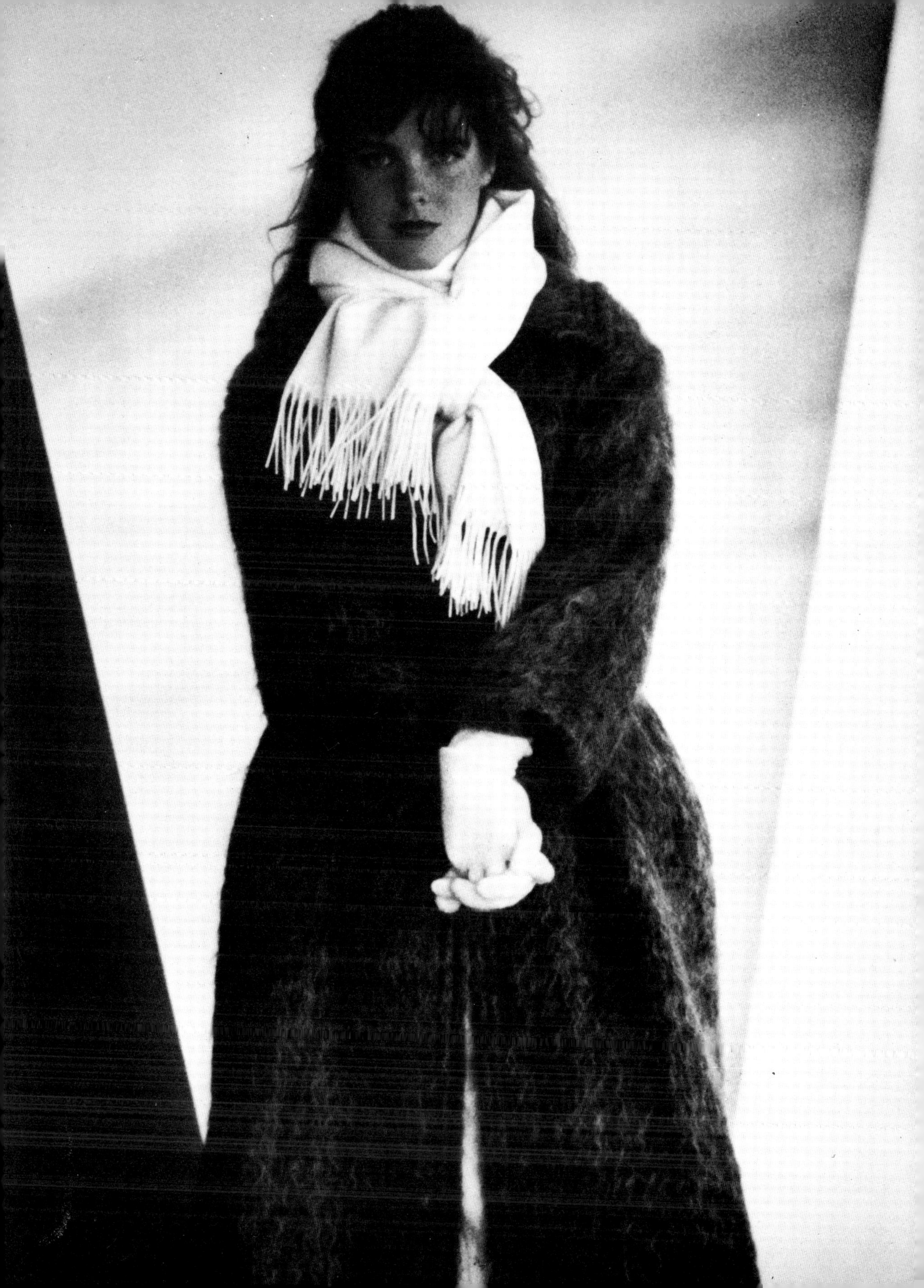

Even More Dash Than Cash

different speeds. They represent the sudden, short-lived trends that come and go; looks that create instant images but leave their mark on mass-produced, chain-store fashion. To a high fashion purist, the commercialized versions miss the main point of the story – the immediateness of it all. By the time the message of new shapes, proportions, colours or prints filters through to alert high street stores, most dedicated followers are well into their next phase. High fashion in its most extreme undiluted form becomes a complete package, a look with a ready-made image. Accepting every craze as it comes along is a form of escapism. It is essential to be discerning: instinct tells you when you are in the wrong clothes. Like every kind of craze, high fashion begins to pall when the novelty fades. It is not worth splashing out on expensive versions every time a new one arrives on the scene, unless you really feel at home in one particular look. When something feels right, it usually suits your style, so take the opportunity to build an image from there and abandon the other gimmicks on the wheel.

There is no final word in fashion; no grand heirarchy that sends down dictates of shape and colour each season. Ideas spring from every level of the empire – from couture to street. Relieved of their rarefied image, the Paris couture collections now provide inspiration for ready-to-wear and mass market fashion. Although salon and high street are separated by an inevitable gulf in price and workmanship, the sense of dressing up, of decoration and ornament, exemplified by Christian Lacroix and Yves Saint Laurent, filters downwards to affect the whole mood of fashion. Evening wear, particularly, has picked up on the extravagance, reflecting couture's rich colour and style. Ready-to-wear collections shown twice a year in London, Milan, Paris and New York have a more immediate impact on what appears in the shops. Like the couture shows, you expect a certain handwriting from each designer in a collection that progresses from the last.

Although designers work in secrecy, they often seem to think on the same wavelength. Each season it is uncanny how a fashion message emerges from their collections. The first impression is that each one has been given the same theme and colour range for their inspiration, but when you look again, each collection bears the unmistakable stamp of its creator. Besides the mainstream, there are tributaries of different styles, particular to individual designers, or even countries. Paris fashion may be full of mini-skirts, Milan with wide palazzo pants, and the most important idea in New York might be a new cropped jacket. The overall feeling is established by key points; the shape of the silhouette, new proportions, lengths, accessories, colours, prints and textures.

The ready-to-wear collections are an important source of inspiration for high street fashion. Trends are interpreted and redesigned to suit

An Individual Style

(opposite) *Paris in full bloom: a crop of summer flowers from Ungaro (centre) and Christian Lacroix*

(below) *Recognise signature style: the unmistakable cut of Yves Saint Laurent (left) and Chanel (right)*

mass production. But success hangs on the style of the prototype – on whether it translates into a cheaper copy without losing its point. The charm of an intricate cut, a mix of textures, subtle colours and special details tends to get lost on the way. The ingenuity of buyers for fashion stores and boutiques varies enormously. Some can be relied upon to find a good interpretation which will appear in their stores at the same time, or only a fraction after, the original arrives in the designer boutique. Customers must be discerning and accept 'knock-off' fashion for what it is. The simplest major shapes – the trousers, skirts, coats – are often hardest to reproduce because they rely on an expert cut which is unsuitable for large-scale production. Instead, it can be easier to imitate the most exaggerated bold shapes, but unless they are cleverly interpreted, these can become badly distorted. They may catch the message of the original but have little value in their own right.

It is wiser to capture the spirit of the clothes, or invest in a key accessory that sums up the new mood. Watch for recurrent characteristics of theme collections: the high-necked shirts, stocks, velvet-

Designer originals are a valuable source of inspiration – suggesting theme, colour, pattern and cut to interpret from cheaper sources. Follow the underplayed elegance of Ralph Lauren (left) or catch the nautical spirit at Kenzo (right)

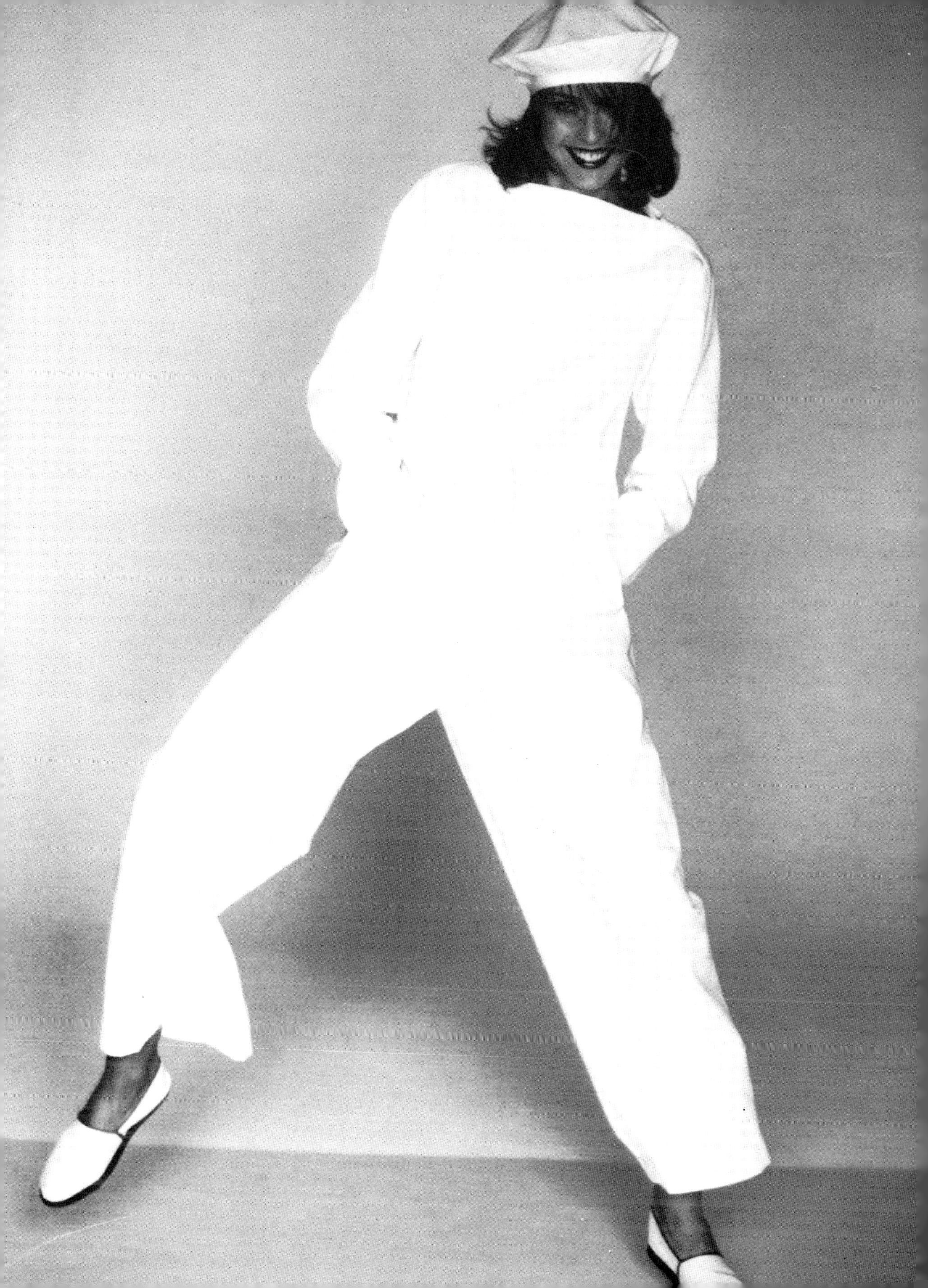

Price apart, designer fashion can be surprisingly simple.
(above) These plain white vests at Zoran can be improvised with cheaper counterparts.
(right) Equestrienne style with a touch of dandy at Chloé – watch for key accessories that capture the look

collared hunting coats, riding boots and bowlers of dandy equestrienne style; the matelot shirts, brass buttons, sailor collars and boaters of nautical style. Highland collections are rich in tartans, kilts, ghillie pumps, sporran bags and berets.

If you take a general theme for your individual inspiration, it is not necessary to buy the expensive designer versions. It is quite possible to make your own look out of the genuine article. Instead of designer cowboys, go to the nearest Western store; instead of Kenzo sailors, make your own rig from proper nautical clothes. If there is a country look, be wary of high-priced fashion tweeds. Track down better quality classics from traditional outfitters and find your checked shirts in boys' departments, not boutiques. Dissect a fashion look; occasionally there will be simple shapes that you recognize, an ordinary white shirt or plain, round-neck sweater, for example. They are bound to be expensive because they carry designer labels, but there is nothing to stop you improvising.

Ready-to-wear fashion filters down the fashion ladder at different speeds and strengths. The alternative system works with the looks that start at street level and are gradually translated into commercial, mass fashion. This process is less alternative than it might seem. To begin with, it usually has an anti-fashion identity as a symbol of nonconformity associated with a particular cult. The punk movement is an example: it started as an aggressive reaction against society and turned into a commercially exploited fashion. Top designers removed it from its origins and punk became posh, to the fury of its originators.

Then there are looks which move from fringe level into everyday fashion, not so much a cult engineered by fortune hunters, more a case of good timing. The quest for a fit, healthy body prompted a demand for fashionable exercise clothes. Boundaries between sport and fashion wear have dissolved, and traditional athletic shapes – tracksuits, racing swimwear, running singlets, sweatshirts and leotards – appear regularly in fashion collections. The anti-fashion inspirations tend to surface as a reflection of hard times. When there is a recession, escapism is more fun than facing up to reality. It is easier to look backwards and sideways than straight ahead, so fashion dives into nostalgia. Anything old is more desirable than anything new, whether it is antique white lace underwear, thirties knitwear, fitted forties suits, rock and roll skirts or psychedelic minis. Sideways fashion leans into government surplus uniforms, ethnic originals or menswear. Inevitably the demand for these escapist clothes grows and inflates prices out of all proportion. Not surprisingly, irony strikes again as crafty manufacturers take advantage of prevailing 'non-fashion' and produce relatively inexpensive versions to fill the demand. These commercial interpretations may appeal to a less

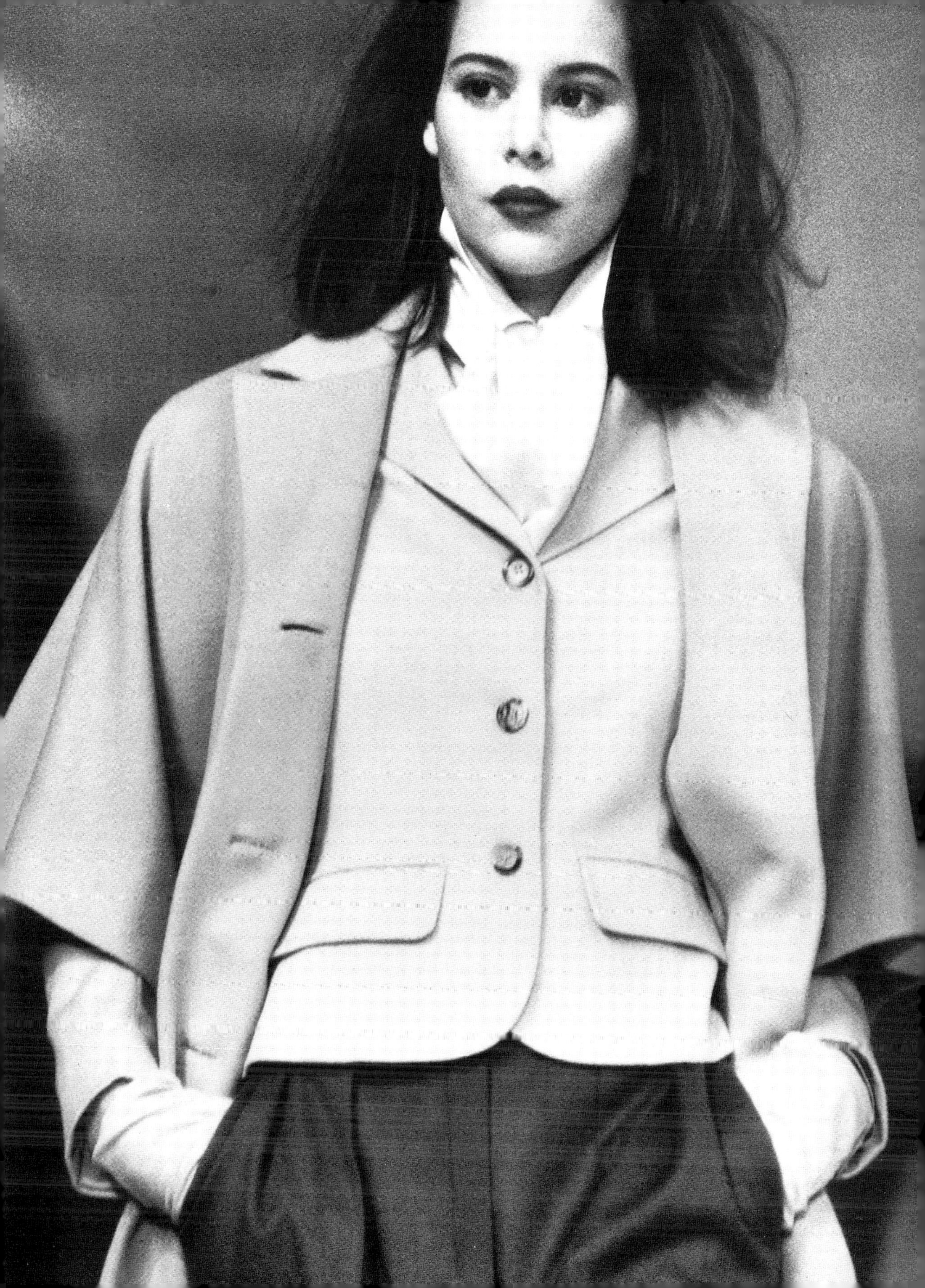

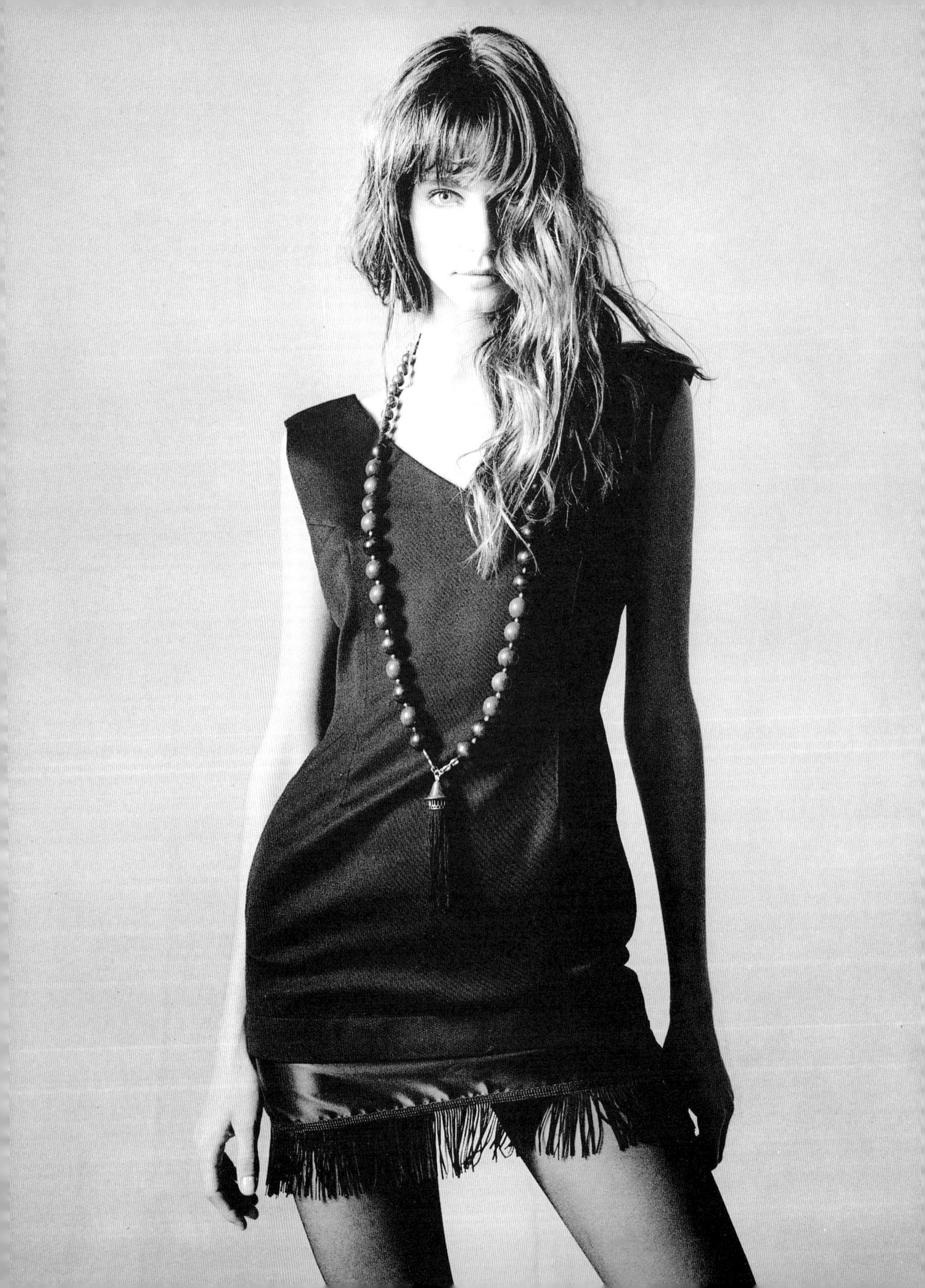

An Individual Style

Alternative fashion: a reaction against materialistic values? (left) Nostalgia for fringed minis and beads swings the cycle back to the sixties. (right) The influence of dance inspires principal boy doublet and hose

discriminating shopper, but invariably spell instant death to the look for its instigators. Escapist fashions thrive on a rarity value that no copy can match in style or quality. Once mass produced and widely accessible, the elite concept of an alternative style dissolves into a gimmick.

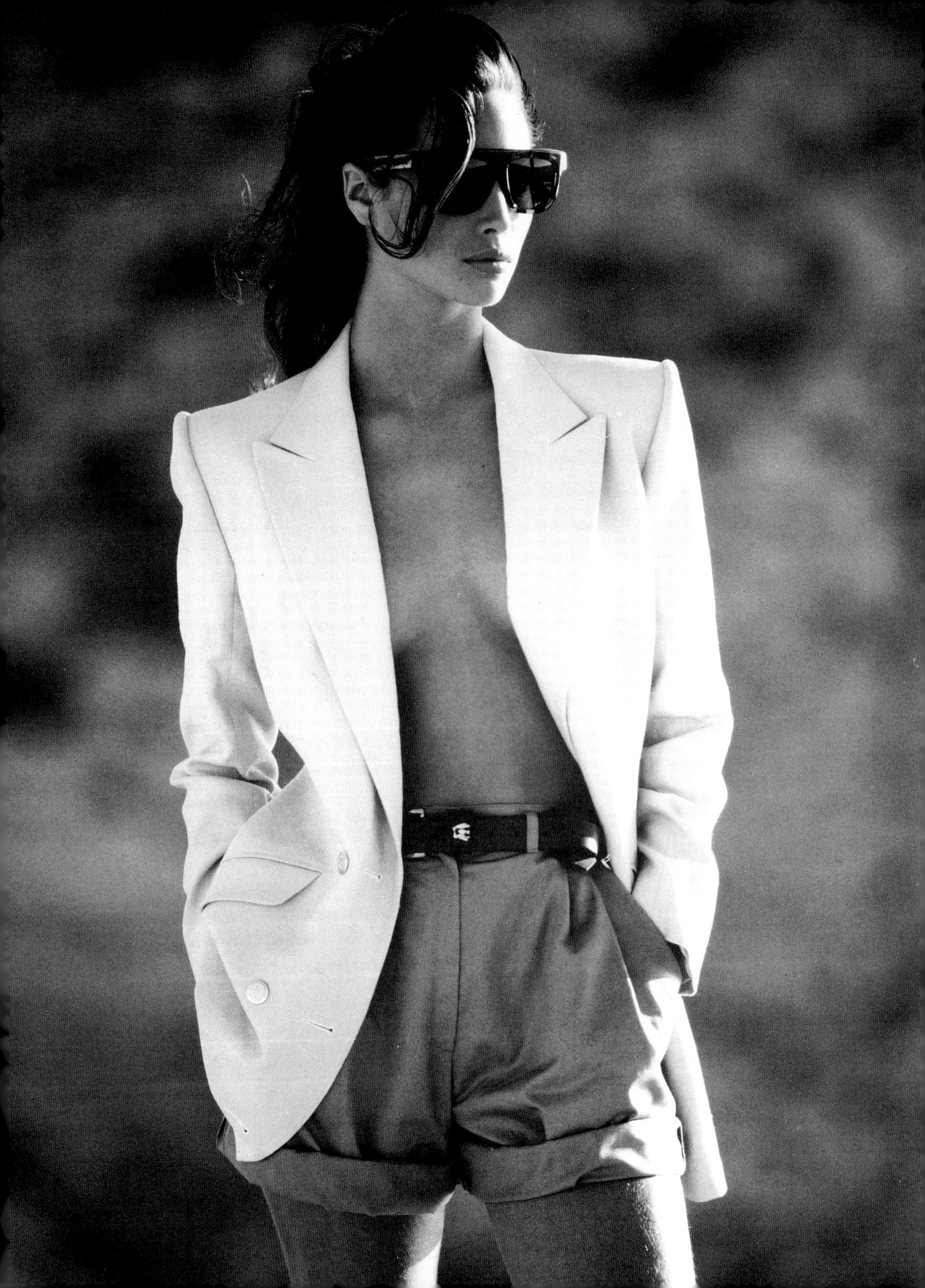

WARDROBE TACTICS

Too many people limit their fashion scope by separating their wardrobe into compartments. Habit and tradition divide winter, summer, day, evening, holiday, town and country clothes into unrelated segments of a total wardrobe. There is an inbuilt fixation that it is wrong to mix clothes bought for different seasons and occasions. Rethink that attitude and look at a wardrobe as a united whole. Not that everything needs to match or come from the same shop; you should be able to see your wardrobe like a family, where everything is related to each other, some elements closely, others more distantly.

Traditional men's fashion is a good example of well-balanced dressing. Because of their limitations and more rational approach to clothes, men, even very image-conscious ones, seem to work on a smaller wardrobe scale, based on logic and necessity; they collect clothes with a long-term approach. Like the argument against a large budget, a small wardrobe encourages a consistent individual style more naturally than an extensive wardrobe of unrelated categories.

With a 'capsule' wardrobe the key has to be versatility. You need maximum options from the minimum amount of clothes. A guideline is how you pack a suitcase (not a trunk) that covers every possible eventuality. Limited space forces forward planning and precise organization, so you prune the selection down to versatile, favourite separates. Necessity may force you to improvise and mix clothes together more inventively than you would at home. If you stay longer than expected, and the only remaining clean shirt happens to be a wrapped silk 'evening' one, then you wear it with jeans and a cardigan in the day. In the evening you change by adding some beads to a lambswool V-neck sweater. Limitation stretches your imagination.

Separates provide more scope for individuality than ready-made, coordinated outfits. A suit, a jacket with a skirt or trousers, is fine if both halves work independently as well. It is a limiting buy if the top or bottom

A wardrobe of well chosen, versatile separates can cover almost every occasion

Seasonless basics (right) *to wear all year round*

Versatile mixes: (below) *satin with tweed and Shetland makes the look work day or night*

A subtle change: (opposite) *dressing up a cardigan with silk trousers*

Night switch: (above) *adding jewellery and hair ribbon spells evening*

look disjointed apart from the other. Well-balanced separates create the backbone of a capsule wardrobe. For maximum versatility they need to be as seasonless and as timeless as possible, so buy clothes in materials that do not restrict their life to a few months of the year. Light wools, corduroy, jersey, suede, brushed or knitted cotton, make more sense than very thick or fine materials. Timeless separates are clothes that can be dressed up or down to suit the time of day or situation.

The contrast between day and evening wear is an individual choice. Obviously the occasion dictates the degree of formality, but there is a definite mood for dressing up, or simply switching the emphasis of your clothes. The transition can be subtle; rethinking day wear by adding higher heels, sheer black stockings, bold jewellery or stronger make-up. Or introduce an element of surprise – pairing a simple sweater or cardigan with extravagant silk pants, faded jeans with a plunging satin blouse.

Evening wear that calls for fullblown glamour is an opportunity to

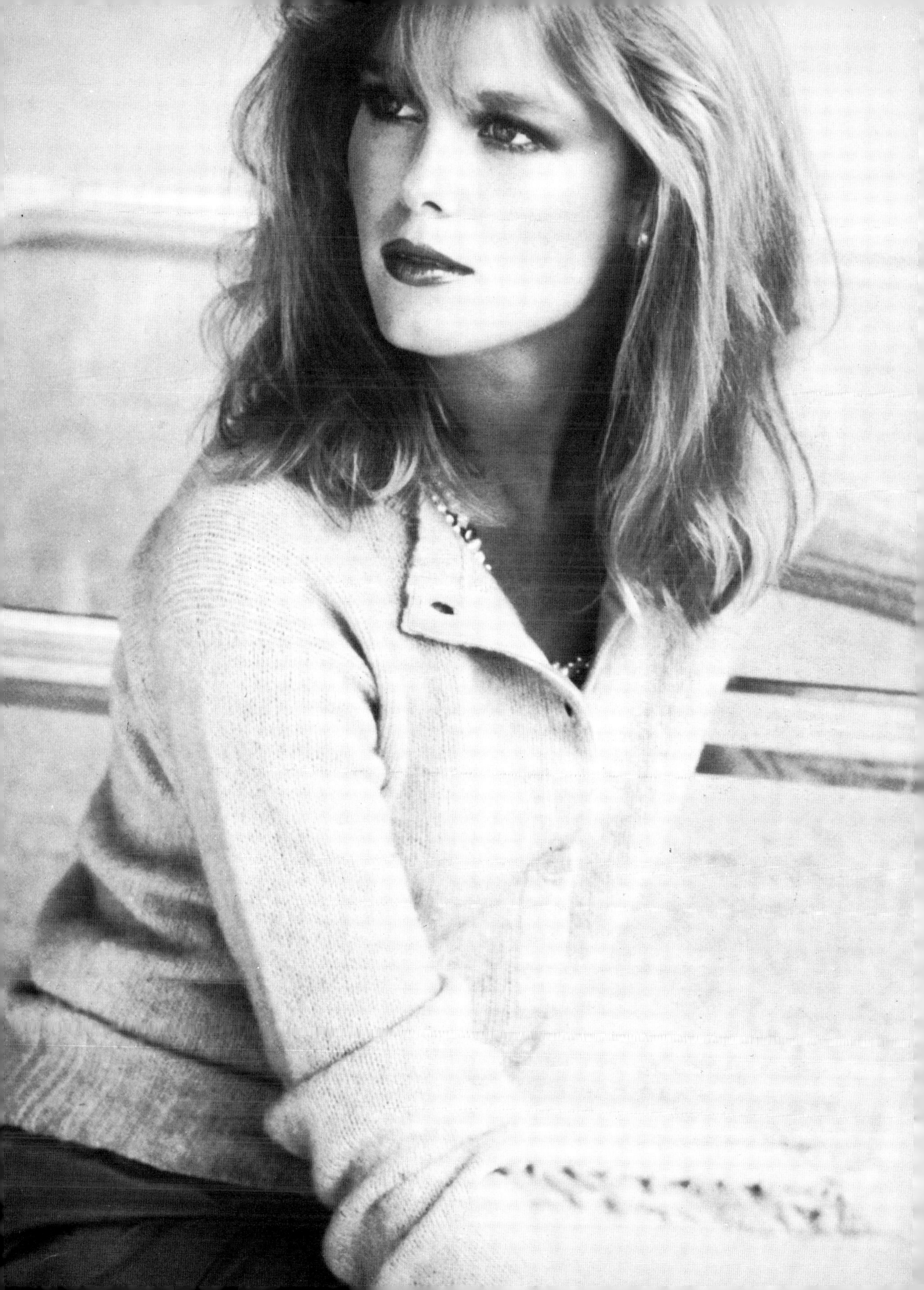

reveal your most adventurous style. Providing you feel happy in the clothes, it is easier to shake off inhibitions and create a stunning impact – the moment to brave shorter skirts, barer blouses, leggings or bodysuits. Colour can also be played up at night, mixing brilliant, even clashing, shades together – magenta with scarlet, lime green with lemon, turquoise with emerald. Luxurious textures of silk satin and crepe de Chine assume a glamorous nonchalance in calm shades of dove grey, mushroom pink, taupe or palest putty.

A BASIC WARDROBE

Basic essentials perform in various guises. A simple, well cut shirt in cotton, linen or silk is invaluable to wear day or night. For variety, collars can be shawl shaped, revered, a classic point or button down.

One underrated basic is a plain white **tee shirt**, round or V-neck. It is an invaluable neutral garment, particularly in summer when it can take you through the day and night. Providing it is white and not yellowing, it looks good with jeans, shorts, skirts, tailored or sporty jackets during the

The all time classic: white cotton poplin with Western detail

day, and can be dressed up at night with a striking necklace and a pretty skirt or silky trousers. In winter, tee shirts provide an extra layer: a round-neck worn under a brightly coloured V-neck sweater is a change from the predictable shirt collar.

A comprehensive **sweater collection** is essential. Shetland, lambswool, cotton and cashmere are investments which, well chosen, never lose their appeal or versatility. A plain V-neck, crew-neck or round-necked 'golfer' cardigan is much more useful than an uncoordinated assortment of fashionable sweaters covered in details or fancy stitches. The key to sweater dressing is the combination of plain shapes with a rich selection of colours and textures. Each sweater must work in its own right, but also add mileage to other separates. For instance, a plain lambswool V-neck can be worn on its own, or over a classic shirt, a tee shirt, a crew-neck sweater, a polo neck, or underneath a V-neck cardigan as a twinset. The twinset image is no longer regarded as dowdy, the principle of a matching cardigan and short-sleeve sweater is an example of flexible dressing. Put your own twinsets together – but with a difference. Experiment with identically coloured sweaters in different thicknesses, a chunky, primrose wool cardigan over a fine, primrose wool slipover. Or try a lambswool twinset in highly contrasting or subtle colour combinations – black with white, or honey beige with cream. There are more options if your sweaters are not all the same size. A mansize, ribbed sweater can be worn casually over trousers, or on its own as a knitted mini-dress with coloured tights.

When it comes to vital mainstay **separates** – a jacket, skirts, trousers, maybe a coat – look for good quality. Paying slightly more than you would normally can be justified: you need value for money, and you cannot expect one cheap pair of trousers to replace the wear of three pairs without looking tatty and shapeless rather quickly. If you want something to last, the quality of the material and cut are crucial. You do have to grit your teeth and pay for a good fit. With tailored clothes, the quality and fit stand out, and any imperfections in the cut are emphasized. But fitting should not mean constricting. Good tailoring means clothes that are softly structured, not awkward to wear. If you cannot afford the price of a tailored style, choose less fitted clothes where the expertise of the cut is not so critical.

A **jacket** can be the most useful coordinating link. It gives unity to separates dressing without the uniformity of a matching suit. Style, colour and fabric should be as versatile and neutral as possible without being boring. A jacket has to add a lift, not just be a top layer. Simple styles free from superfluous fashion notes are essential. The shape itself depends on personal choice; perhaps a traditional blazer, a double breasted boxy or cropped bellboy jacket, a thick knitted cardigan, classic windcheater, jeans or safari jacket. Whatever the shape, there are key

Shawl collared white linen for indisputable style

Sweater dressing: keep to simple shapes and natural fibres for year round wearability

(opposite) Seasonless separates guarantee great fashion mileage

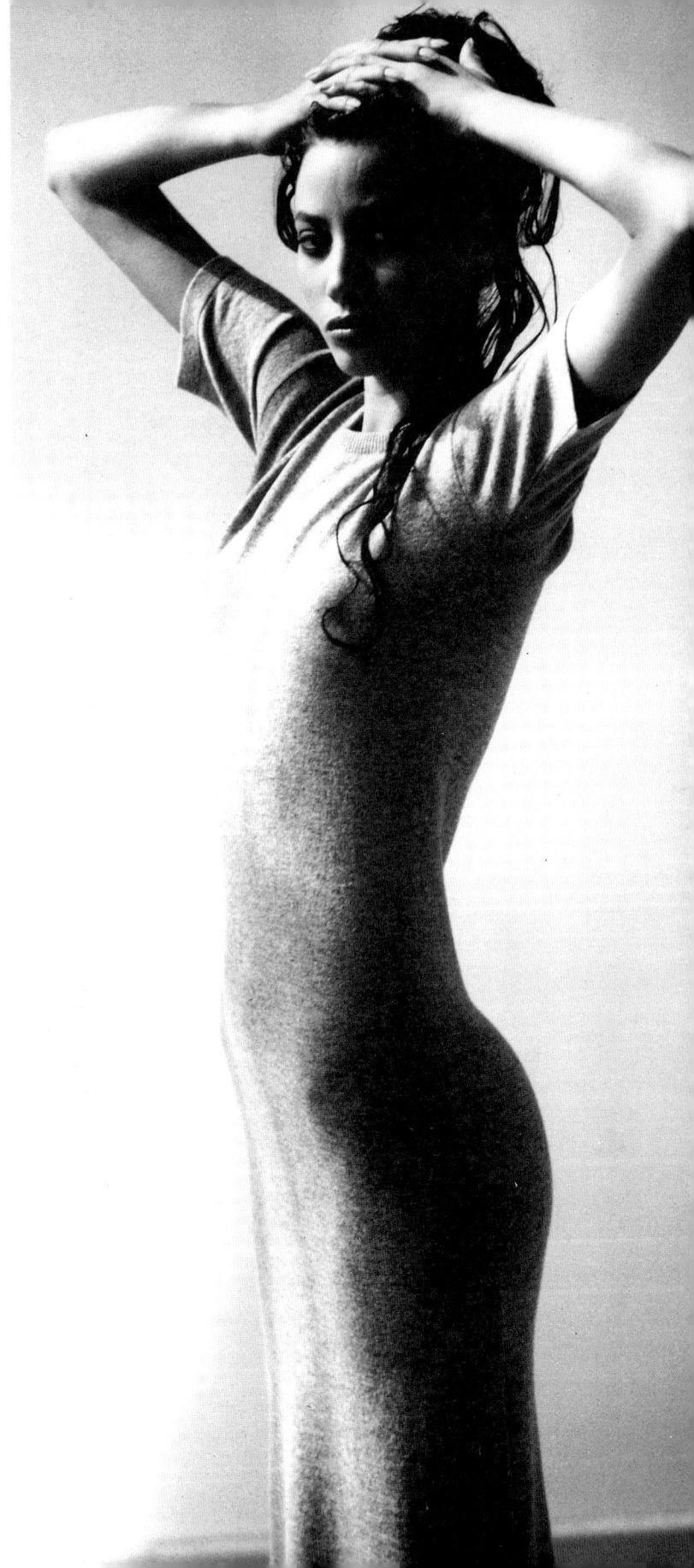

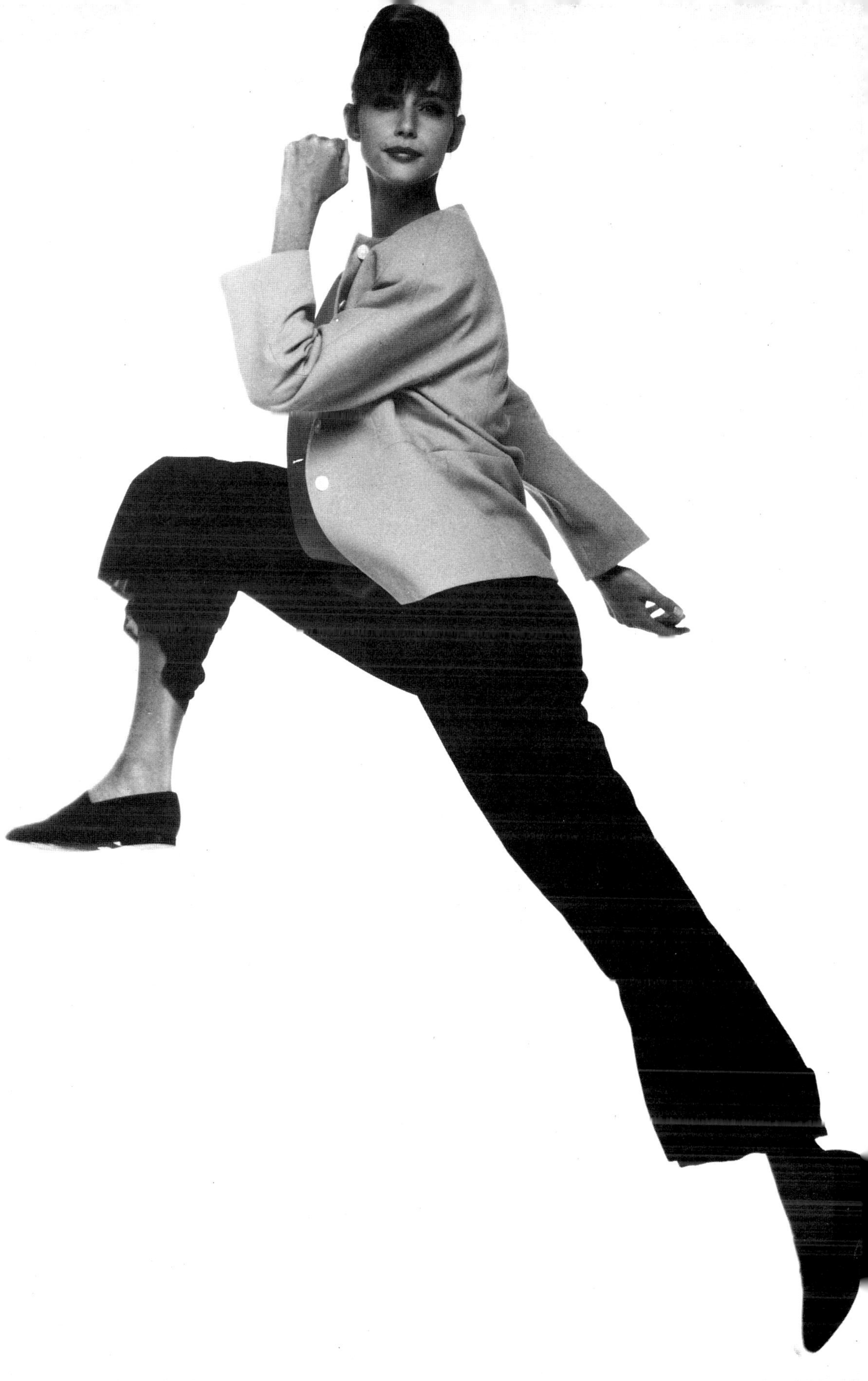

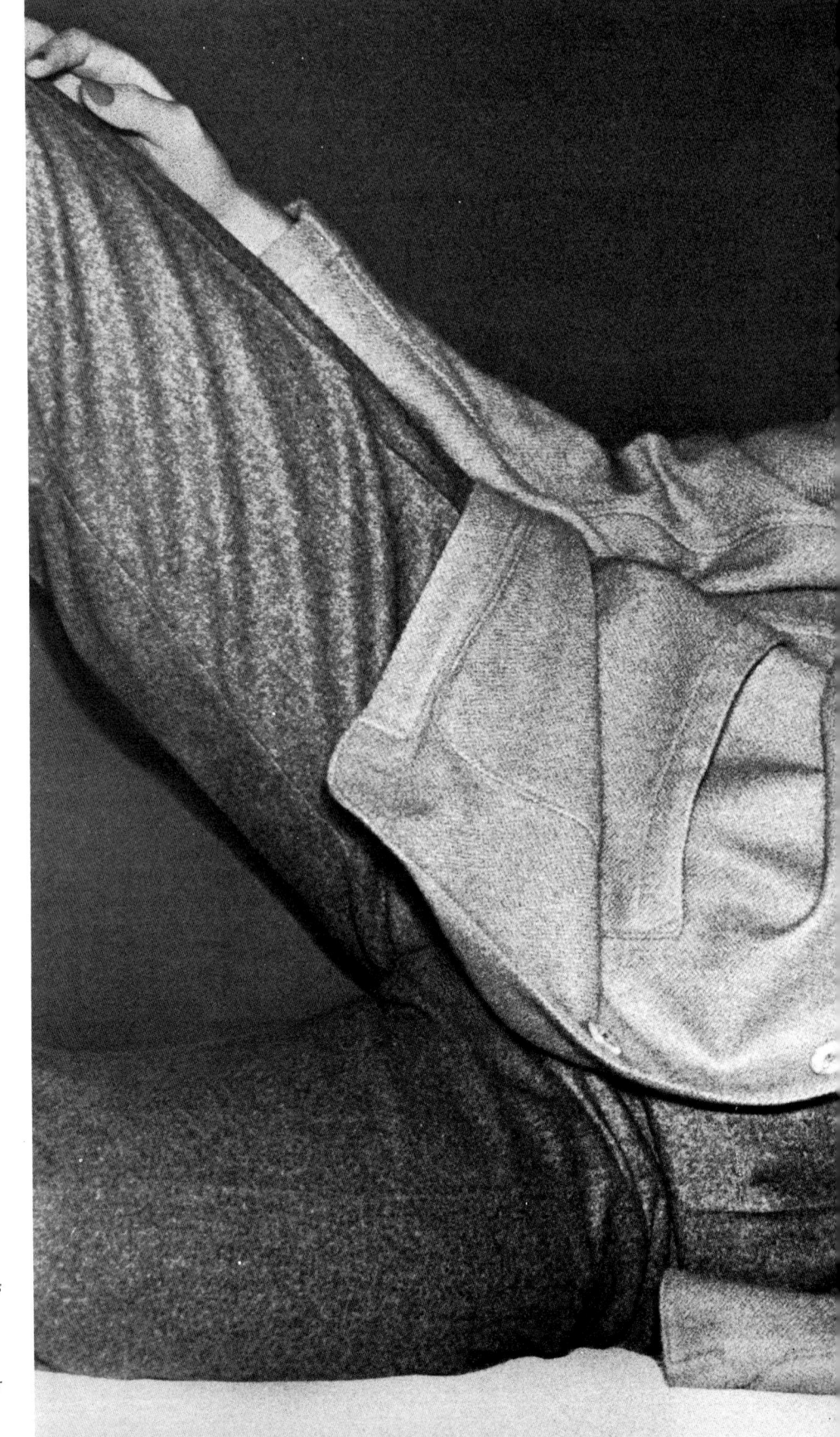

Jackets are useful during inbetween weather; an obvious bridge for spring/summer and autumn/winter dressing, when it is not cold enough for a coat, or warm enough to go without. And a jacket is not just for wearing outside; it has an inside life in cold weather, and can be worn like a cardigan over a shirt or sweater

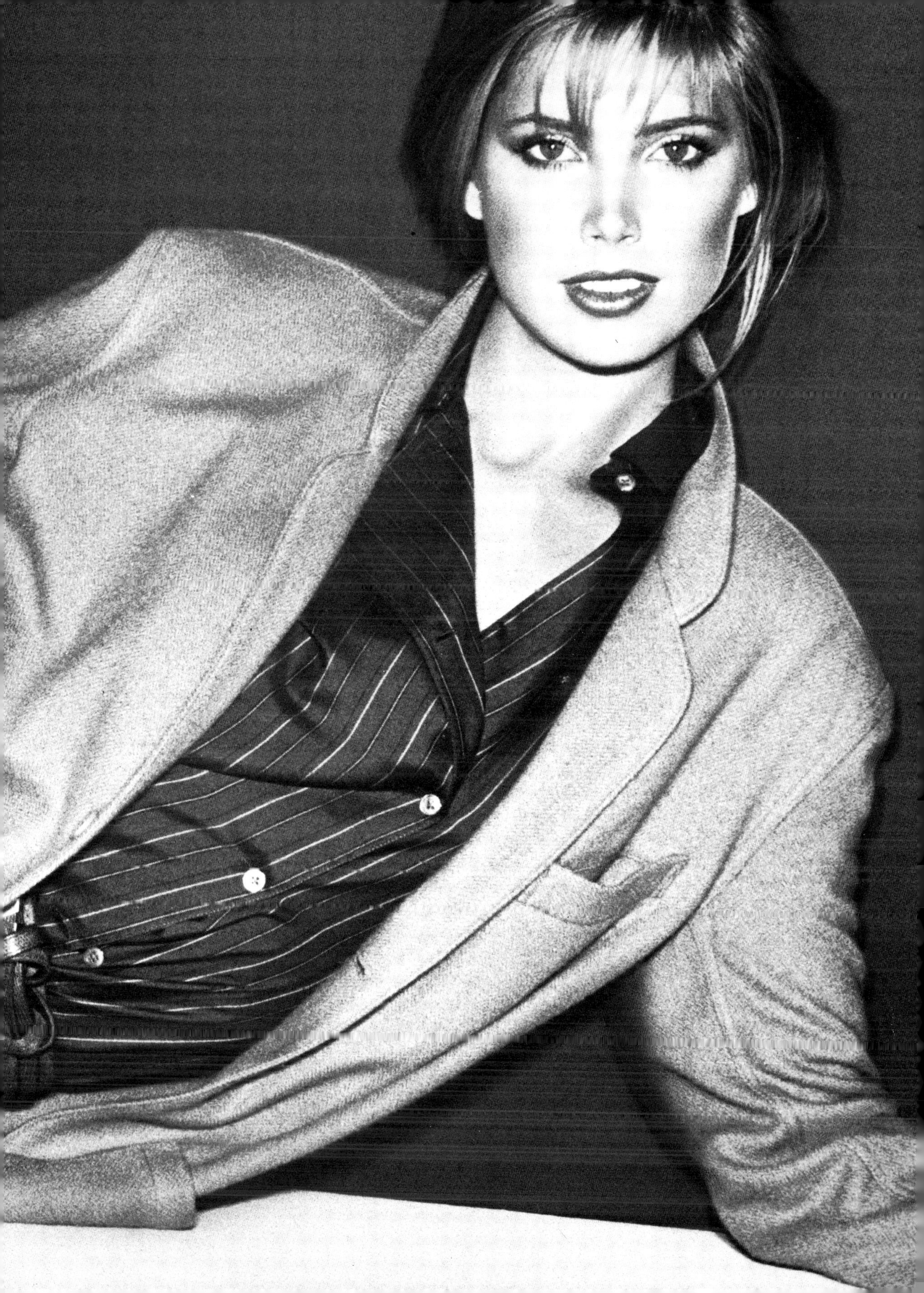

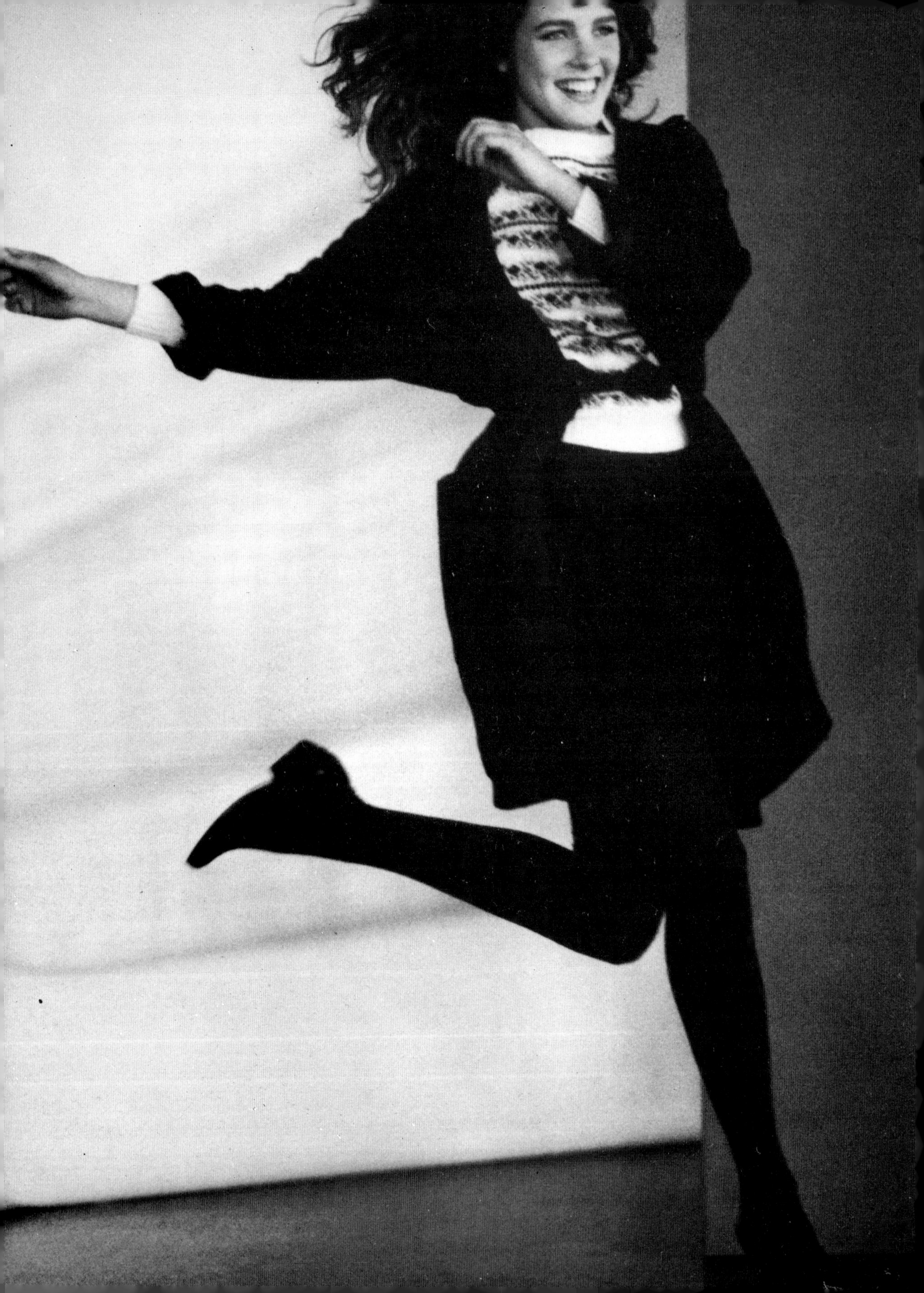

Wardrobe Tactics

Rules of proportion are determined by individual style, but the relation between hemline and heel should be a balanced part of the whole silhouette

points to check: avoid an exaggerated collar and revers, wide shoulders, unnecessary stitching or contrast piping, large pockets and drawstring waists, hems or cuffs which tend to look messy, and change buttons that look cheap or too obvious. Provided the weight of the material is correct (wise choices are wool gaberdine, suiting, knitted wool, flannel, suede, leather, denim), jackets serve a year-round purpose. They are invaluable for inbetween weather, and a useful bridge between spring/summer and autumn/winter dressing when it is not cold enough for a coat, or warm enough to go without. A jacket is not just for wearing outside; it has an inside life in cold weather and can be worn like a cardigan over a shirt or sweater.

A balanced number of skirts and trousers gives variety to a wardrobe, although if you feel or look better in one there is no reason to own both for the sake of convention. Trousers during the day or evening can look as smart as a skirt and are no longer a casual alternative. The only relevant guideline is that cheap skirts look less obvious than cheap trousers, where the cut and fit are important – especially in woven fabrics like flannel, tweed, gaberdine, corduroy, linen or denim. As a general rule, heavier materials justify a higher price because you are paying, you hope, for a good shape. Lightweight cotton, silk or jersey adapts more successfully into loose pyjama trousers and full skirts with elasticated or drawstring waists. Cotton or woollen jersey leggings are an inexpensive

Everyday jackets: (below) *a denim blouson,* (right) *tartan-lined combat jacket. Trouser shapes* (far right) *where quality really matters*

(opposite) *It is not always the shapes that change each season, but how designers balance the proportions*

Silhouettes to choose from: (top left) *Armani,* (right) *Chanel,* (below left) *Gianfranco Ferre,* (centre) *Calvin Klein,* (right) *Claude Montana*

(below) *A coat should be a classic – completely timeless with minimum fashion detail*

alternative to tailored trousers or jeans. Blended with lycra they have a stretch that is comfortable as well as flattering.

While the shapes of classic trousers and skirts remain constant, it is their proportions that change, updating a look from one season to the next. Hemlines remain a wavering issue with skirts – whether straight, wrapped, dirndl, or pleated – and are acceptable from ankle to mid-thigh. There are no hard and fast rules to follow any more except that a skirt length should be a balanced part of the whole silhouette; one that considers the depth and position of the waistline, the cut and fit of a jacket, the height of heel and density of stocking.

The rule of proportion is determined by individual style, but more important, by the shape of your figure. Recent designer collections contradict the classic pairing of cropped jackets with short skirts, introducing a longer jacket over shorts or mini-skirt, that camouflages wide hips and makes briefer hemlines less challenging. The line of a long, full skirt is flattered by a fitted peplum jacket or cropped cardigan style. But unless you are very tall, a long jacket over a long, straight skirt is difficult to carry off.

Heel heights are the key to the balance, enhancing or spoiling the final effect. Wearing high heels with short skirts and flat shoes with long skirts can be taken as an optional guideline. Trouser shapes also need to be balanced by a well-proportioned jacket and heel height. The most flattering equation is to put a long jacket or three-quarter length coat over slim tapering trousers, and a fitted, cropped or cardigan shape above wide Oxford bags or palazzo pants. Heel heights work in proportion to the width of the trouser. A tapered style can take the lift of a higher heel, while wide legged shapes need the balance of a flat pump or slipper.

The waist is an important focus that can alter the balance. A deep or raised waistline, especially on loose, wide trousers, often needs to be paired with higher heels. Defining the waist with a wide, stretch belt has an elongating effect on the legs, particularly if trousers, tights, shoes and belt are kept in a similar dark colour.

Buying a **coat** is a substantial outlay in any wardrobe, one choice where real value for money is esential. Value in terms of wear: you must be able to live in it for at least six months of the year. It has to work with all your clothes and meet every demand, without being too smart or too scruffy for certain occasions. A coat should be a classic – simple and timeless. Any style that is a fashion statement is limiting. It is remarkable how the traditional, understated cut of a man's overcoat never looks out of place. There is nothing exaggerated or pretentious about the classic double-breasted line, the immaculately proportioned collar, revers and pockets. It is an example of perfect simplicity. The key that turns a basically masculine shape into a feminine coat is softer, less structured

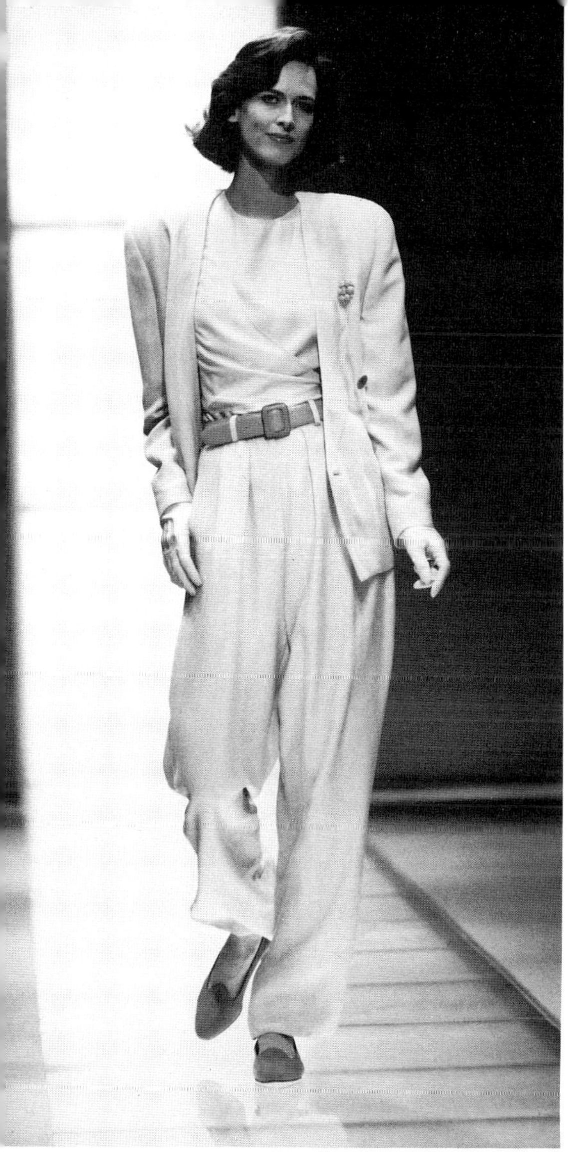
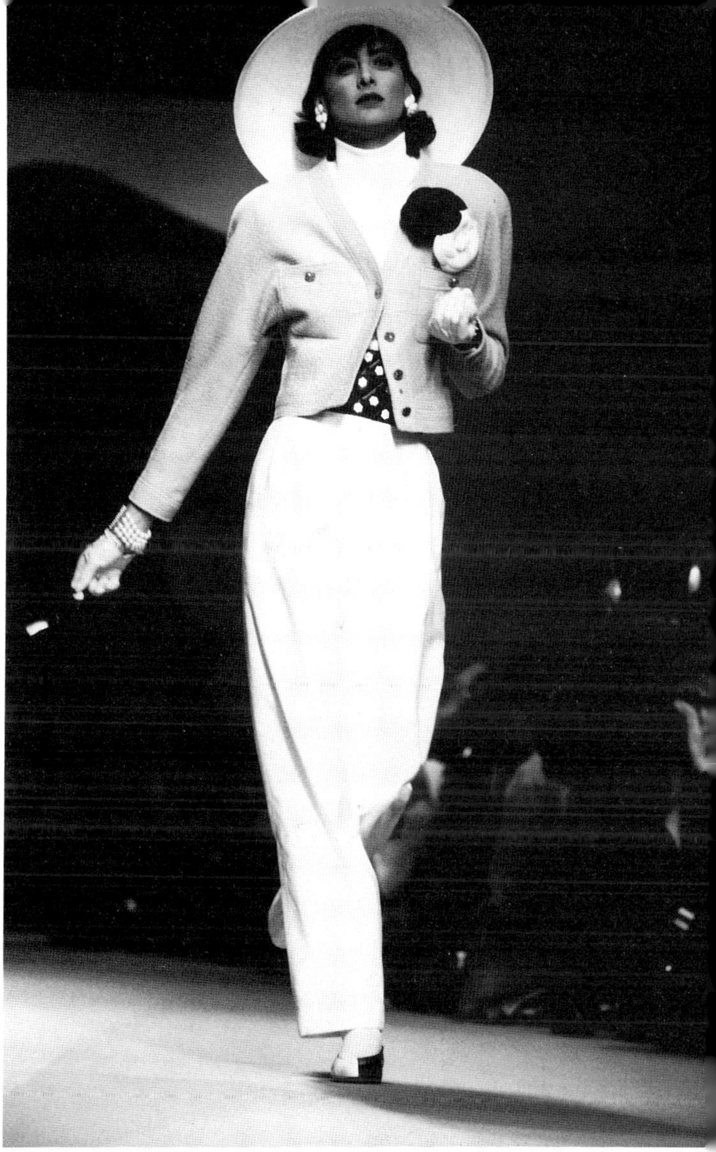
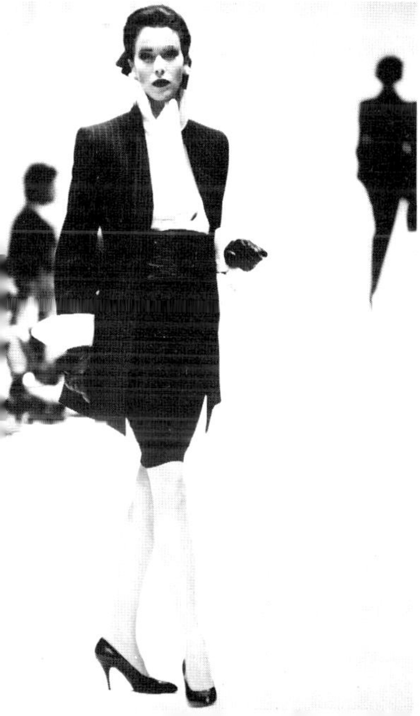
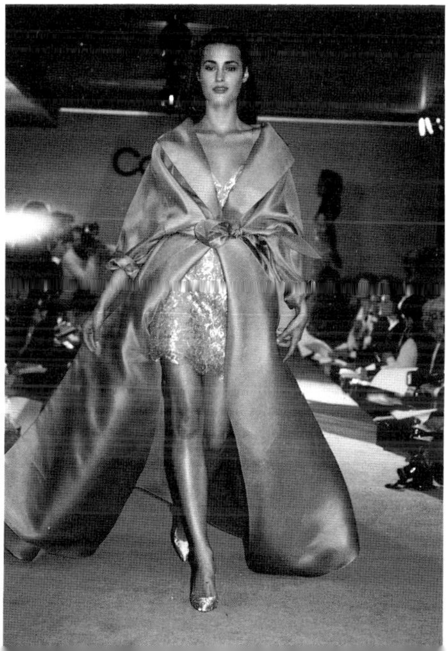
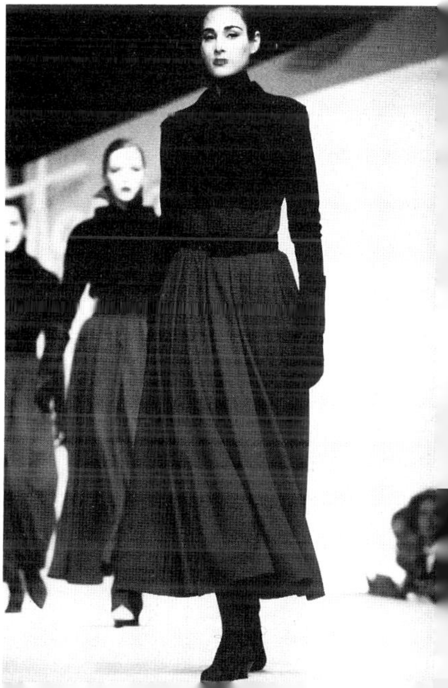

tailoring. But a winter coat is not an essential buy; it is better to go without if you cannot find one you love. A **raincoat**, especially one with a detachable warm lining, can take its place. It needs the performance of a winter coat, plus a seasonless quality that fits your clothes all year round, not just in the rain. Well-worn raincoats have much more style than brand-new looking ones, but you do need the right shape to start with: the traditional trench coat or single-breasted mac. Fashion raincoats look tatty, not stylish, after five years.

Accessories cannot be counted as part of the wardrobe backbone, but they do qualify for an important share of the budget. They bring change and variety to a limited range of clothes. Without a choice of accessories a mathematical style can become monotonous. As they have such diverse tasks to perform they can be divided into basic accessories and switch accessories. **Basics** are everyday essentials like shoes, belts and a bag, which for practical and economical reasons have to work in shape and colour with all your clothes. **Switch accessories** are vital extras that transform one set of clothes from being casual to dressed up, or from day to evening. They set a mood. It may be the addition of a beautiful necklace, a pair of drop earrings, an armful of copper bangles, a patent leather belt, or a switch from loafers to high-heeled courts.

A change of **shoes** is the most obvious way to dress a look up or down. They spell a mood more instantly than any other accessory, and for that reason it is essential to treat them with the importance they deserve. They should never be an afterthought: the wrong shoes with new clothes ruin the effect completely. The key point is quality. Unfortunately leather and suede are expensive but it is worth saving up for one good leather pair rather than buying several cheap pairs. Cheap shoes are false economy. A well-cared-for leather pair will look smart long after cheaper ones fall apart. Suede is labelled as impractical and hard to maintain which is untrue. Providing it is protected immediately against the rain, it is no more difficut to care for than leather.

The simplest shapes are the most versatile, especially in neutral colours like tan, black, navy, chocolate, that can be worn in every season. Providing you will not tire of brilliantly shod feet, there is no reason to avoid scarlet, sapphire or fuschia pink shoes, if they pay their way as key accessories, transforming one look from day into evening. Brightly coloured leather, suede or gros grain looks stunning at night, worn in summer with brown legs. Keeping to classic styles increases their wearability. Flat ballet pumps double as summer and evening shoes; low-heeled loafers look as good with bare legs as they do with thick socks. If resources are low, your most treasured suede and leather pairs can be set aside in summer, and replaced with canvas lace-ups, espadrilles, plimsolls or bright cotton pumps.

A change of shoe dresses a look up or down. Low sling backs or grosgrain pumps would switch this holiday style into something smarter

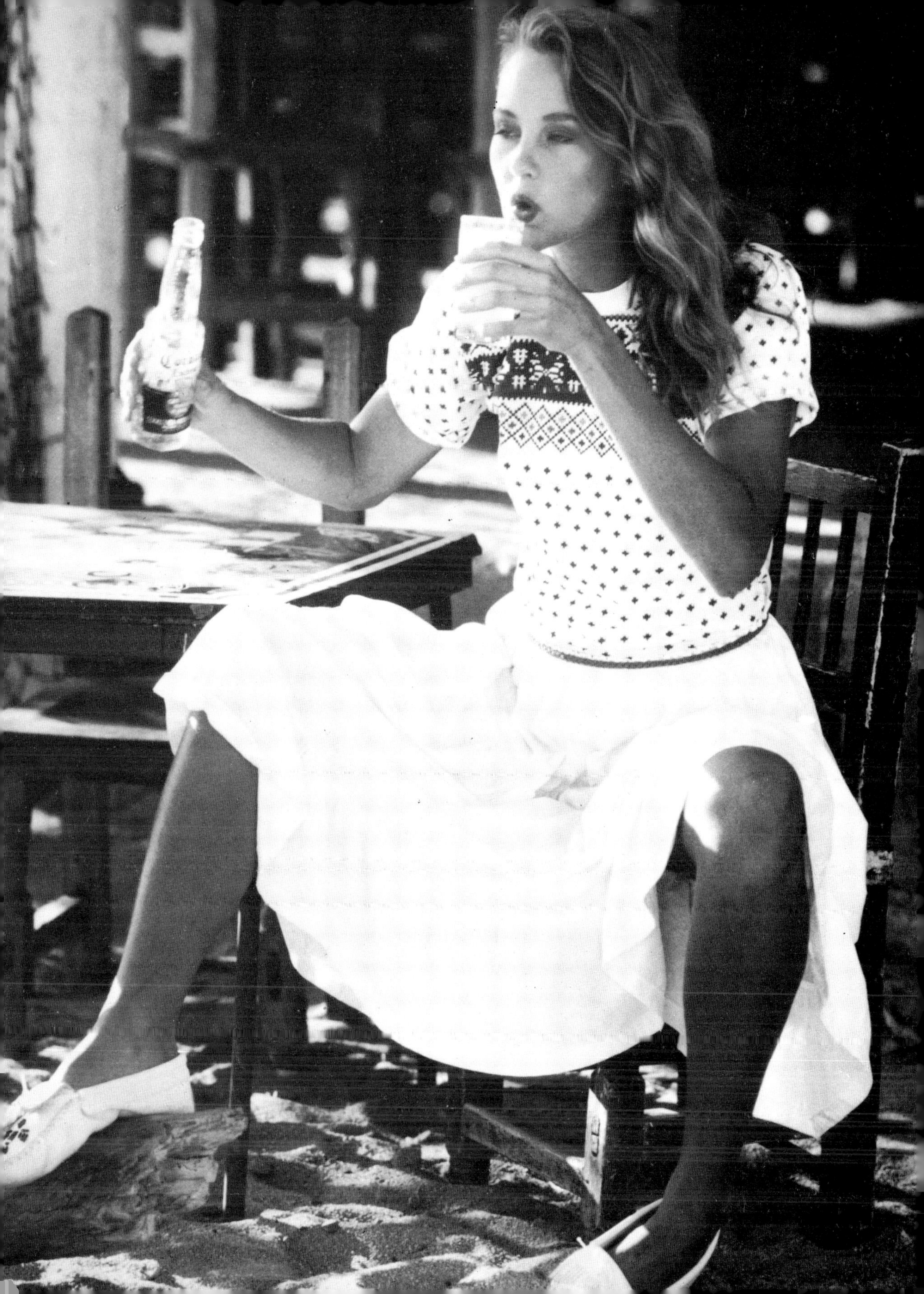

Accessory impact in a brilliant palette of magenta and gilded scarlet

(overleaf) When evening calls for full-blown glamour, consider burnished brown and gold for a striking combination

Bags are often more of an afterthought than shoes. There is no need for a wide selection. A simple shape in a basic colour – tan, navy, black, wine – should work with all your clothes. When budgeting for special occasion dressing, a bag, like shoes does need to be included. A groomed appearance can be ruined by a bulging, oversized bag. A small, tailored shape looks smarter and also doubles as an evening bag. For all but the most disciplined, a capacious holdall bag is an indispensible investment; a classic shape on the lines of a saddle bag, duffel, brief case, bucket or tote. When necessary, evening essentials can be contained in a slim clutch or zip purse inside the larger bag. Consider tapestry, velvet, wicker, canvas, straw or thick cotton.

When it comes to balancing finances, one critical area that is too often overlooked or hard done by is **underwear**. It is not an overstatement to say that what goes underneath is just as important as what goes on top. Badly fitting or badly shaped underwear can ruin the final effect – however well put together the clothes may be. Take time to shop around and find underwear, especially bras, that suit your figure. Many people wear a wrong size or incorrectly fitted bra. It is worth being properly measured and fitted by a trained saleslady who will check the strap adjustment and cup size if you know yourself to be inbetween standard chain-store or brand sizes. A common mistake is to shorten the straps which pull up the back of the bra and pushes the bust forward unnaturally.

Underwear ridges caused by bulges from tight pants are another terrible letdown in appearance. The answer is to wear a larger size, but make sure they lie smooth, or to find shapes that enhance the outer garment. It may mean something more substantial than tiny bikini briefs, but more surface area does not imply heavy-duty corsets. The latest foundationwear fabrics are light and comfortable with subtle stretch properties for smoothing stomachs and hips. Under fitted trousers and jeans, eliminate the chance of a ridge by wearing waist-level boxer pants with high cut legs.

The variety of **stockings and tights** in the hosiery department can be confusing, but it is one area where quality definitely pays. If you choose sheer tights, they should be as sheer as possible in fifteen, ten or seven denier plain knit. Avoid micromesh which gives uneven colour coverage. Tights or stockings worn with open-toed or sling-back shoes need to be extra fine with a sheer sandal heel and toe. Opaque tights are a useful and economic alternative in a more durable sixty denier blend of cotton and nylon. An addition of lycra adds to the price, but gives a sleek fit that smoothes ankle and knee wrinkles. Dark opaque tights in black, navy or chocolate flatter less than perfect legs, and worn with a matching skirt, have an elongating effect on the appearance.

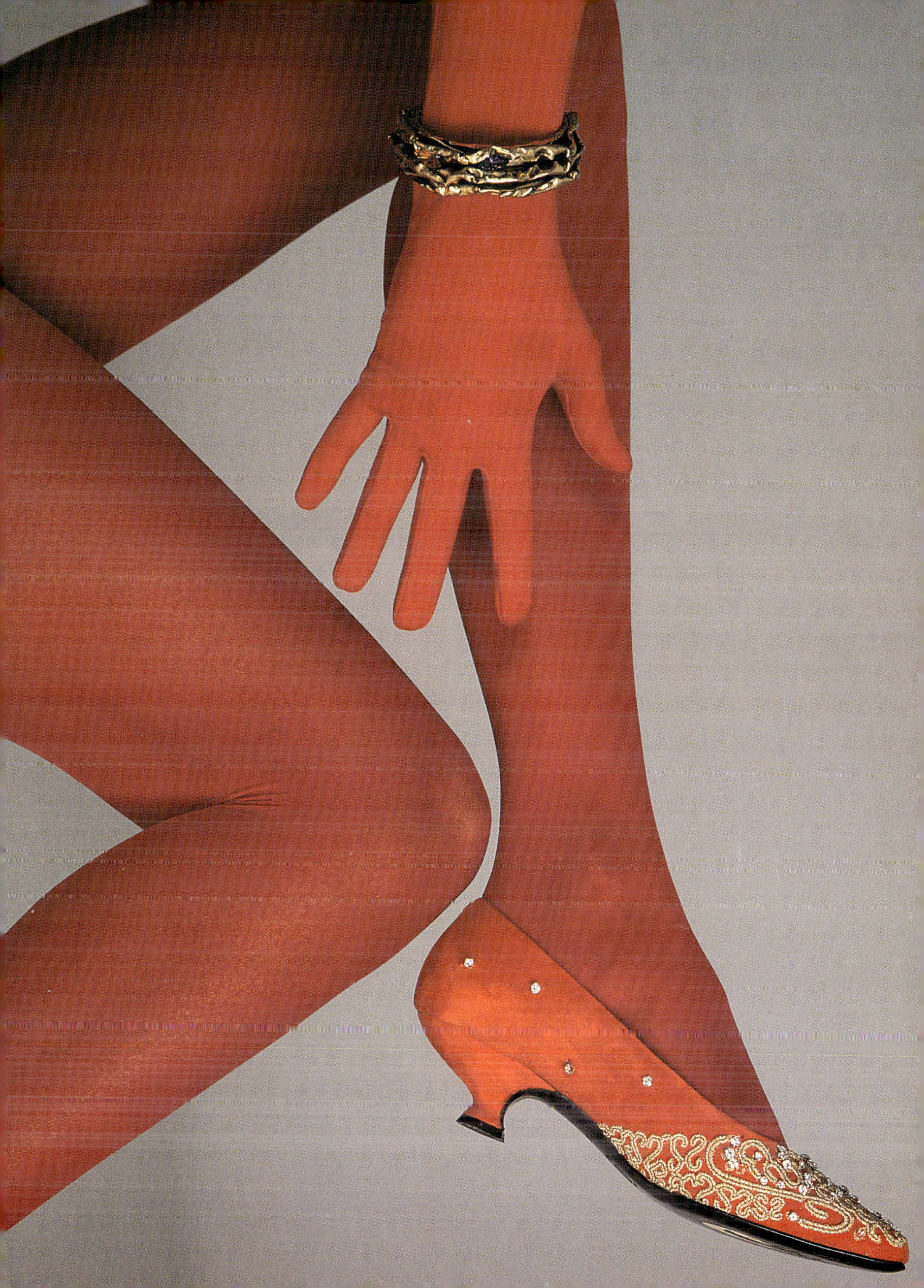

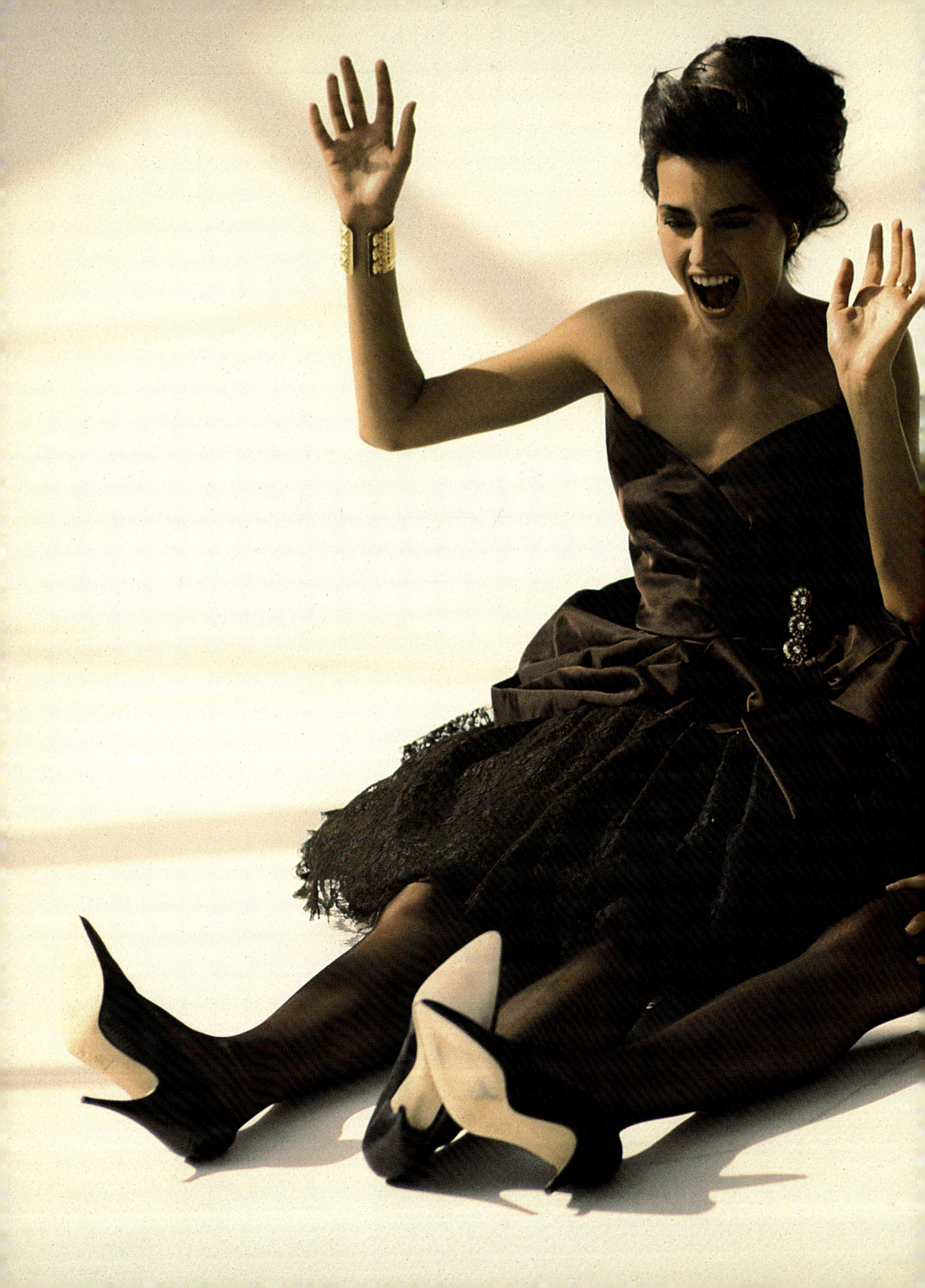

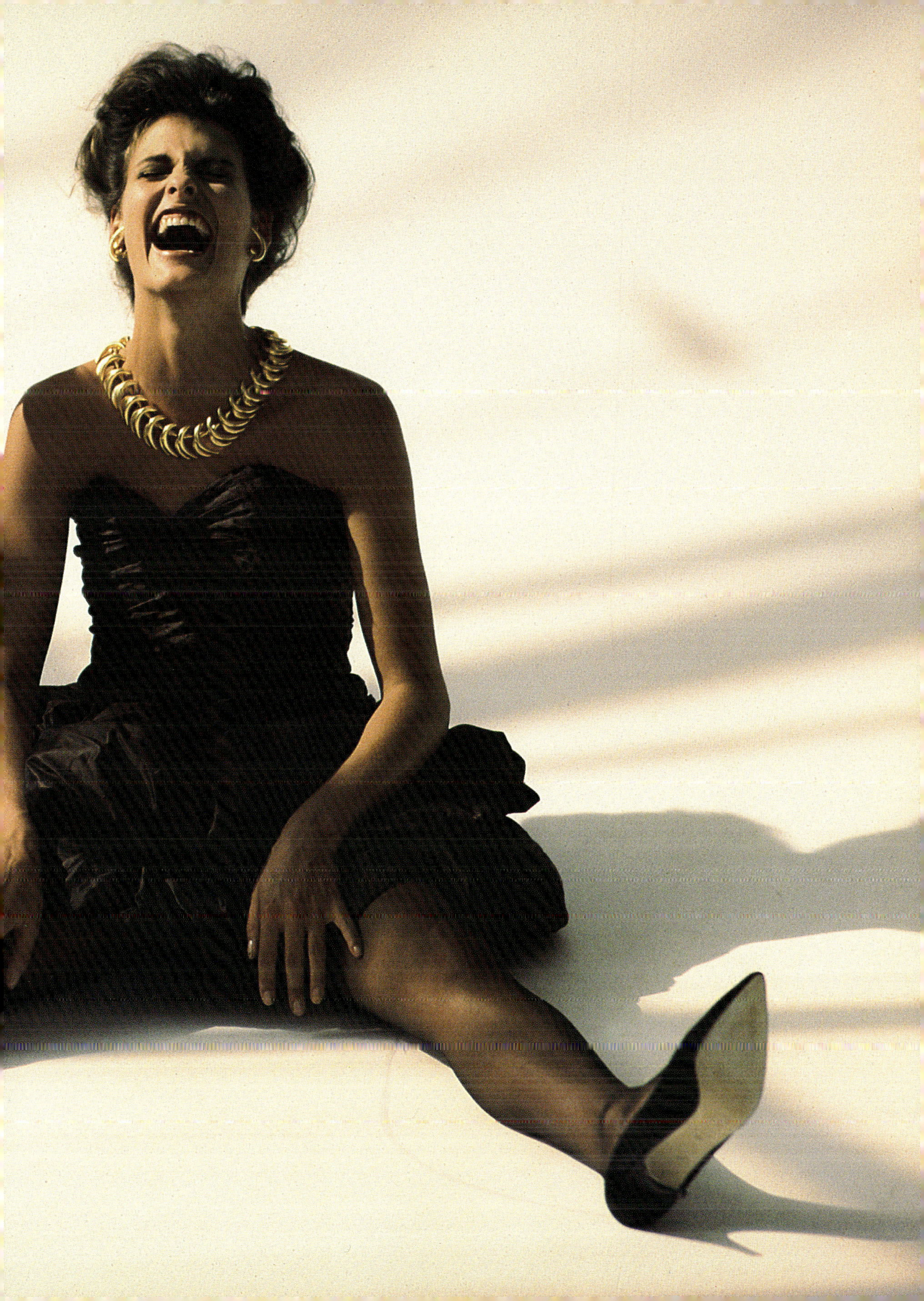

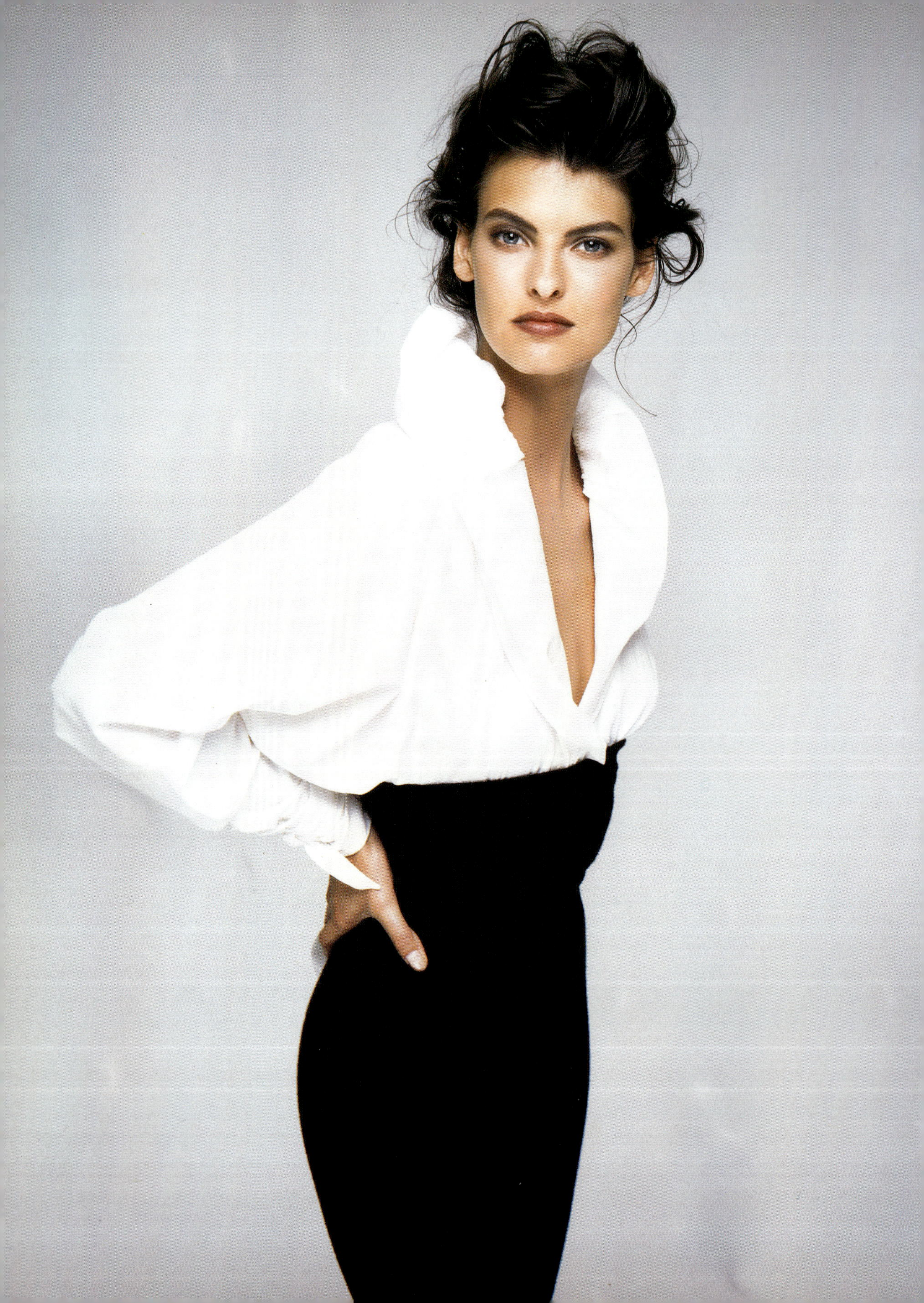

COLOUR-WISE

The **colour** of clothes in a small wardrobe is as important as the shapes. It makes sense not to limit the possibilities with a random colour scheme. The most workable wardrobe is based around a coordinated system where every garment has some link in colour as well as shape. The colour you choose is an entirely personal decision: be single-minded and wear what you love and only what suits you. Unlike fashion, colours never change, and there is no obligation to be in step with each season's 'right' shade. The most versatile approach is to use one neutral colour as a backdrop for everything else and build from there with related and contrasting colours.

A neutral colour like black, grey, tan, taupe or burgundy provides a **base** for a palette of bold primaries, subtle related tones or delicate pastels. Each neutral has its own colour family, or families, where the shades complement each other. Black is a classic base for day as well as evening. It is timeless and seasonless with the ability to upgrade cheap clothes. Too much unbroken black can have a deadening effect on the complexion (unless tanned), and needs lifting with white, with brilliant tones of red, fuchsia, yellow or china blue, with earthier tones of brick, sand, camel, chocolate or olive, or with soft neutrals like cream, dove grey, stone, taupe, dusty pink. Grey as a backdrop (all shades from silver to charcoal) works with ginger and rust, and with crimson, primrose, white and lilac tones. Navy works with white and scarlet, with dusty pink, cream, taupe, yellow, grey and olive. Burgundy (which needs to be a rich, cherry tone) works with cream, taupe, gold, pale pink, navy and black. Dark brown makes a neutral base for pale yellow, fuchsia, shell pink, camel, gold, black and scarlet. The taupe (or beige) spectrum has an understated look that can be difficult to bring alive. It needs a lift of white, vanilla or peach to prevent the quiet colours looking monotonous. Accents of navy, olive, black or chocolate add depth to the related tones of camel, stone, ivory and bronze.

The danger with **colour planning** is to fall back on habit. It is easy to grow narrow-minded and stick with certain colours as a security. Some of the blame can be laid on sweeping generalizations which declare certain colours unsuitable for different hair types. Those old-fashioned rules presuppose that each hair colour has a standard skin colouring. Your hair colour, unless it is very extreme, is unlikely to clash with your clothes. It is skin tone that makes a colour look sensational on one blonde while doing nothing for another. It is worth trying on colours that you think are incompatible; they may well suit you.

Combination advice can only be very vague because everyone is so different. The pale skin that often goes with blonde hair and blue eyes

The classic match of black and white works day or night

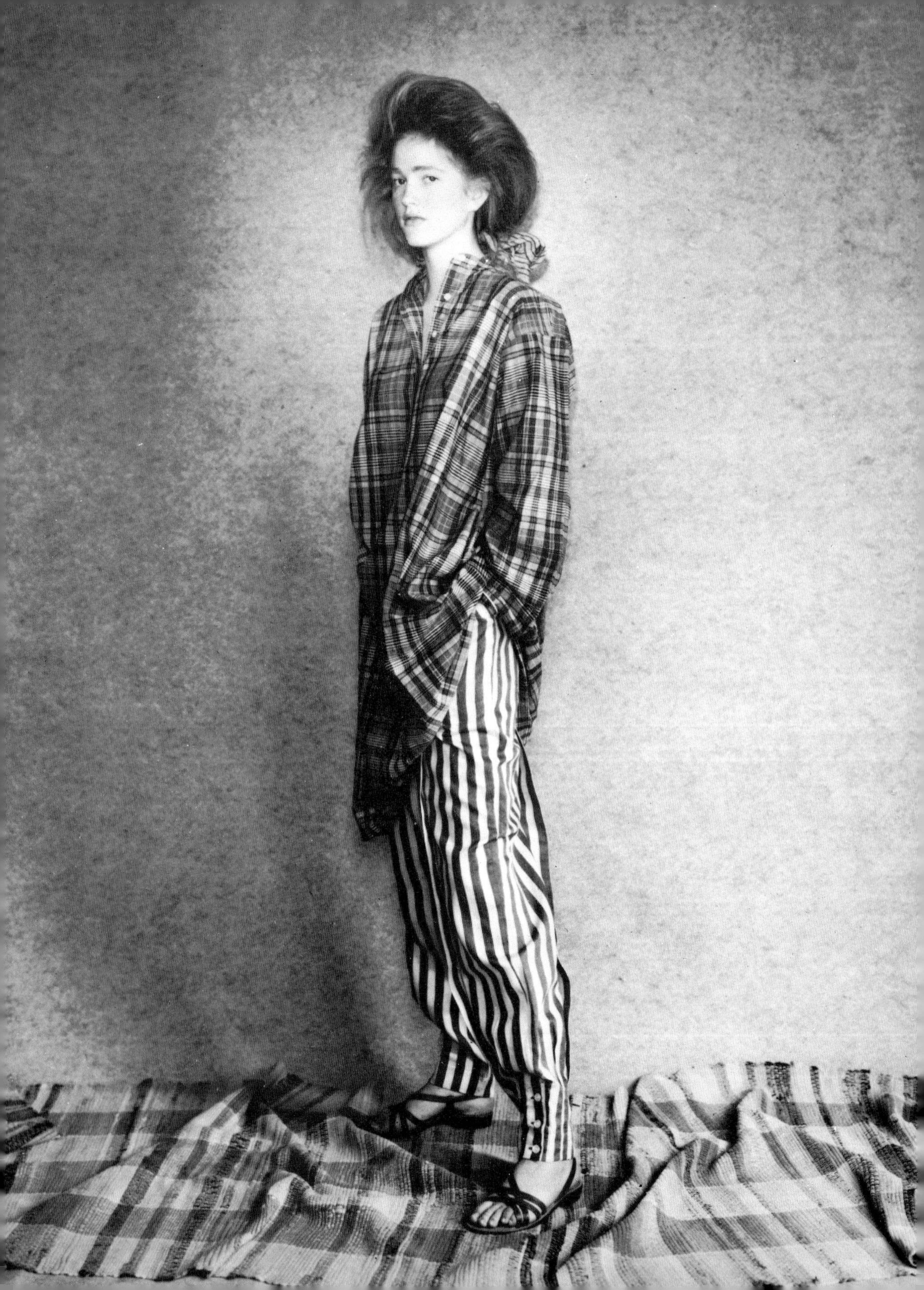

Wardrobe Tactics

needs warmth from a careful balance between soft colours which, if overdone, can look insipid, and dark strong colours which can drain colour from the face. The grey spectrum is particularly flattering for fair hair. Redheads often look good in the beige spectrum, with the emphasis on the peach and olive shades. If a skin tone is high (prone to red blushes) avoid hot colours like red, bright pink and ginger tones which accentuate the complexion. Some of the most flattering colours for every skin tone are shades of plum, claret and cherry red from the burgundy spectrum. Scarlet looks marvellous against medium and olive skin tones. It is surprising how much colour can affect your mood. Some days you need cheering up with a flash of something bright or luxurious. Maybe a shocking pink cardigan or a pair of primrose socks.

Certain combinations are guaranteed to look striking: navy and white, black and white, and navy, red and white. But there is also the danger of looking too predictable and over coordinated. The evenness of an outfit with white earrings and necklace, a navy shirt, white skirt, navy shoes, white bag, navy and white scarf is overdone. To avoid such a self-conscious balance, let one of the colours dominate or introduce an unexpected third colour: sand or olive green to navy and white, for example. With some experimenting, mixtures that were traditionally out of bounds, like green with blue, brown with black, brown with navy, pink with yellow or red, can be striking. Alternatively wear one colour. It has great impact providing you pick the right one. A total look in navy, light beige, black or cream is extremely elegant, but the same quantity in a bright yellow or hot pink is overpowering. Knowing where to draw the line is important. The quickest way to look overdone is to carry a strong colour through to all the accessories, especially tights. With a red dress and red shoes, sheer natural tights are more effective than sheer red ones. With thick or opaque tights, the density and bright colour become a definite part of the look, rather than a backup to the main colour.

A coordinated colour system does not exclude **patterned clothes**. A print is a clever way to introduce related colour and liven up plain separates. Prints are another matter of personal taste, but the most flexible designs are variations on stripes, checks, paisley themes and spots: classics that you can never tire of. Too many people have a mental block against mixing prints and textures. It requires skill and a good eye. It is not advisable to mix more than two different prints together and there must be a harmony between the design; if they conflict, the clothes look muddled. Learn how different stripes, or spots with stripes, can complement each other. As a guideline it is better to distinguish the different patterns in different materials. A softly striped cotton shirt with a Fair Isle wool cardigan looks pretty, but a striped wool sweater under a Fair Isle cardigan looks a mess. When you mix two prints, it is best if the

Mixing prints is easiest and most effective if you keep to versatile unimposing patterns. Two unfailing classics together are stripes and a Madras plaid

There should be a harmony of colour and texture between each print. Paisley, tartan, checks and Fair Isle all blend successfully

dominant one belongs to the more important garment. If you put a striped jacket over a check shirt, the stripes should be bolder than the checks. Mixing prints only really works with simple traditional patterns. Strong, fashion-inspired prints are less flexible; the design or motif becomes the focal point and overpowers the shape and style of the garment. There is nothing wrong with bold prints if you love the design and will not be tied by it, but it is not sensible to buy a mainstay garment in a print that has a limited appeal or versatility.

DRESSING YOUR FIGURE

Obviously the colours, prints and shapes you choose to wear are influenced by your figure type. If you have a large build, there is no reason to camouflage yourself in insignificant clothes, hoping that they will make you look smaller. Dress for your size, not to hide your body, but flatter it, even celebrate it, with the right colours and proportions. It helps if you understand how colour behaves on the body. In the same way that dark colours make you look smaller than light colours, hot colours – red, yellow, orange, yellow-based pink and ginger tones, all expand on a body, while cold colours – blue, green, purple, brown and grey, all contract. Since few figures are uniform, buying separates means you can find the right coloured and sized tops and bottoms. Avoid fitted shapes and go for clean lines in loose, but not baggy, separates. Watch the line where the garments meet: it becomes the most eyecatching area. Keep the colours in related tones instead of a stark contrast and avoid a glaring demarcation line. Unless you really want to show off a tiny waist, it should be defined, but not accentuated, with a loose narrow belt. One slimming illusion is to extend the colour of a skirt; if it is black, carry the colour through with sheer black tights and black court shoes. Other tricks are to hang your shoulder bag on a long, narrow strap, to wear a lightweight, narrow scarf instead of a bulky muffler; to restrict jewellery to long necklaces and simple, but bold, earrings.

If you are petite, you need to balance your clothes to your smaller frame. It is a mistake to wear fussy elaborate styles in place of simple shapes scaled down to your size. Avoid large prints which can swamp petite figures, and go for small, but never fiddly, patterns instead. Bypass high necklines and too many frills and ruffles. The most successful colour scheme revolves around warm, bright shades and pastels, especially cream, white and scarlet. Short legs can be elongated by keeping shoes and tights in the same colour tone. For accessories, choose small definite shapes; neat earrings and simple bangles.

It is rare to meet anyone who, given the chance, would not change the shape and size of at least one part of their body. The overdone concept of a 'perfect figure' turns those inevitable, usually inherited characteristics like a tiny or large bosom, a thick waist or broad hips, into major defects. You cannot change the basics of what you are born with. The only answer is to accept your body and learn how flattering the good points can divert attention from the not so good.

The trick with wide hips is to play up your top half, and if you have one, to accentuate a small waist. Eye-catching ruffled, lacy or embroidered blouses, V-neck tops, sweaters and softly padded shoulders all draw the eye upwards. It is wise to avoid jackets, shirts or sweaters that come to the broadest curve of the hips. For a thick-waisted figure it is better to keep away from fitted clothes with waistlines. Instead, go for unstructured, generous shirts, smocks and sweaters that can be belted loosely into a low-waisted tunic shape. Again you need to draw the eye upwards with the help of light or bright colours and striking accessories – scarves, bold earrings or chunky necklaces. Keep away from gathered or drawstring skirts and draped bloomer trousers which enlarge the waistline. Bust sizes are a perpetual source of envy and dissatisfaction. Small busted figures can wear most shapes successfully except for low-cut, off the shoulder or boned dresses that need a full bosom to carry them off and keep them up. With a large bust, what you wear depends on how much you want to emphasize. Anything very fitted or clinging, or jackets and shirts with bust-level detail like patch pockets, zips, bright stitching, all exaggerate the size and shape. The best minimizing lines are softly draped loose clothes; lean cardigan jackets with slim lapels, worn with narrow skirts or gently tapered trousers.

SHOPPING LOGIC

In spite of good intentions and logic, shopping expeditions can turn into frustrating ordeals. When you are in need of one specific thing, it is nowhere to be found, and when you browse with no intention of buying, you find something irresistible. Then there is the confrontation between heart and head. Despite the warnings from fashion pages, impulse buys often turn out to be successful because they are natural, instinctive buys. You are blinded by love for your find, which is the best possible motive to buy it. Even if you resist temptation at the first sighting, there seems to be a strange force that draws you back to the shop again.

If the object in question is not outrageously expensive and will belong in your wardrobe, there is little point in depriving yourself. It is better to buy clothes on that basis; all the fun goes out of shopping if you only buy from necessity. Some people like to buy their clothes in occasional sprees (often essential if you live away from a town), others prefer to shop at a slower pace and collect one thing at a time. The spree shopper needs to be strong-minded not to catch buying fever: it is easy to get carried away. If you buy one pair of shoes, why not have two? If you buy a new skirt, wouldn't it be fun to have something new to go with it? You let yourself be persuaded by an eager shop assistant to buy a top that may well go with the new skirt, but back home goes with nothing else. (The good shopper knows there are several things in her cupboard that will go with the new skirt, otherwise she would not buy it.)

There are disadvantages with a batch of new clothes. The novelty wears off at the same time and you need to avoid that rather clinical first-term, school-uniform look that a complete outfit of new clothes can have. They do lose the obvious freshly bought stamp when you mix them with established favourites from your wardrobe. Most new clothes take some wearing in before you feel at home in them and they look a part of you. If you can resist wearing all your new clothes the minute you buy them, it is worth keeping something back for a month or two. One new sweater can pep up a well-worn group of clothes.

The single-buy shopper needs a photographic memory of her wardrobe, so that every time she is tempted to buy, she knows how and where the new find will fit in. There are times when you find something that turns out to be invaluable, making you wonder how you ever managed before. It may be the simplest thing like a perfectly shaped bra, a great pair of jeans, shoes that are made for your feet or an irresistible lipstick or eye colour. If, when you discover the find, you can be convinced of its value it is definitely worth stocking up. It is exasperating to set your heart on an extra replica and find a month later that the shop has sold out, that the line has been discontinued or was a trial run in limited supply.

When the shops are full of a new season's clothes, it is a good idea to go on a shopping exercise with a notebook instead of a chequebook. The impact of many new possibilities can be bewildering and it is easy to make the mistake of buying something just to mark a new season, without being sure how much you like it. Browse through as many shops as possible, noting down the colours, shapes and prices you like, before buying anything. Try on everything, even tee shirts, unless you know and trust the brand. If you are looking for a skirt or trousers to go with a specific jacket, or vice versa, take the jacket with you. When you buy something that is going to be a mainstay, take it on approval, if at all possible, to check how well it works with the rest of your clothes, and whether your opinion of it stays the same for twenty-four hours.

Shopping during sales times can be dangerous: few people are strong willed enough to ignore a bargain, and sales fever increases the temptation to buy something unnecessary because the price has been slashed. It is always worth considering the reason for such drastic reductions. Perhaps an original blouse or a pair of distinctively cut trousers are being virtually given away because they have hung, unbought and possibly unwearable, in the shop all summer long, or perhaps they are the last and least saleable of a disappearing fashion craze. It makes sense to invest in genuine reductions – quality articles like knitwear, leather shoes and bags, at a fraction of their original cost – providing the styles are simple. Sale pitfalls are high fashion or gimmicky clothes in unwearable colours; however smart the label, it is no reason to buy something you are not convinced about. It is wiser to buy more mundane essentials such as underwear, nightwear, socks and tights.

The timing of winter and summer sales does have advantages. Retailers keep half a season ahead of the buying public and fill their shops with summer dresses at the end of February and winter coats in August.

If you have the patience to wait until December for winter clothes, and July for summer clothes, you can buy everything at sale prices. Obviously the cream of the stock is snapped up when it arrives at the start of the season, but the shops are forced to reduce the remaining clothes to make room for new deliveries. Before you invest in an expensive coat, find out when the sales start. Next week the same coat might be half price, and there is nothing more infuriating than someone else's bargain.

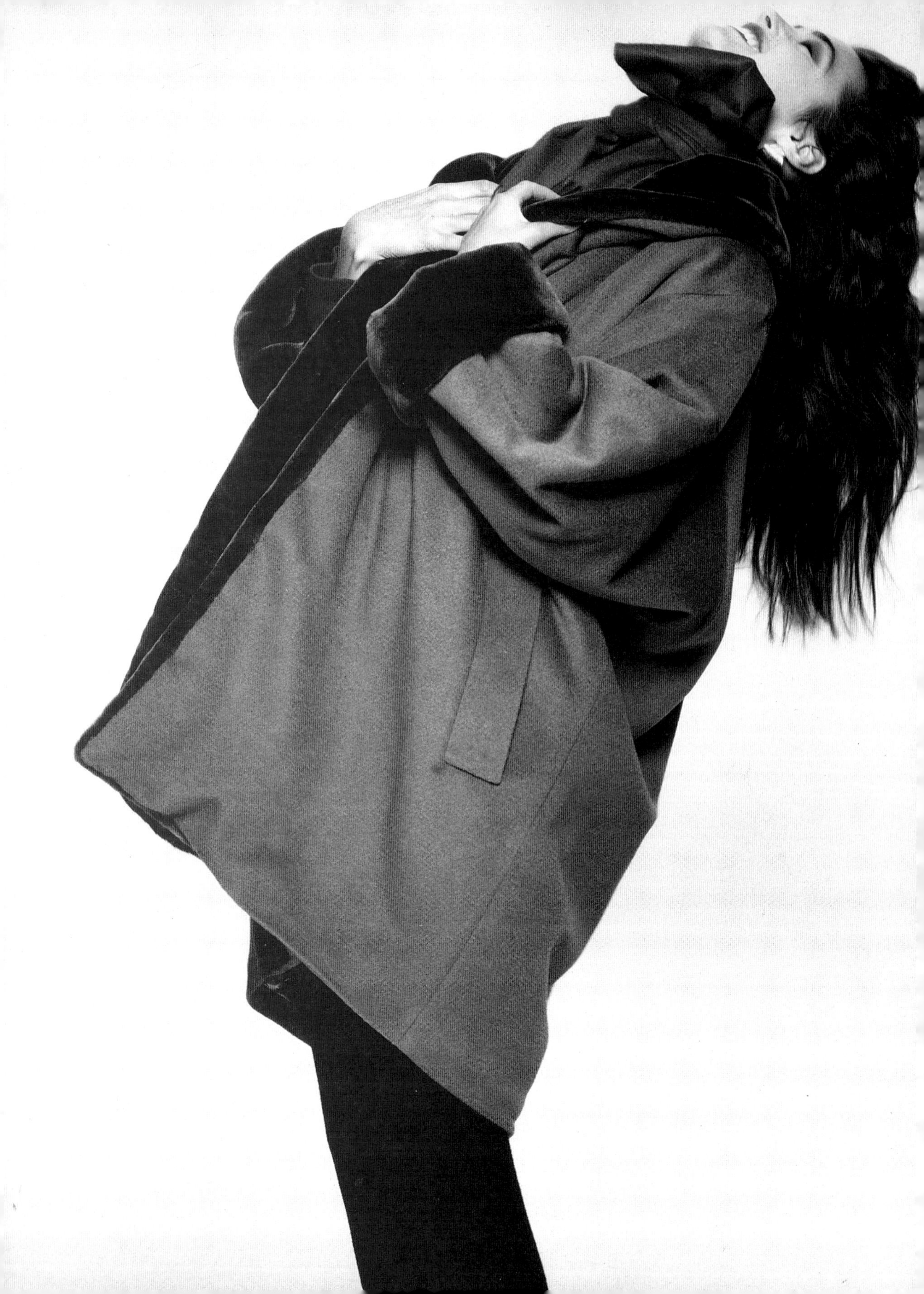

THE CLASSICS

Classic fashion: an investment in timeless style

Classic is a fashion term too often used to describe the kind of clothes that are not in the swing of high fashion. It is a definition of simple, low-profile dressing, but has unfair overtones of dull, rather prim clothes. The classics in this chapter are fashion legends. They stand aside from the turbulence of high fashion with a timeless style. True classics last until they fall apart, rather than fall out of fashion.

So what makes a classic? The magic quality is a pure design with perfect proportions, free from any moods and extremes. Classics are completely natural and unimposing clothes for everyone to wear. As quality is a key point, these clothes may cost more than their counterparts, but they are investments that justify their price. Their style is not a uniform. There are classics in every type of dress: sporty, sophisticated, surplus, ethnic, country or jumble sale. Classic buying is a simplified approach to choosing fashion; it demands an instinct for the best colour, material and cut.

The vital point about a classic is **shape**. True classics have a permanent place in fashion because their shape can never be bettered; they are invaluable starting points for designers. The trouble starts when unnecessary detail is added to the basic shape. One of the best things about a classic is the way details and extras are pared down to an absolute minimum, so that every button, zip, seam, or pocket serves a purpose. Leading classics are legendary shapes that inspire copies at every price level. Top billing can be shared between the traditional Burberry-type trench coat, the plainest, small-collared man's shirt, the kilt, the Western jean, the twinset, the polo neck and the cardigan.

The 'British look' is made up of underrated classics. Every ingredient is a classic in itself: the traditional textures of tweed, tartan, fine cotton, corduroy, flannel, sheepskin, Shetland, cashmere, Fair Isle and Argyll-checked knits, all in pure natural colours, worked into shapes which

(bottom left) Easy country classics

(bottom right) Perfect tailoring – a fresh look at the most undesigned shapes

Classic elements: (opposite) a silk satin blouse that slides into tailored gaberdine

could not be less designed if they tried. Their potential tends to be overshadowed by their stuffy image, but take a lesson from cosmopolitan interpretations of the British style, which mixes such clothes with an essential dose of wit and originality. The bonus about the British look is that it is well interpreted at lower price levels. Each time it is reinstated from the borders to the centre of fashion, there is a crop of tweed coats, jackets, kilts, corduroy skirts and trousers, traditional knits and trench coats to suit different pockets; an opportunity for the discerning shopper to find the best quality and style for a low price.

Modern classics are the kind of basic clothes that have become indispensable. Blue jeans are a prime example. From being a symbol of anti-fashion, they have become a classic trouser. The need for much of fashion to be functional as well as decorative promotes casual sporty clothes into contemporary classics. A plain sweatshirt, a white tee shirt, a polo shirt, a tough leather motorbike jacket, butt cotton chinos, a leotard and leggings are all modern classics.

How you wear the classics is as important as what you wear. Classic clothes have a neutral quality which does not impose on your character.

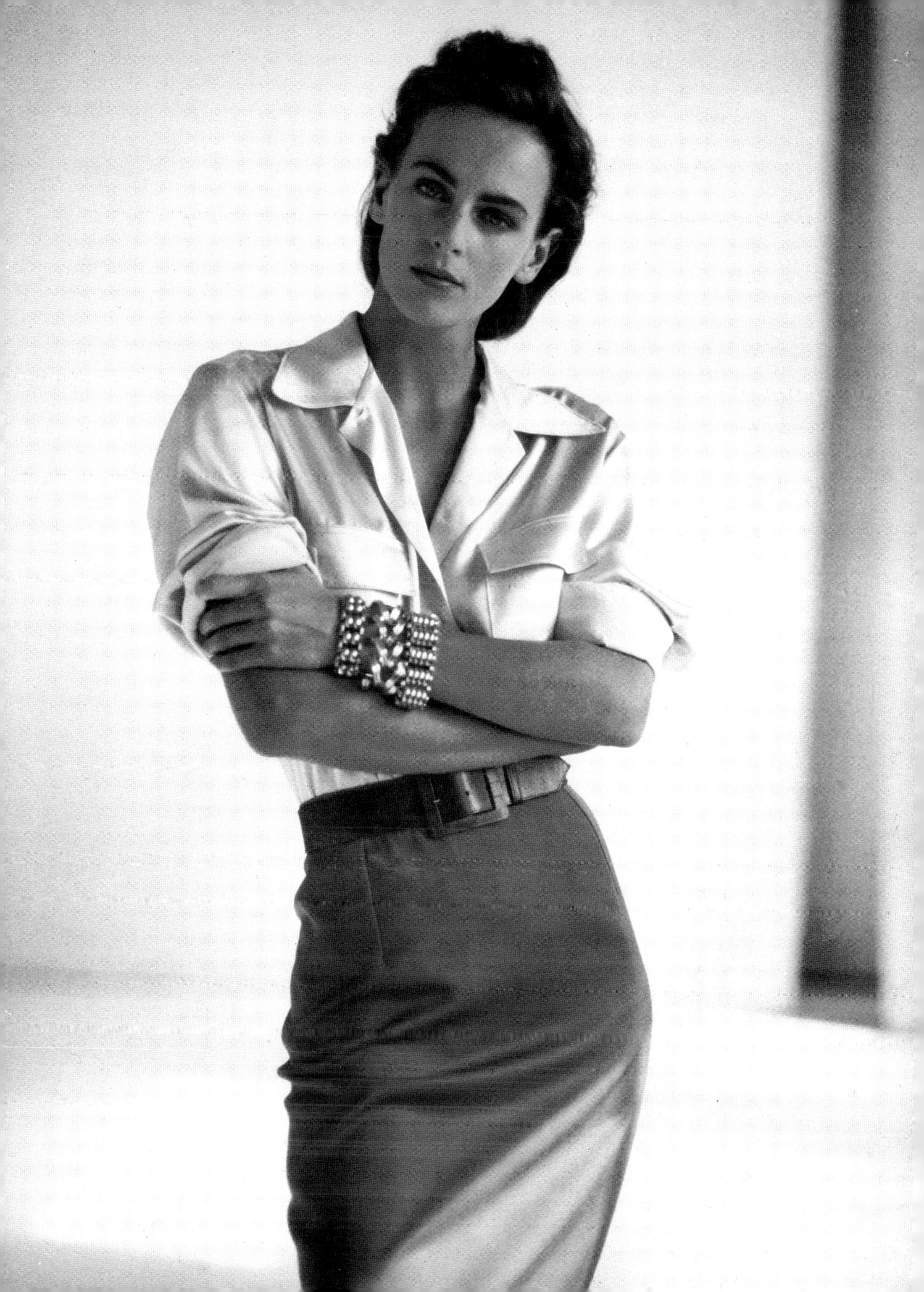

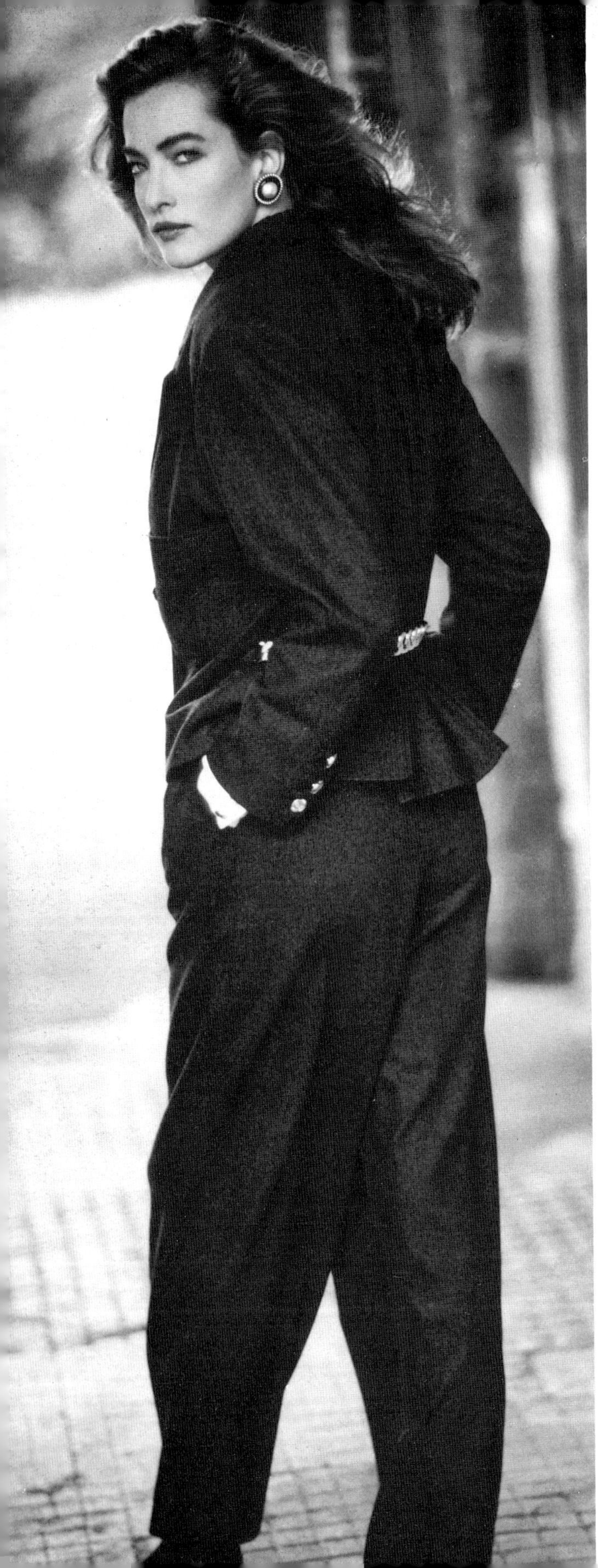
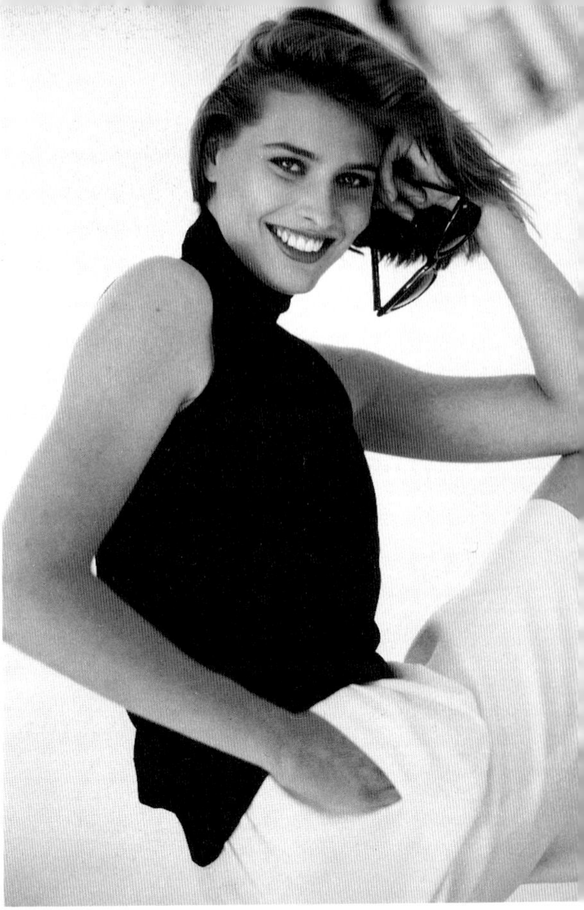
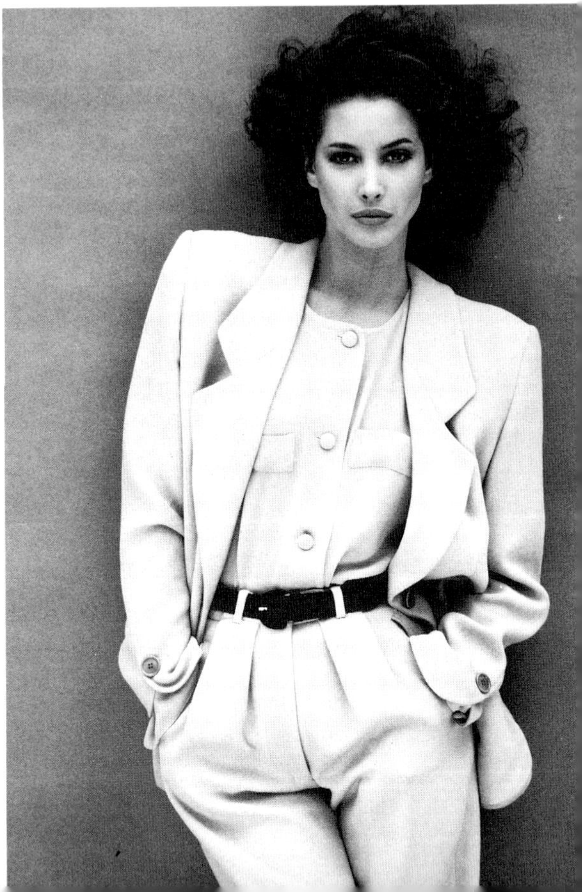

Sheepskin, leather and denim (right): enduring textures for town or country

Impeccable suiting: (far left) grey flannel and gilt by Karl Lagerfeld for Chanel; (bottom left) the restrained cut of an Armani wool crêpe trouser suit; (top left) the essential black polo neck – in cut-away silk for summer

Classics have timeless versatility the instant rapport between silk satin, suede, denim jeans, tooled leather belt and heavy-duty Rolex

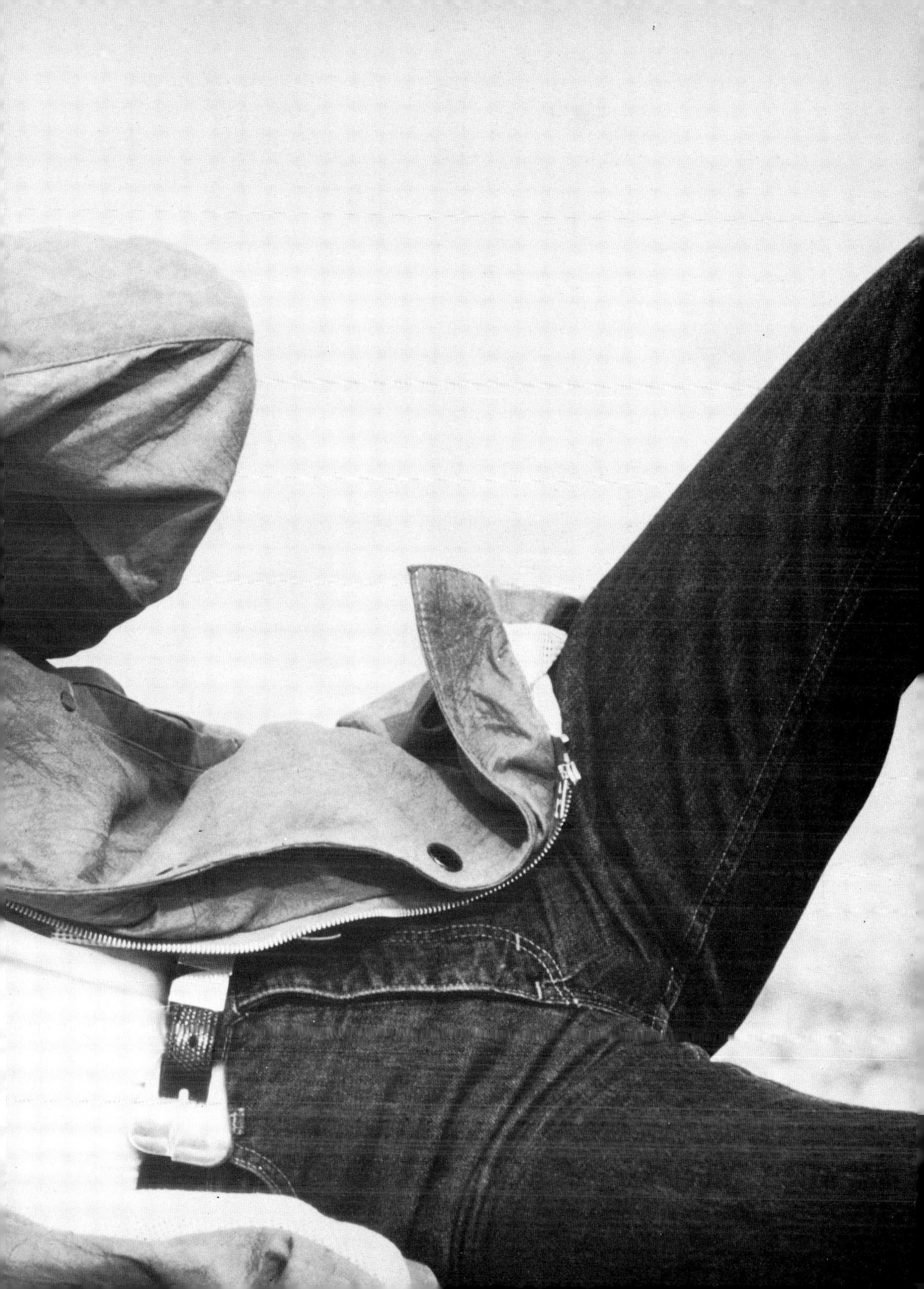

Elements of surprise: (above left) understated tee shirt and plimsolls softened with silk chiffon and easy trousers

New proportions: (above right) cropped tweed jacket with mini-skirt and high heels

(right) The flattering ease of a more generous cut

You have to take the initiative to create your own style from the perfect ingredients. Their charm is versatility, they look right in any place or situation. It is as if all the classics speak the same language and have an instant rapport with each other – even if one is an exquisite tailored shirt and the other is faded jeans, they still look good together.

To get the most from these clothes you have to see them from different angles. Develop unexpected combinations: create a surprise by mixing tough and soft clothes together; a thick ribbed sweater over a fine cotton skirt – or a tough leather jacket over a fragile silk camisole; by mixing old and new together, like an antique white lace blouse with sharp pinstripe trousers; by mixing formal and informal together – a cotton singlet with satin trousers, or a Shetland sweater flung over your shoulders with a silk dress. Try out certain things in a larger size than you would normally wear. A more generous cut, particularly with tailored jackets and shirts, relaxes the formality of the clothes and makes you feel more at ease and less 'dressed up'; and draped clothes are more flattering on the body than a tight fit. In the same way you can pull your clothes about until they feel right and look a part of you – make the most of the little details like pushing up sleeves and turning back collars and cuffs.

Use colour to make the classics live. Detach yourself from what you expect and what others expect to see, and try to use colour with a fresh eye unchannelled by tradition or practicalities. Of course you should usually buy clothes in a sensible, versatile colour, but one that gives you pleasure each time you wear it. It is a surprise to find an established classic in an unexpected colour combination: a kilt in pastel tartan, pebbly Harris tweed in bright red or hunting green, a sheepskin coat in a crazy colour. Some combinations are unbeatable, like blue denim, green loden, cashmere-coloured cashmere, grey flannel, white cotton. Others tend to go together out of habit. There is certainly no reason why raincoats always seem to be a depressing shade of beige or black.

THE FINER POINTS

What does a classic wardrobe include? There are no fixed rules, just flexible guidelines of shapes, colours, materials and patterns to follow. The material of the clothes is a critical point. There is something superior about natural fibres. They feel more comfortable to wear than man-made, they fall better, and most look good as they age. Synthetics tend to lose their original colour and texture, although a small addition of man-made to natural fibres *can* be undetectable, improve the wear and maintain the shape of the garment. The inferior synthetic image is vanishing while textile technology advances to produce replica silk, cotton and linen which look and feel natural enough, but have the advantages of being easier to wash, crease resistant and quick drying.

Pure wool is incomparable. It comes in such a range of textures that there is almost one suitable for every kind of clothing. Light woven weights like wool crepe, wool gaberdine, wool jersey and thin flannel are perfect materials for seasonless skirts, dresses and jackets. Tweed comes in a wealth of traditional and modern patterns, and a wide variety of thicknesses, some chunky enough for substantial overcoats, others fine enough for light trousers and tailored skirts. The most classic tweed patterns are the traditionals: hound's-tooth, herringbone, Prince of Wales, Harris fleck, Glen checks, Donegal speckles, all with a chameleon nature that makes them fit in with contrasting materials. A tweed jacket looks quite in place over a delicate lace blouse. And classic tweeds can go anywhere; the same jacket can look as good in the middle of a field as it does in the high street. Knitwear prices vary depending on the quality and type of wool. Luckily it is still possible to buy inexpensive pure wool knitwear, and as acrylic, the man-made alternative, lacks the characteristic warmth and texture of wool it makes perfect sense to do so.

Cashmere is the ultimate in knitted luxury. It is the rarest natural fibre,

Natural fabrics have seasonless, go-anywhere style

combed from under the fleece of cashmere goats from Inner Mongolia. One sweater takes two fleeces, which proves how special and luxurious cashmere is, although the sheer joy of wearing it easily justifies the expense. The different grades and thicknesses (or plys) of cashmere are reflected in the price, which ranges from being expensive to quite out of the question for most people. The lowest priced cashmere sweaters which you may find in chain stores are not the most superior quality, but they are still well worth the investment. Pure cashmere does need special care because the fibres are so soft and fine. It is more resilient and cheaper when mixed with a percentage of lambswool. Shetland and lambswool have become general labels for two types of wool, and the top qualities of each can cost the same as cheap cashmere, but you can find both at surprisingly low prices. These do not feel quite as soft as the expensive brands, because they are knitted from medium- or low-grade fleeces, but they are still pure wool. The shaping of the sweater is often a criterion of its quality. It should be fully fashioned – knitted as a whole, with the sleeves properly set in, not sewn together from separate pieces. The best classic knitwear comes in the simplest old-fashioned stitches – cable, Aran, ribbed and plain knitting – in solid colours, or the most classic Fair Isles, Argyll checks or pale intarsia rose patterns.

Leather and suede are examples of perfect classic materials that improve with age and are hardwearing; a quality that helps to justify their initial expense. But leather is not limited as an outdoor material. Fine suedes and leather can be as supple as light wool, and adapted into unstructured, simple shapes; easy drawstring trousers, wrap skirts, soft cardigan jackets, even shirts. The crucial point about suede and leather clothes is that the shape should be simple. They have a habit of accumulating unnecessary details – overdesigned touches, such as extra zips, stitching, contrast piping or a pretentious lining – which kill the charm of the material.

Silk is another quality fabric that tends to be treated as something wildly extravagant, but the wide choice of types, textures and cost of silk, make it as accessible, pricewise, as wool and cotton. The silk family includes crepe de Chine, satin, raw silk, organza, taffeta, chiffon, and vaious blends with wool or cotton. It is also remarkably strong and not as difficult to look after as some people imagine. Part of the charm of silk is the strong definition of colour, whether it is bright, pastel or muted. Unlike a synthetic equivalent, drab silk is hard to find.

Linen is a classic summer fabric, woven from flax. It is revered by some and avoided by others for its tendency to crumple. But once experienced, the upkeep and expense of pure linen are rewarded by its understated style, supple drape and comfort. Plain coloured linen does need to be immaculate, but a patterned or slubbed weave has a more casual image

Classic textures: (top) *the seductive luxury of cashmere and silk satin;* (above) *silk crêpe de Chine and pearls;* (right) *evening impact in black silk grosgrain*

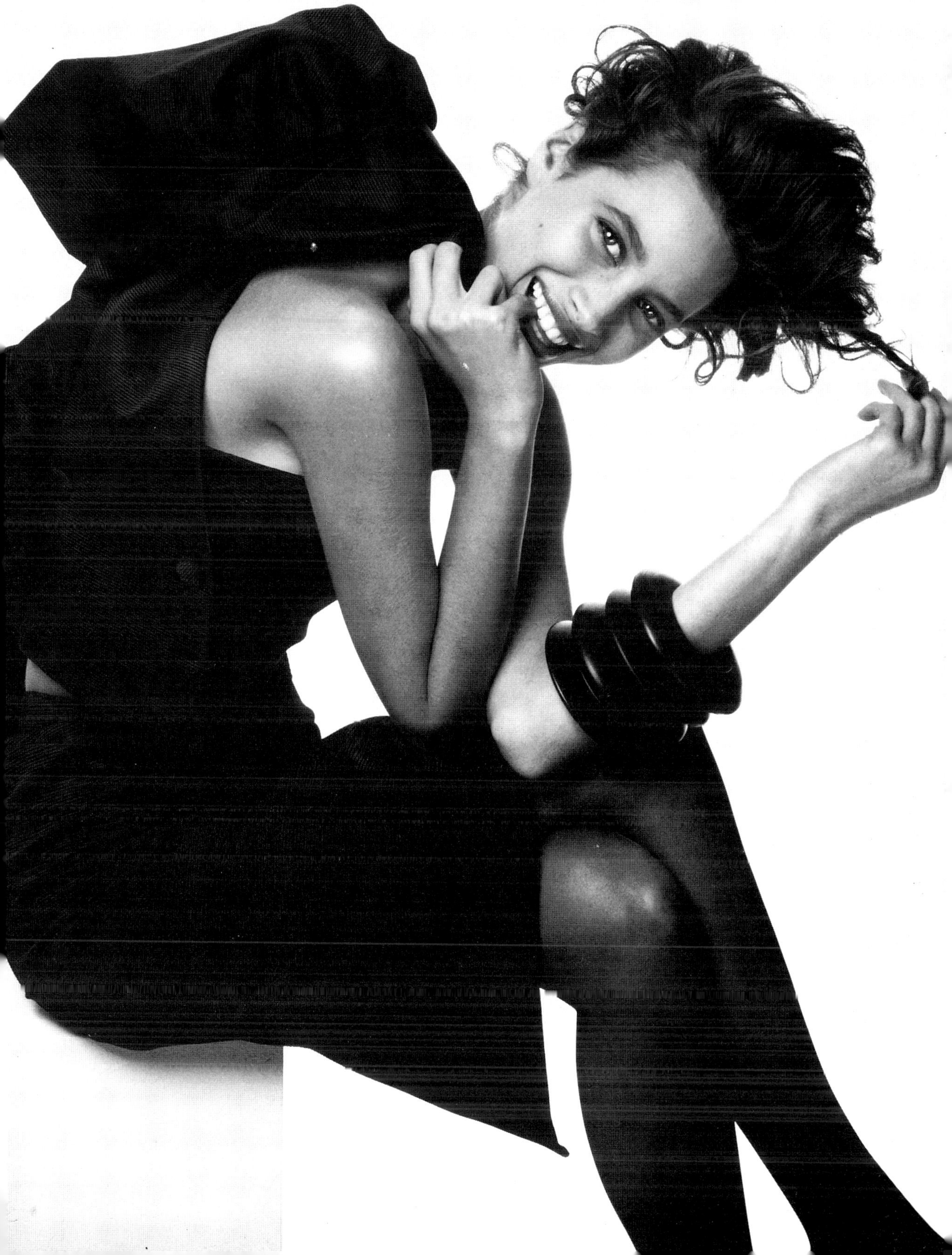

that is often enhanced, especially as a jacket, by looking soft and well worn in.

Cotton is the cheapest of natural fibres. It is a beautifully comfortable fabric that comes in a wide range of woven and knitted textures; cotton lawn, voile, shirting, denim, mercerized, cellular, corduroy and velvet are all definite classics. Most cottons are hard wearing, but it does pay to buy the best you can afford. Cheap corduroy, for example, tends to go bald and limp after several washes.

Denim must be the most well worn and famous version of cotton; it is certainly one of the most comfortable and cheapest materials (in terms of wear for money), and one that grows in style with age. A great pair of jeans depends on the quality and weight of the denim as much as the cut. The colour fastness and behaviour varies from brand to brand. If jeans are not preshrunk, they are likely to shrink about 8 per cent in the waist and leg. Sanforized denim means the jeans should shrink only 1 per cent. Indigo denim, which is dark blue, can be uncomfortably stiff at first, but softens and fades gradually with each wash. Pale blue, washed-out denim looks best in sunny countries, or chopped off as beach shorts; it still hasn't quite recovered from the strong links with frayed flares, slogans and patches. When denim is promoted sporadically from being a basic to an essential element of fashion, it becomes more than a pair of jeans, and features in skirts, shirts, dresses, jackets, hats, bikinis, shoes and bags as well. When the designs of these denim fashions are pure and simple, they too rank as modern classics.

But for guaranteed style, jeans outweigh the alternatives. It is easier to look great in a pair of jeans, if you can find a pair to fit, than a jeans skirt. Jeans shopping is no more a question of Levis or Wranglers. The shops are swamped with different labels at different prices, all making claims to be the ultimate fit. At the top end there are designer jeans with a higher price that reflects the smart label on the pocket, more than a guaranteed superior fit. The problem with the middle-priced, traditional Western jean is that it suits a male shape better than a female one – cut for bodies with slim hips and no waist. Luckily the competitive market has spurred manufacturers to produce jeans that flatter a waist, fit round the hips and elongate female legs. Long skinny legs can take the cut of tapered jeans, but shorter legs look better with a high-waisted, straight jean. Once you find a shape that suits you, it is worth sticking to that brand. Jeans rank as a classic only if the styling is minimal and functional – after all they are the archetypal utility garment. They should be well constructed with double stitching on seams, pockets and flies, reinforcements on stress points (pocket corners, the zip base, belt loops), have a heavy-duty metal zip to last with the jeans, and at least five tough belt loops for a close fit at the waist.

Denim, the utility classic: (right) *a mansize jeans jacket goes over almost anything;* (left) *daily denims, chambray shirt and inimitable 501s;* (below left) *cropped black denim, easy tee shirt and long black legs*

SURPRISE CLASSICS

Another key point to classic style is the surprise of taking a traditional shape into an unexpected material. It is the same principle as switching colour combinations. You expect to find the classic jeans shape made up in denim, instead you find jeans made in silk or soft leather. Or take a man's singlet, a perfect natural shape, thought of as underwear or sportswear in knitted cotton, but with the twist of a different fabric like a chunky cotton knit, cashmere, silk jersey or linen, it turns into an individual classic. The same applies with tee shirts. The pure shape of a round or V-neck tee shirt translates perfectly into fabrics other than knitted cotton. The round-neck golfer cardigan, which you expect to see in knitted wool, adapts naturally into flannel, gaberdine, velvet, tee shirting, suede, and so changes from knitwear into a jacket.

Accessories are vital extras that add originality to classics. If ten fashion-conscious girls were given identical basic clothes to wear, but freedom with the accessories, each one would look totally different from the next. Their choice of shoes, belts, bag, socks, tights, jewellery, the mix of colours and textures all have a critical effect on the final appearance. For instance, the accessory permutations with one fine-checked cotton shirt are almost endless. It can be worn buttoned to the neck and left plain or decorated with a brooch or polka dot scarf, or it can be worn unbuttoned with a necklace or cotton kerchief. The sleeves can be rolled up to show off a loose steel watch, or two polished wooden bangles, or rolled down with bright cufflinks and a striped armband. The pocket might be discreetly monogrammed or contain a lace or spotted hankie. Each accessory has a character that influences the image of the shirt.

Accessories have to look like natural extensions of the clothes, not last-minute afterthoughts. With each outfit there is a perfect balance to gauge between the clothes and the accessories. Because classic clothes are essentially so simple, the danger is to feel underdressed and pile on too much of everything else to compensate. The result is a muddle with accessories competing against each other; it is much more striking to focus on one area. If a necklace is bold, there is no need for a belt with a dramatic buckle, and dangling earrings. Creating a focal point with your accessories is a subtle way to emphasize a particular part of your clothes. Use earrings to play up a collar, bracelets or rings for pretty cuffs, a necklace for a décolletage, or a belt to accentuate the texture of a sweater. Accessories tend to get pigeonholed into day and evening wear; casual, neutral colours and materials for day, glitter and vibrant colour at night, but this limits the scope of classic clothes. Everything has to be interchangeable – you *can* put a thick leather belt round a flimsy chiffon dress, and diamanté earrings with a sweat shirt.

Belts are essential. A classic collection should include belts that are striking enough to be the focal point of a look – perhaps a black patent cummerbund, a wide buckled suede in a delicious colour, a studded cowboy belt with a tooled silver buckle – and belts that add an unobtrusive finish; simple stamped, smooth or plaited leather and suede in colours that work with all your clothes.

Scarves are such versatile accessories that they verge on being classed as clothes. Depending on the size and material, a scarf can be a winter shawl to wear instead of a coat (travel rugs also double as winter cloaks), it can be twisted into a bikini top, wrapped into a straight skirt or into a dress if sarong size. A scarf is an interesting way to add colour, introduce a pattern, or soften a severe neckline. It takes some experimenting in front of a mirror to tie a scarf that looks effortless. A silk square, unless large enough to drape nonchalantly round the shoulders, usually looks like a headscarf that has slipped from under the chin. Wool, cotton and lace scarves are easier to control than silk. Bright-coloured, checked and tartan mufflers or pastel cobweb mohair scarves can be twisted and knotted at the neck or in the hair. A large printed wool square folded into an oblong is an alternative to a knitted muffler. Plain, cotton squares add a surprise flash of summer colour, worn at the neck as a kerchief, or

Striking accessories add character to an appearance

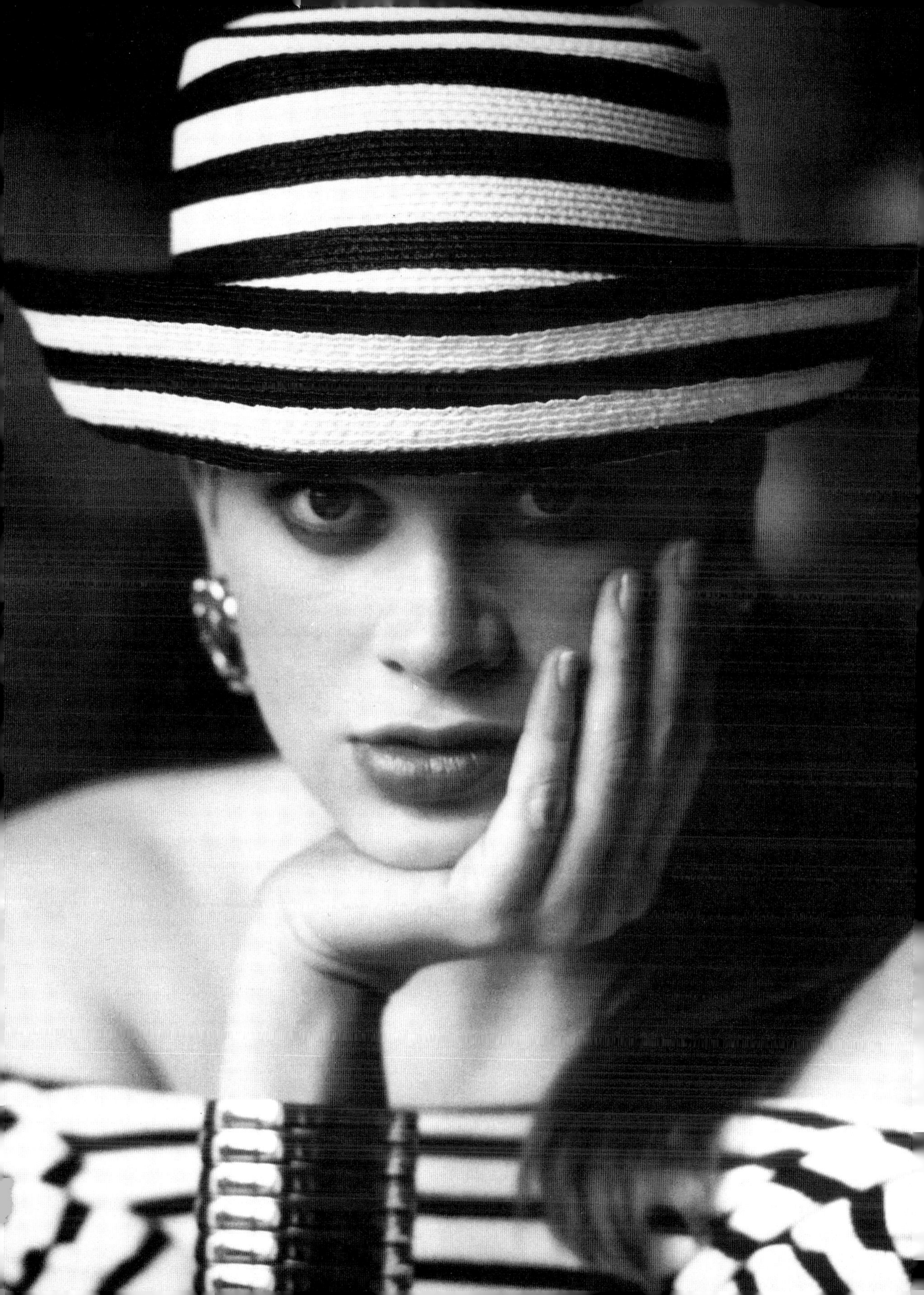

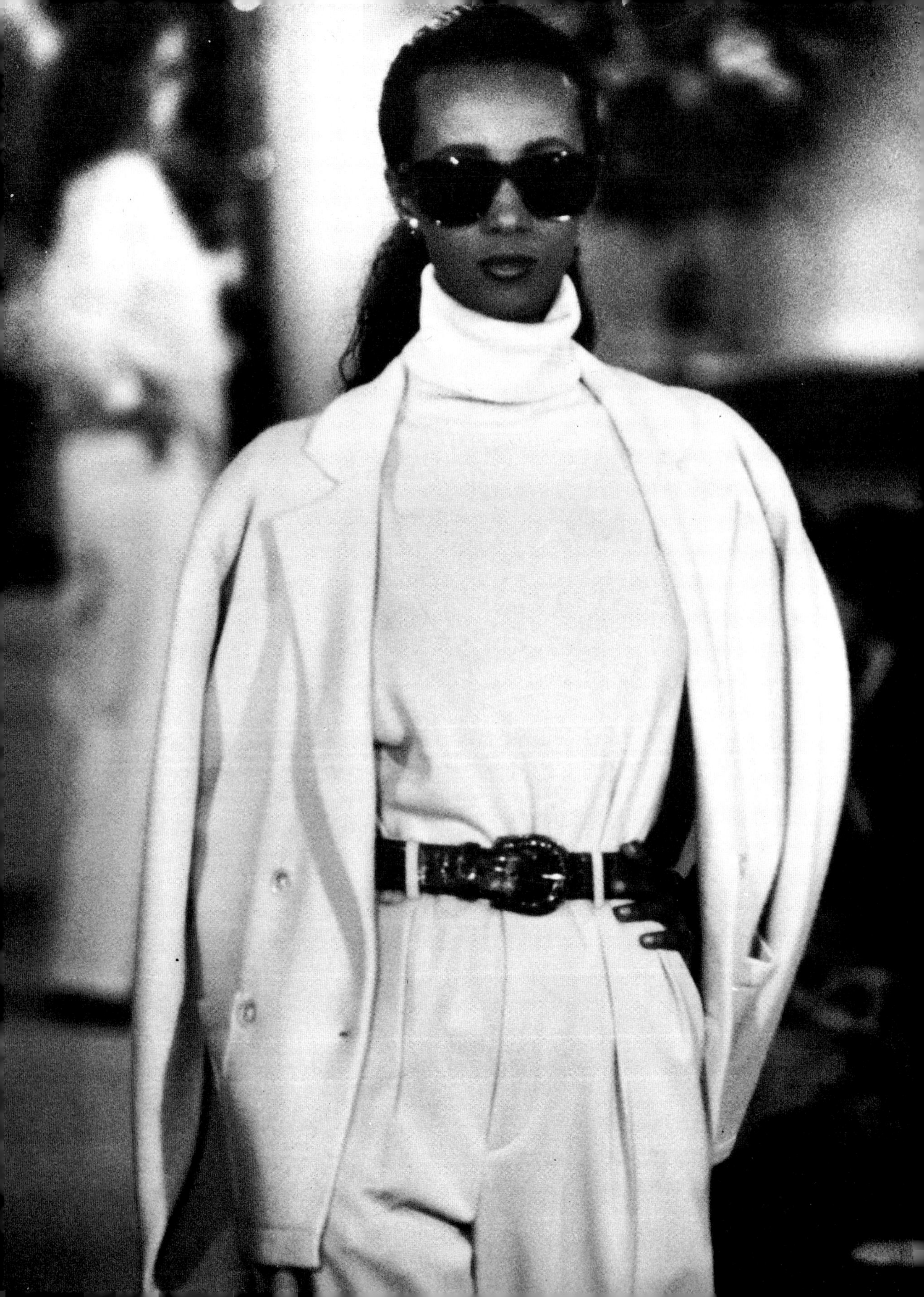

wound into a belt.

The idea of a classic **shoe** makes some people think of a sturdy lace-up brogue, or a Sloane Ranger slip-on trimmed with gold chains. But the classic definition applies to a shoe that is a perfectly simple design; a shape that is naturally flattering. Again the key is a lack of exaggeration or unnecessary detail; a heel that is not too unwearably high, spiky or wide; a toe that is neither too pointed nor square; straps that enhance the shape of the foot and line of the leg (thick ankle straps and elaborate lacing can make the legs look stumpy). From these guidelines, the most timeless shoe shapes are the court shoe, the low-heeled loafer, variations of the ballet slipper, lace-up walking shoes and the riding boot. Certain classics have inimitable style, like a Chanel-style correspondent in navy and white or taupe and beige.

When it comes to **jewellery**, there is a mental division that separates real and fake jewellery. There are no rules against mixing different kinds. Combinations of real, fake, ethnic or home-made beads, earrings, necklaces and rings, can look highly original – especially worn in surprise circumstances; ethnic silver with a twinset, and delicate pearls with a leather jacket. Fake jewellery is fine, providing it is not blatantly plastic. The best fakes are the kind that can be mistaken for the real thing: pearls, coral, turquoise, amber, lapis, jet, jade, silver, gold, copper, brass, or diamanté impersonating diamonds.

It takes confidence to wear a **hat** as an everyday accessory. But providing you feel comfortable, not self-conscious, hats do add individuality and wit to a classic wardrobe. The most important point is choosing one that suits and flatters your face, and one that is large enough. Whatever the style, it should fit generously over the crown of your head, not perch insecurely on top. Classic hats are investments that last for years, especially in natural straw, felt or fur. Timeless winter styles are variations on a man's bowler, a trilby, beret, cloche, toque or Davy Crockett fur with a tail. For summer, a deep-crowned sunhat with a wide straight brim is almost universally flattering, or consider a flat-topped boater or shallow cartwheel. To vary the line of a summer straw, a wide soft brim can be caught up at the front, back or side with a pearl hat pin. Feathers, silk or fresh flowers, tulle and veiling can all change the look of a hat to suit the clothes and occasion.

Your style of **sunglasses** makes a strong impact. Depending on the colour, density and shape, they can add a sense of glamour, mystery or fun to your appearance. As it makes sense to invest in good quality lenses, the frames should be a simple shape that flatters without overwhelming the shape of your face. Timeless classics are dark-lensed Raybans with black or dark brown frames, rounded tortoiseshell frames or gold-rimmed aviators.

Classic clothes are a perfect backdrop for strong accessories

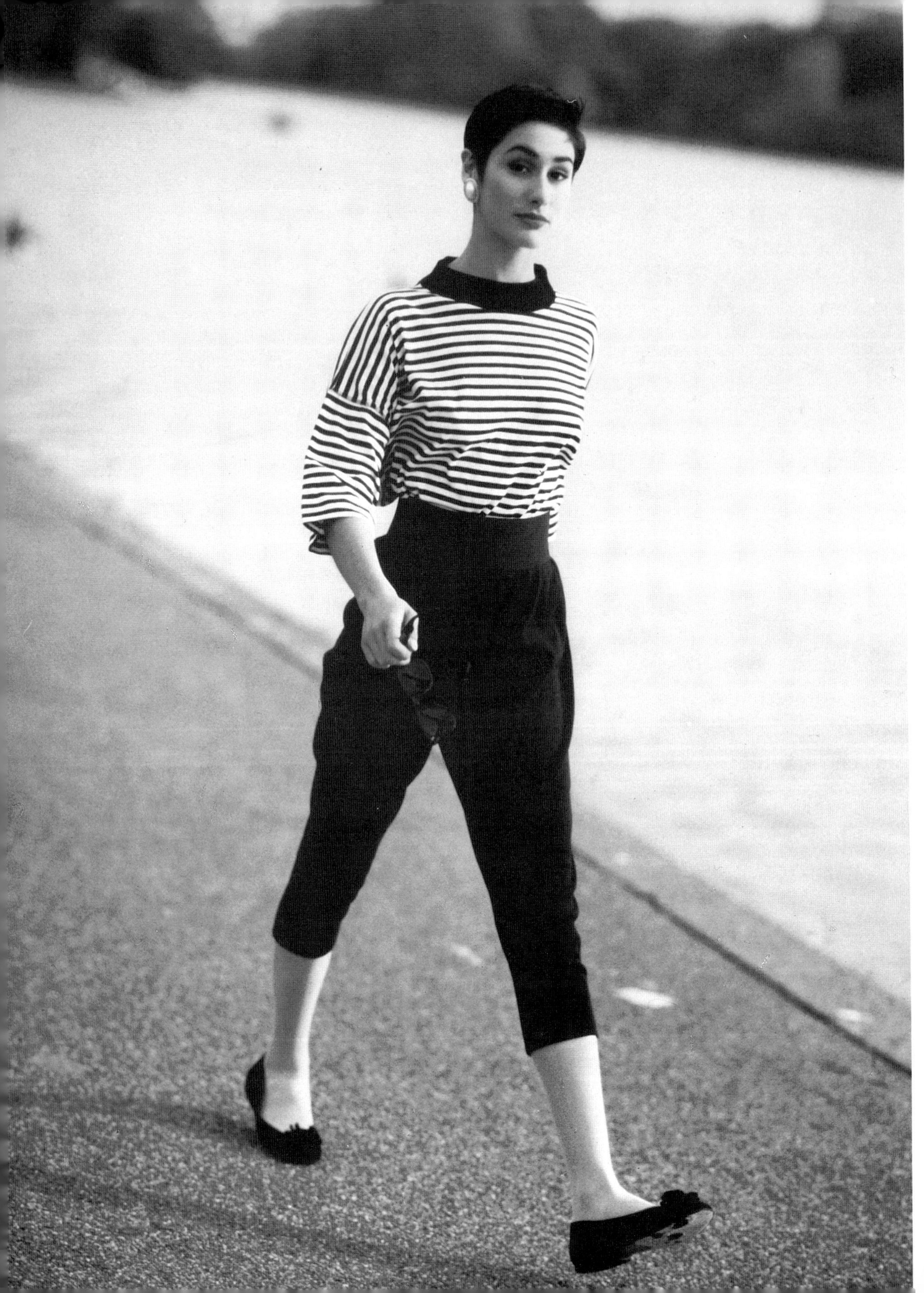

OUTSIDE INSPIRATIONS

Fashion reflects the spirit of the day like a barometer, darting capriciously from one mood to another. It is affected by catalysts at different levels. The economic atmosphere plays a large part, with gloomy times inspiring nostalgic and escapist cults. The media have a more direct influence; films, television programmes, styles of art and pop music trigger off new and revival fashions.

The reaction to fashion influences has changed enormously since Hollywood days, when movie star styles and faces were idolized. Clara Bow personified the twenties flapper girl; Greta Garbo was adored for her elusive elegance and glossy page-boy hair; Joan Crawford prompted the craze for crimson, bow-tie mouths and square-shouldered clothes; Marlene Dietrich was worshipped for her cool sophistication and her sensational legs; the Veronica Lake vamp hairstyle covering half the face became a wartime factory hazard; Hedy Lamarr spread a wave of jet black hair after her starring role in *Samson and Delilah* and Marilyn Monroe's voluptuous figure was a symbol of glamour and female perfection. Other film stars have promoted specific fashions: Rita Hayworth popularized mannish forties suits with broad shoulders, nipped-in waists and straight skirts; Esther Williams, the champion swimmer who appeared in the 1944 film *Bathing Beauties*, gave new impetus to beach fashions; Lana Turner, the original 'sweater girl', boosted forties knitwear, and the large-scale imports of Italian knitwear in the fifties were attributed by some to admiration of Gina Lollobrigida; Brigitte Bardot with her admired vital statistics and air of knowing innocence brought fame to blue denim, pink and white gingham and broderie anglaise; Audrey Hepburn provided the contrast to the sex kitten image and started the flat-chested gamine look in *Roman Holiday*, later echoed by Leslie Caron's French schoolgirl style in *Gigi*. The fashion explosion in the middle sixties was accelerated by Julie Christie as the full-lipped, mini-skirted model in the 1965 film *Darling*. Two years

Gamine glamour: stove pipes, ballet pumps and matelot stripes – in Audrey Hepburn mood

later, in *Bonnie and Clyde*, Faye Dunaway briefly reinstated the gangster beret and draped thirties knitwear. *Doctor Zhivago* prompted Russian-inspired fashions, and *Viva Maria*, helped by Brigitte Bardot and Jeanne Moreau, led to a brief Mexican-style revival of ruffles and flounces. *The Great Gatsby* brought back a feel for the twenties Jazz Age, with a sudden crop of Mia Farrow bobbed heads, slim wispy dresses with dropped waists and handkerchief hems, cloche hats and long beads.

Recent films have revived a nostalgia for colonial fashions – or an idealized, more glamorous version. Following the preoccupation with the Raj, underlined by *A Passage to India*, *Gandhi*, *Heat and Dust*, and *Jewel in the Crown*, Africa stepped into the limelight. Meryl Streep as Karen Blixen in *Out of Africa* brought back the perennial appeal of feminine safari dressing with her crisp white shirts, sweeping skirts and wide-brimmed hats. The elegant langour of thirties fashion was evoked by Kenya's Happy Valley set in *White Mischief*, and by Kristin Scott-Thomas as Evelyn Waugh's heroine in *A Handful of Dust*.

Musical films often influence fashion by triggering retrospective revivals. Nostalgia for the fifties and sixties are recycled by classic college movies, *American Graffiti* and *Grease*. *Absolute Beginners* looks back to the fifties, while *Hairspray* and *Shag* – complete with its own dance craze – remember the sixties. Each musical cult has its influence on fashion, inspiring clothes that reflect the music's identity. Some are transient phases, while others take root and surface at appropriate intervals. The punk movement is just as likely to be revived and made respectable, following in the wake of the reinstated hippy.

Nostalgia for the late sixties summer of love and its non-materialist values has inspired the children of the original flower power movement to re-establish a fashion for ethnic caftans, beads, afghan coats, thonged sandals, psychedelic colours and smiley badges. Hippy fashion is an escape from reality, in total contrast to eighties power dressing. But second time round it lacks the urgency of an anti-establishment cult, and is given credence by exalted designers like Christian Lacroix, Giorgio Armani and Romeo Gigli who have interpreted the ethnic influence into their collections.

The image that pop stars project can be strangely pervasive. Madonna became a cult figure whose raunchy appearance in provocative bustier, mini-skirt; skintight jeans, jangling earrings, crucifixes and bow-tied blonde mane was a catalyst for teenage look-alikes all over the world. Pop music has also created the androgynous look. First came cross-dressing; an ambiguous style of gender confusion, championed by idols Boy George and Marilyn who flaunted make-up, long hair and dresses. In reverse there was Annie Lennox who exchanged the pop star stereotype for a conventional man's suit and bleached hair, short back and sides.

Fashion influences: (top row) *Greta Garbo, Joan Crawford,* (middle row) *Marilyn Monroe, Brigitte Bardot,* (bottom row) *Madonna, The Princess of Wales*

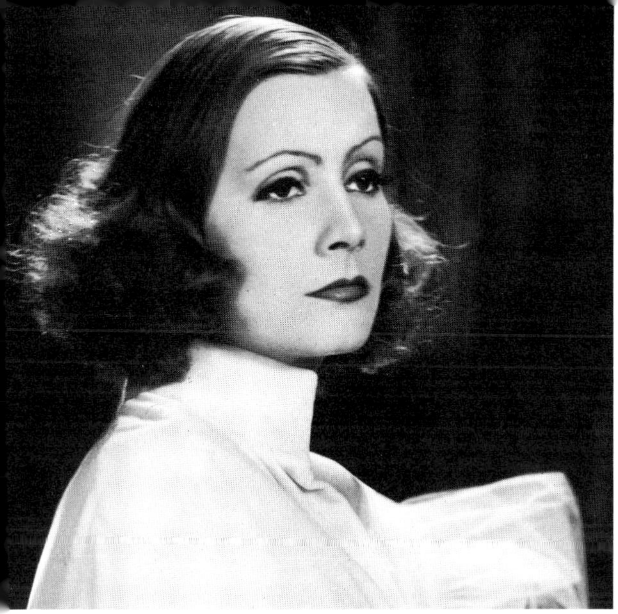
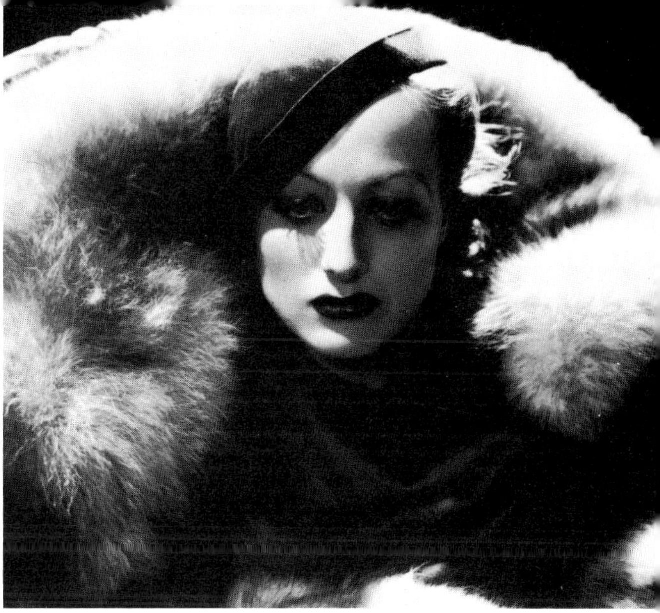
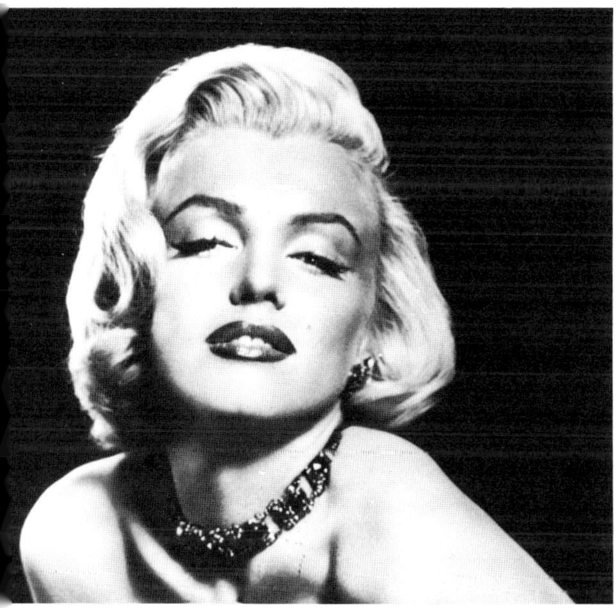
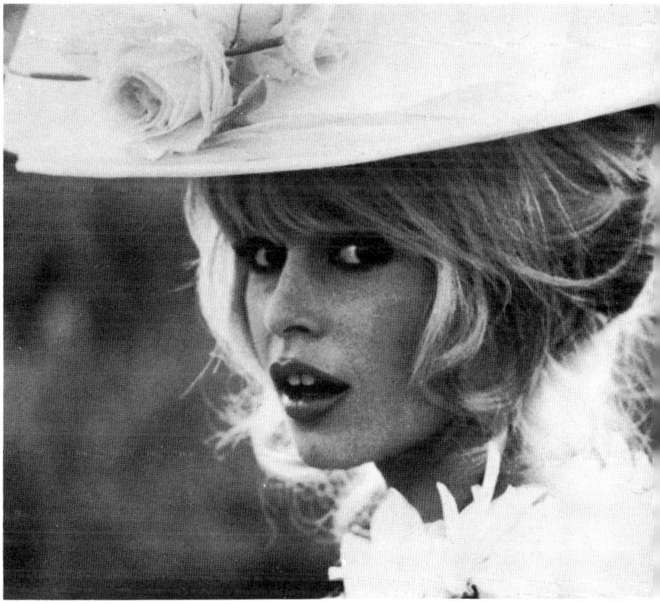
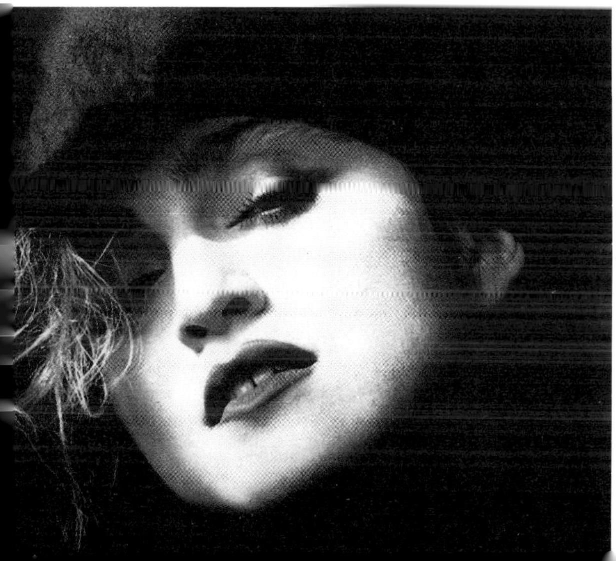
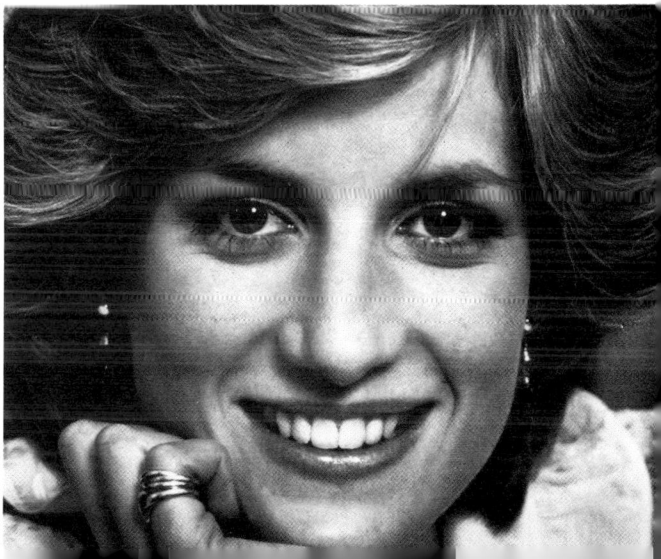

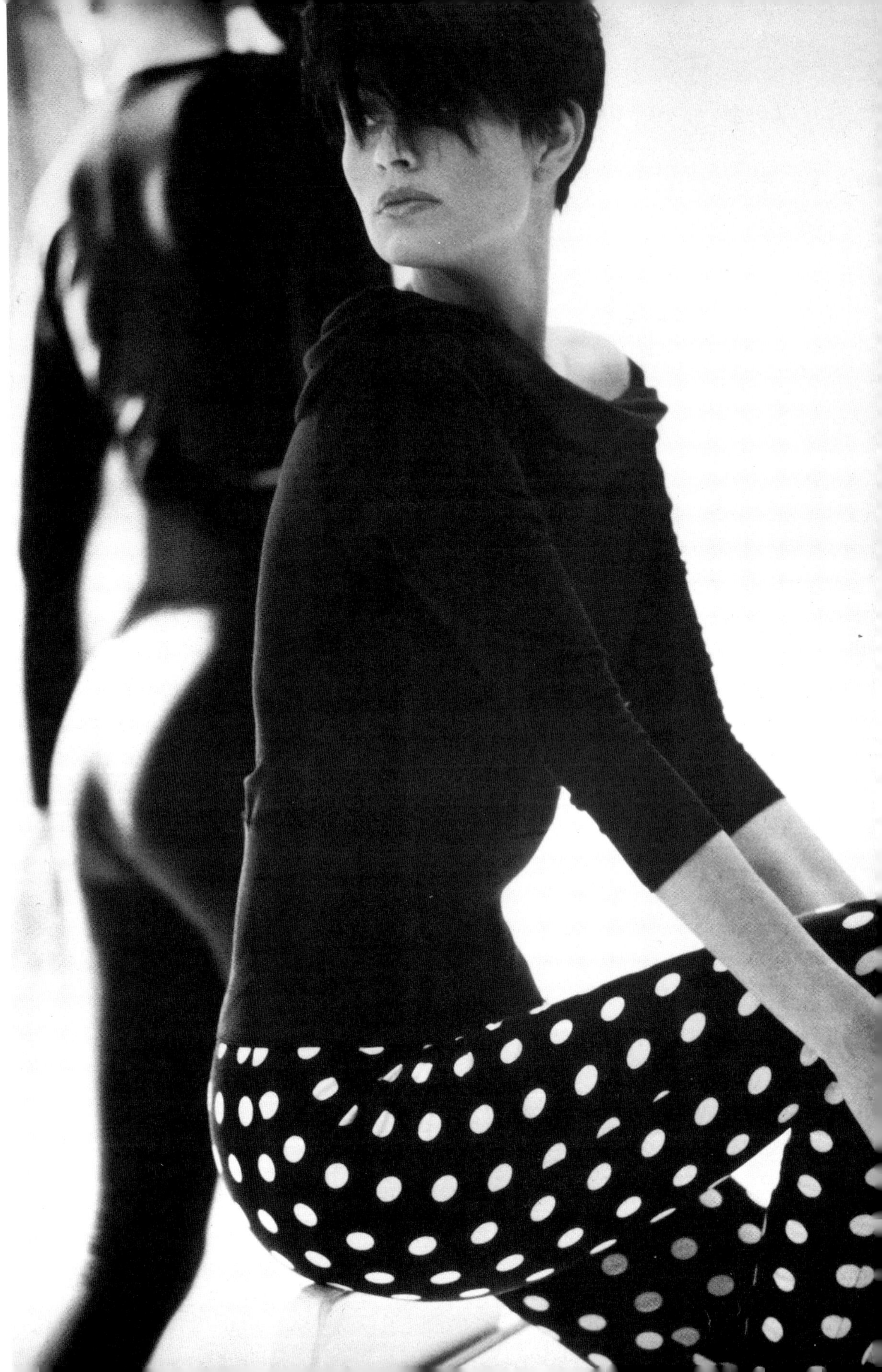

Outside Inspirations 73

Now, in the late eighties, such extremes have calmed down into an accessible low key appearance that stays clear of any outrageous statement, conforming to leather jacket, jeans, white tee shirt and Doc Martens, as worn by heroes Bruce Springsteen and George Michael.

The change in direction in the eighties towards a more groomed elegant appearance has been accelerated by a fascination for the younger royals. The most obvious fashion influence is the Princess of Wales, whose image from hairstyle, tuxedo, spotted socks to flat shoes has been copied by a devoted public and mass manufacturers throughout the decade. Proving it possible to appear ladylike without looking

(left) *High energy dressing: fitness clothes are an integral part of fashion*

(right) *New Wave hippy with bell bottoms, ankle boots and hoop earrings*

dowdy, the younger royals have reinstated the finishing touches of hats, gloves, bags and extravagant jewellery. It may have been Karl Lagerfeld who relaunched Chanel's hair bow, but it was the Duchess of York who spread nationwide bow fever across shoes, hats, tights, earrings, gloves and hair accessories.

At the opposite end of the spectrum lies the influence of street fashion – the initially subversive clothes that gravitate from street to designer status. The seeds of cult style have sprung regularly during the seventies and eighties from Vivienne Westwood's fashion mecca in the Kings Road. Her shop with its changing name and content has housed some legendary fashion extremes. At first sight many have appeared outrageously out of step, but proved to be innovations ahead of their time. The original shop, 'Let it Rock' opened in 1971, selling Teddy Boy clothes. In 1972 it was 'Too Fast to Live Too Young to Die', and sold rockers' biking leathers; in 1974 it was 'Sex', and full of rubber and leather pre-punk uniform; in 1977 it became the official punk H.Q. Seditionaries. Since 1980 the shop has been 'World's End', pioneering collections of Errol Flynn piracy, savages, Buffalo girls, Hobos, mini crinis and not-so-traditional Miss Marple tweeds, fashioned like armour.

The body-conscious shape of mainstream fashion reflects our preoccupation with health and fitness. As exercise in various guises – aerobics, gymnastics, dance, swimming – becomes an integrated way of life, the feeling for sleek second-skin clothes increases. The simple shape of exercise, swim and dance wear have become recurrent pieces in influential collections from Azzedine Alaia, Romeo Gigli, Giorgio di Sant Angelo, Jean Paul Gaultier and Donna Karan. Their innovative, well-timed focus on wrap tops, bodies, tube skirts, leotards, leggings and bicycling shorts has percolated through to high street fashion. Stretch is the key property of these clothes. Combining lycra or spandex with cotton, jersey, wool, silk and gaberdine creates a fabric that moulds the female body without disguise; a style of dressing that is liberating, yet revealing, in tune with the quest for comfortable, flexible clothes.

The stretch properties enhance and support the curves of a full, well rounded body that no longer needs to be boyish or rake thin. Day wear is exercise based, with essential black jersey leggings, high waisted lycra skirts, bodies, cropped vests, wrapovers and polo necks in black, neutrals and an occasional stripe. Evening style combines shine with stretch in the shape of sequinned vest dresses, lace skirts, satin bustiers and thonged minis baring glimpses of well-toned thigh.

Body dressing marks a reaction against the aggressive contours of Dynasty-style shoulder pads that distort the natural female line. It was also the perfect antidote to enveloping Japanese fashions of the early eighties that shrouded the figure in baggy monochrome layers.

An Oriental influence inspires rich embroidery and texture, especially at night

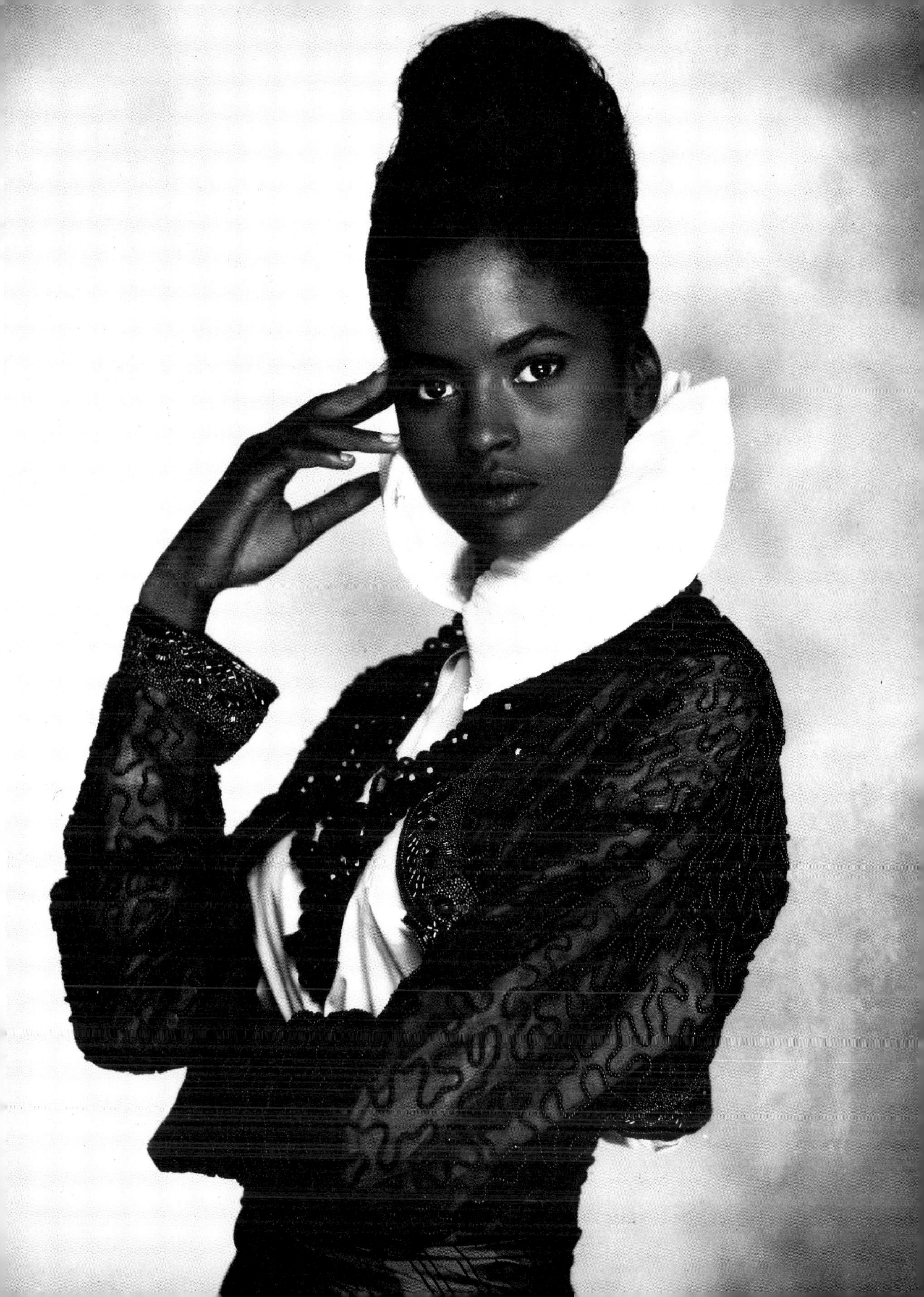

Black lace mantilla and bows: in Latin American mood

(far right) Gilding the ethnic tradition with crushed velvet, sequins and beads from Christian Lacroix (top), *Romeo Gigli* (centre), *Martine Sitbon* (below)

FASHION ROOTS

While these cults have a varied and transient effect on fashion, the inspiration that comes from national dress is constant. Many of the shapes, patterns and colour mixes that recur are based on the traditional designs of different national costumes. The styles survive the passing of time because they are deeply rooted in the origins of their country, based on timelessly simple and practical shapes and made from naturally available materials, coloured and patterned to reflect the environment. National costume is a rich source of fashion in its purest sense. Taken too literally it becomes fancy dress – no one needs to dress up as a bona fide Hungarian folk dancer, or an Indian squaw in full war paint – but there is a wealth of tradition that can be borrowed and translated into contemporary fashion.

Too often, designers have to take the lead and show a Russian- or Oriental-inspired collection before anyone is brave enough to experiment with or see the potential in any authentic clothes they may be hoarding – the ethnic souvenirs you buy and wear on holiday that feel out of place back home. Ingenious designers cast new light on national costume by

Outside Inspirations

giving it modern treatment. They juggle the pieces unexpectedly; adjust the proportions slightly, add some contemporary details, rethink the colours, yet retain the hallmarks that give it a definitely Mexican, Chinese, jungle, or wherever look. When the clothes of a particular nationality come into fashion, there is an inevitable epidemic of ethnic imitations in the shops. These mass-produced versions (unless they spring from the country of origin) often lack the charm of the genuine article because the traits that characterize the style are scaled down for commercial success. Obviously the actual designer clothes that spark off each ethnic look are desirable because they are originals in their own right. After all, who would say no to a genuine Kenzo peasant dress, or Saint Laurent matador? But the authentic thing, besides being much cheaper than a designer label, does have winning qualities. It is the look in its purest form, without the fickle lifespan of anything stamped by fashion.

Historical and contemporary dress from the Orient has had an enormous influence on fashion. The perfect simple shapes, the rich colours and traditional prints, the sumptuous embroideries and materials tempt designers to take their inspiration from the East. Collections with a Chinese or Japanese feeling invariably reflect the native cultures: Chinese dragon prints; Ming porcelain colours; lotus blossom designs that contrast with swashbuckling Samurai warror styles. The kimono influences the cut of contemporary coats, jackets, cardigans, blouses and dresses. Its soft, unconstructed lines epitomize the freedom that belongs with the most wearable modern fashion; an easy wrap instead of zips or buttons. An obi sash, the traditional kimono belt, reappears as a key accessory in Oriental collections.

Other characteristic shapes are the mandarin jacket: slim, single breasted with a small stand-up 'Mao' collar; the cheongsam, a narrow, asymmetrically fastened tunic, often worn over wide-legged drawstring silk or cotton coolie pants. Quilted and padded clothes come from the Orient, and have been interpreted to form a permanent and practical side of fashion.

Besides the inspiration from the basic shapes and textures of Asia, the genuine articles are definitely worth investigating. Shops with Oriental stock are full of surprisingly inexpensive finds. Look out for embroidered silk or cotton pyjamas, smart enough to wear in the evening with beaded velvet Chinese slippers, or fine silk embroidered petticoats to wear as sundresses. Cotton kimonos make useful dressing gowns, but they also adapt into summer wrap dresses or beach robes.

Another Eastern influence on fashion is the recurrent feeling for peasant clothes that stems from regions like Mongolia, Tibet and South America. They inspire cold weather clothes in layers of mixed patterns and textures: sheepskins, alpaca, blanket shawls, woollen dirndl or tiered long skirts, homespun knits, flat suede or leather boots, thick ribbed leggings, headsquares under bowlers and Davy Crockett hats, all in a random jumble of vivid stripes, paisleys, florals, plaids and checks, coloured with the richness of a brilliant tapestry. Peru is a great source of peasant knitwear, renowned for the distinctive Inca sweaters in garish green, pink, yellow, turquoise combinations, decorated with stripes and paperchain cut-outs; and the more sombre brown and cream alpaca knits patterned with primitive Aztec and animal motifs. The appeal of these sweaters is the texture and colouring which is not easy to imitate. Machine versions tend to be wishy-washy and too uniformly designed.

The influence from India is revived regularly, inspiring designers to produce ethnic collections of sarong skirts, sari tops, dhoti pants, Nehru jackets and coolie trousers. Bypass the Western-priced designer versions for Indian originals, keeping to well-made separates in pure cotton or silk. Choose simple shapes that enhance the characteristic embroidery and crinkled texture of the fabrics. Traditional Indian colours reflect their origins; hot spicy shades of cinnamon, saffron and paprika woven into Madras checks and batiks, some threaded with bronze glints. Indian silk dyes to vivid shades of turquoise, magenta and emerald which shine beautifully at night. Indian classics can be worn together for a thoroughly ethnic look, or diluted with simple shirts, knitwear or jeans. Key pieces are embroidered muslin skirts (to wear in

Hints of hippydom with shaggy coats, ethnic beads and flowers at Romeo Gigli (left), Rifat Ozbek (centre), Armani (right)

Tribal style, black on white: muslin bandolier, turban and cuffed ethnic silver

The Fair Isle tradition (opposite) *handknits in soft Scottish colours*

(Next spread, right) *Folkloric knitting in exuberant colour and pattern*

(Next spread, left) *Russia's peasant colours – one Saint Laurent blouse among the ethnic brilliance*

Nordic knitting: woolly reindeers and snowflakes at Kenzo

layers or below a shorter beaded skirt), drawstring cotton smocks, shirts, afghan waistcoats and zouave trousers – cut like draped bloomers falling in dhoti-style folds to the knee or mid-calf. They look best with a wide belt to define the waistline, a soft shirt or sweater, bare legs and flat sandals. Indian history has left its mark on two recurrent fashion shapes. Jodhpurs are named after the state of Jodhpur; the Nehru jacket and hat are a legacy from the first post-Independence prime minister Nehru. Indian silk scarves make versatile accessories to drape over shoulders, twist into belts, turbans or bandeau tops. When saris are unravelled they stretch for yards, but a child-sized one could be worn as an exotic evening wrap, or as a bandolier sash secured on the hip with an ethnic brooch.

Some of the crispest cottons come from Mexico. Their starchiness inspires voluminous skirts, dresses, puff-sleeve blouses, nightdresses, wedding dresses, with rows of fine pintucking, lace panels and ruffles. In white, the clothes are the nearest contemporary fashion to antique white lace, but in the characteristic stark black, scarlet, turquoise and magenta, they are strongly Mexican and can be just as dramatic.

The Spanish matador tradition inspires a strong seductive look, characterized by schemes of black and scarlet. Hallmarks are cropped bolero jackets embellished with frogging, embroidery or beading; full flamenco skirts with wide corset waistbands, gathered over black lace petticoats, or cut straighter with asymmetric flounces; gold hoop earrings and black sombreros. The gipsy look is related, but less tailored. Its more bohemian mix of colour and pattern is distinguished by off-the-shoulder blouses, laced belts, tiered floral skirts, fringed shawls and a headsquare knotted under long Romany curls.

Ethnic knitwear is a constant influence on fashion. The Nordic theme inspires chunky sweaters dotted with snowflakes, reindeer and Arctic variations. The traditional colouring is navy and white, but some of the most original adaptations come in iced pastels. The influence from Irish knits is in the texture – knubbly mixes of blackberry and diamond shapes in thick, creamy wool which translate perfectly into short, cotton knits in every colour. Fair Isle patterns are the most classic ethnic knit, and as a result are probably the most copied on a commercial scale. Because it is such a traditional style, even the mass-produced Fair Isles have a certain appeal, but they seldom have the old-fashioned blend of muted colours that distinguishes a genuine Scottish Fair Isle from the copies. Nostalgia for traditional sweaters has revived the knitted-by-Granny look, particularly anything reminiscent of a thirties or forties handknit. Unless you have an industrious granny, these handknits are prohibitively expensive because each one is unique. The cheapest answer is to invest in a sleeveless sweater which works over everything, or on its own, day and night. If you are a knitter, look out for back copies of women's

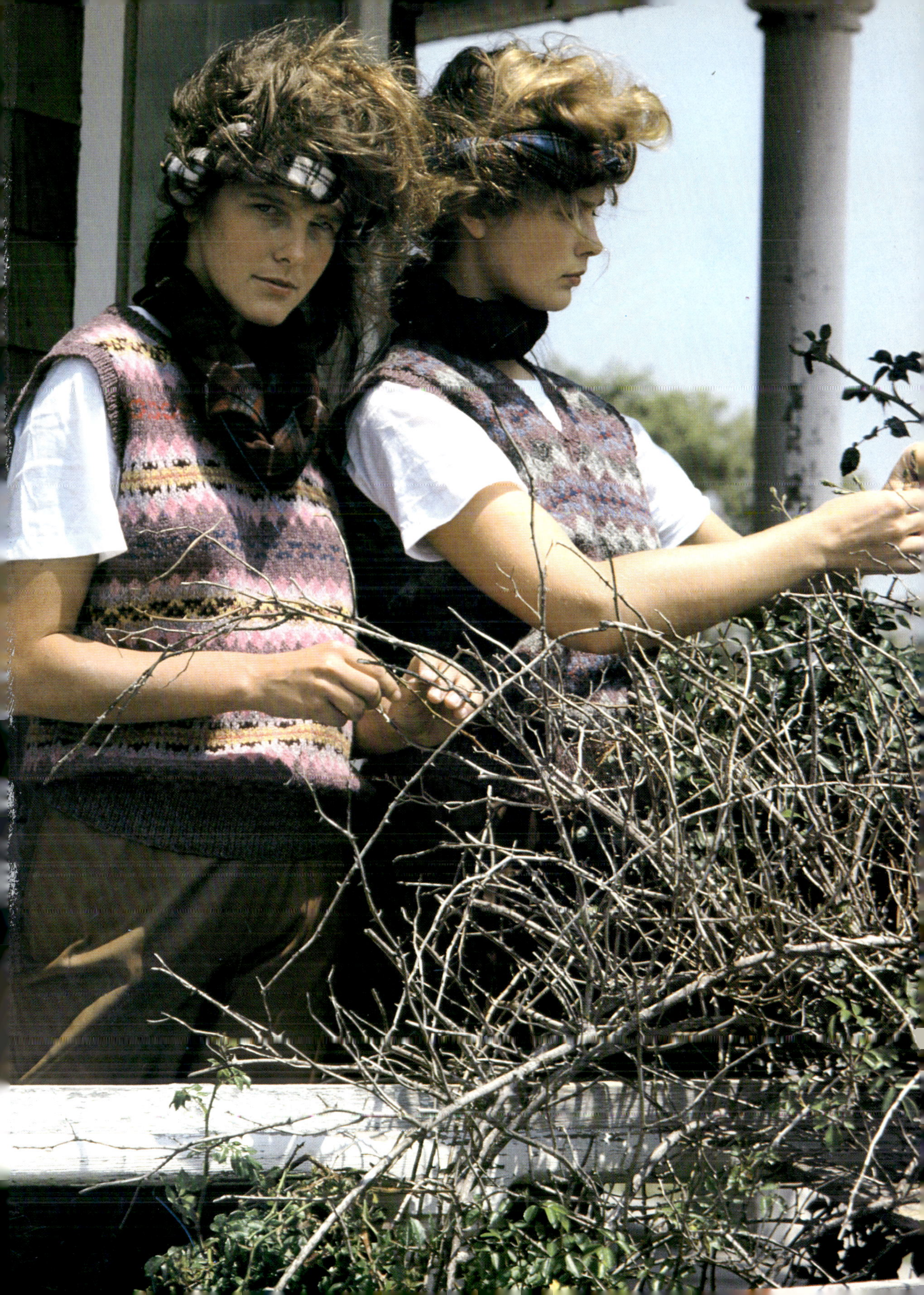

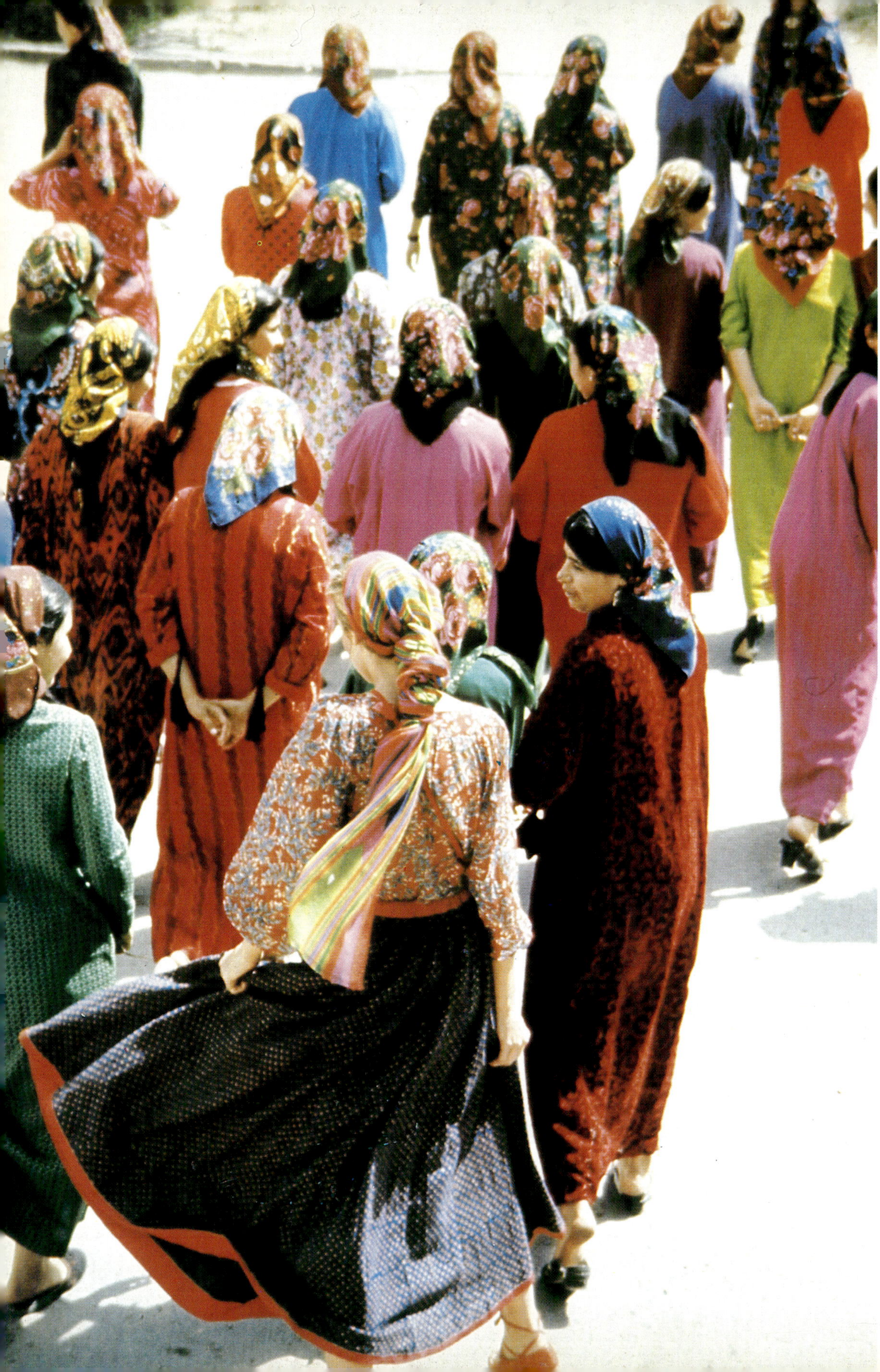

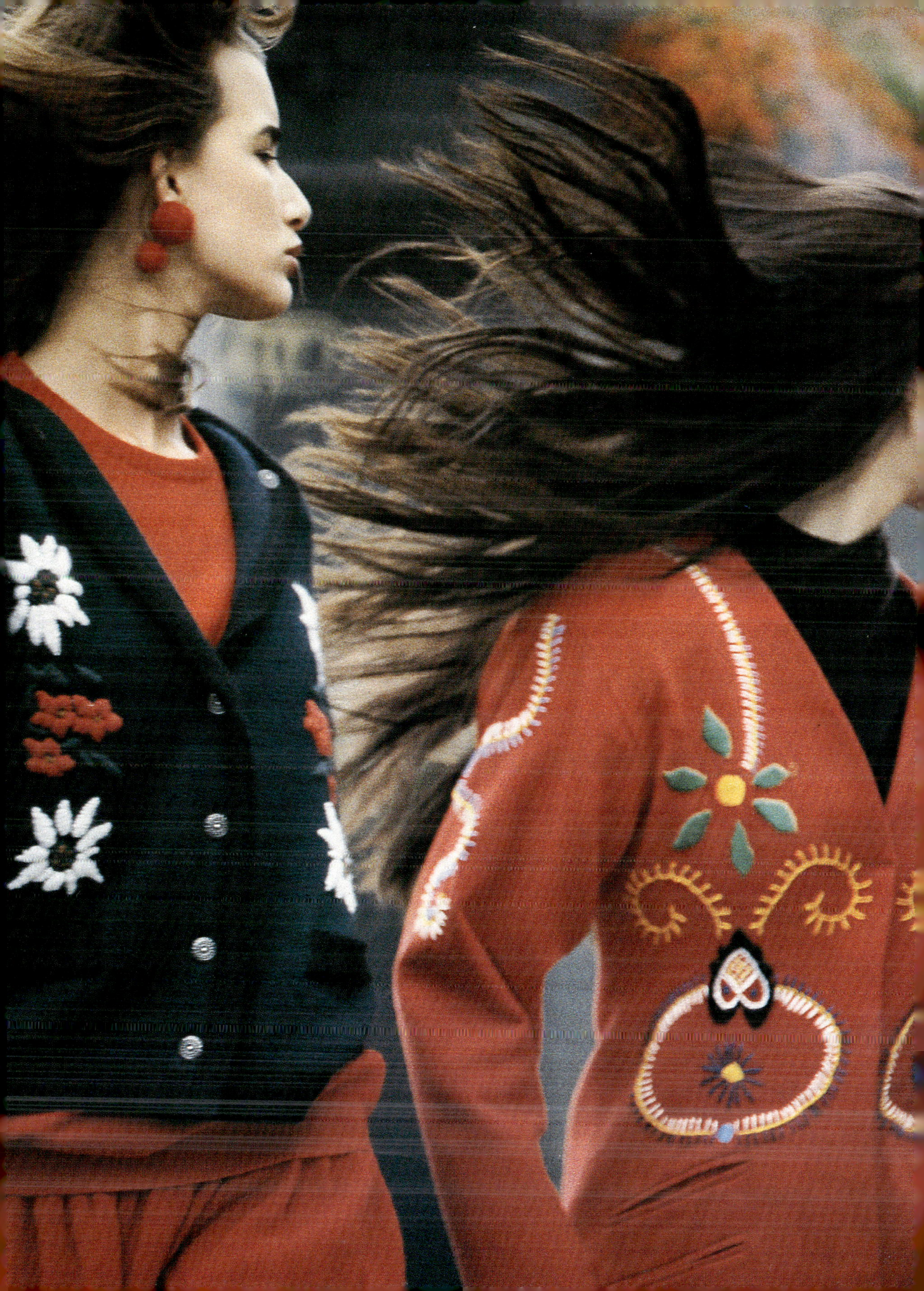

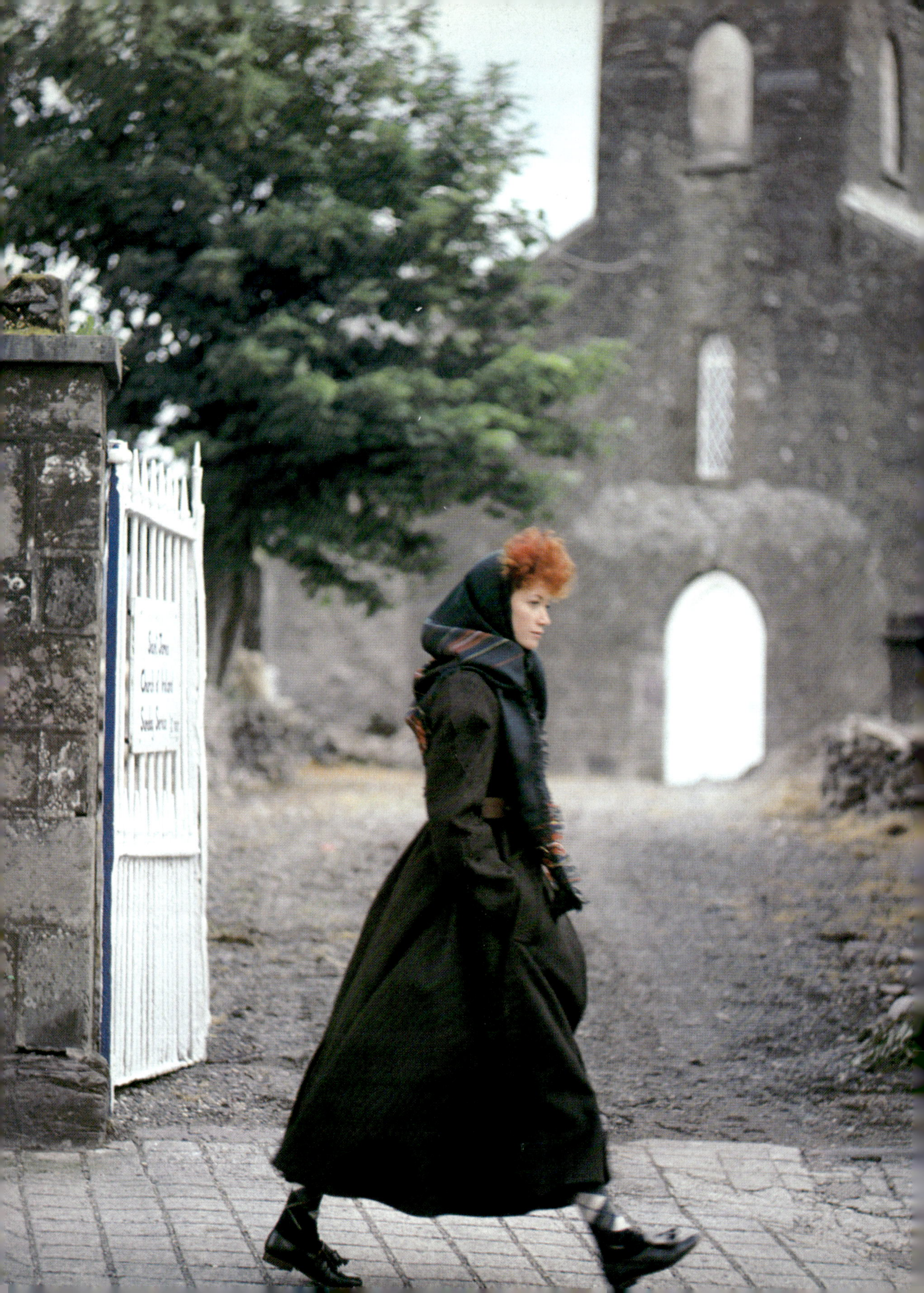

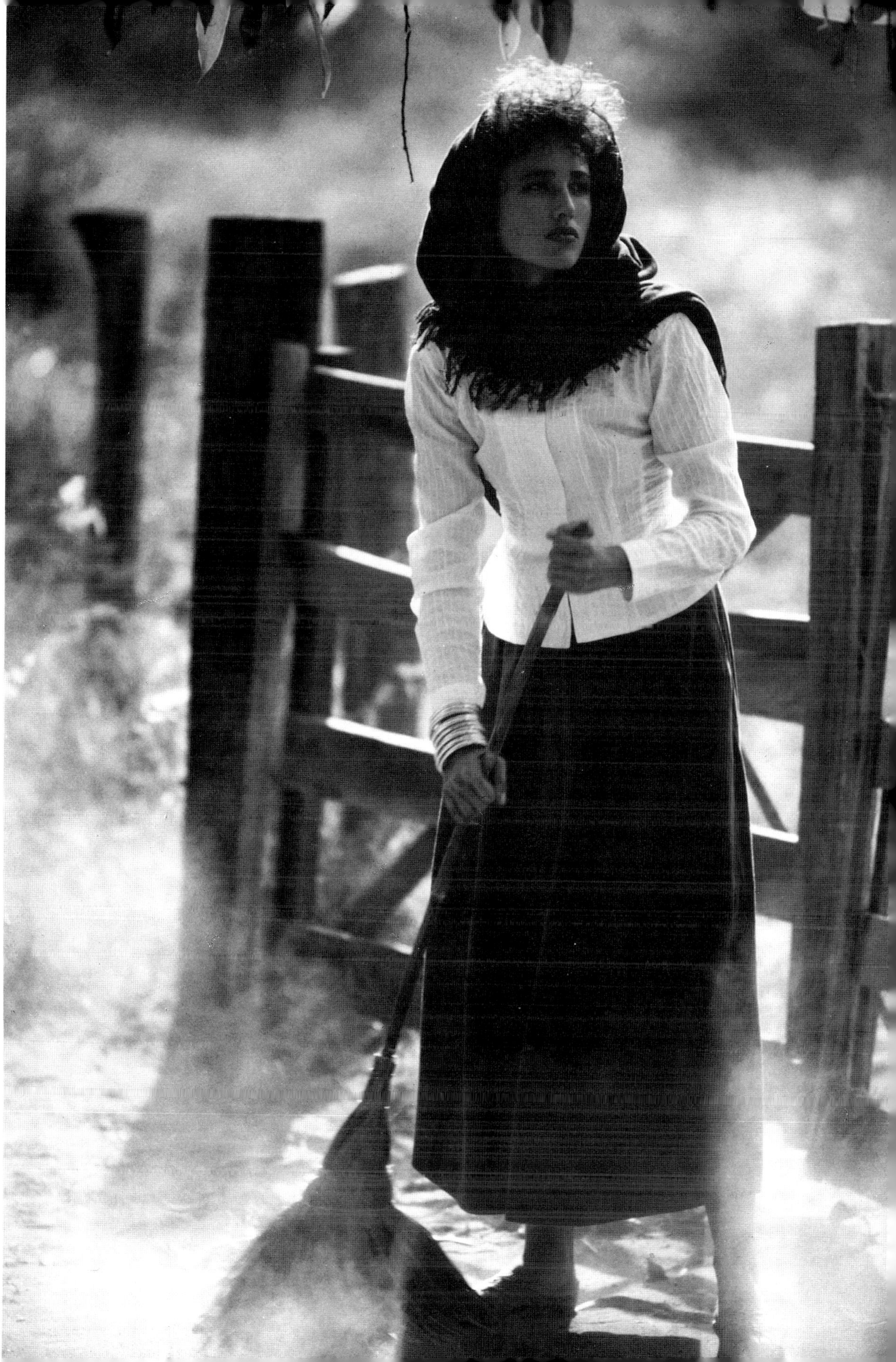

magazines. Amongst the recipes and romances you may come across some covetable contemporary-looking forties-style knitting patterns.

The kilt must be one of the most fashion-orientated pieces of national dress. It never goes out of fashion, but comes into its element when designers produce collections with a Highland theme – accompanied by a rush of tartan and plaid shawls, sashes, mufflers, tam o'shanters and white, high-neck frilly blouses. It is a look to take up in moderation, as a surfeit of sashes and sporrans looks like a Highland reeler in full rig. Scottish dressing requires individuality. A genuine kilt is a wonderful classic, but needs relaxing with non-Scottish, feminine coloured knit-wear and informally ruffled shirts. Kilts can look original worn above the knee with bright coloured thick tights and flat loafers. It is difficult and almost criminal to cut off a hem, so it is worth investigating children's departments for junior sizes in short lengths.

The folkloric influence is another inspiration; loosely based around fairy tales and children's book pictures of Hansel and Gretel characters in immaculate Tyrolean walking outfits. Lederhosen and braces apart, the fashion pointers are embroidered, white cotton drawstring blouses, appliquéd boleros, circular felt skirts with decorated borders, feathered Tyrolean hats, and cropped, forest green or scarlet jackets edged with braid and silver buttons.

The Russian influence is also based on folklore and the arts. Russian peasant fashions are reminiscent of the traditional wooden mama dolls, painted with brilliant flowery headscarves and multi-striped skirts, petticoats and long aprons. The voluminous cossack style stems from Tolstoy heroines. Anna Karenina silhouettes of dramatic black cloaks, braided, fitted velvet coats with swirling skirts, over high-buttoned lace blouses, with fur toque hats, deep fur muffs, cossack boots – all reflecting the romantic wintry associations of Russia. Colours are usually rich and sombre; mainly black, wine, bottle green and dark navy in a sweeping mix of fur, thick wool, velvet, brocade and lace. The Oriental costumes of Diaghilev's Ballet Russe still inspire modern fashion. The Arabian Nights theme of *Scheherezade*, the most visually exotic ballet, is a literally fantastic source of rich colours, textures and patterns. It recalls sumptuous fabrics, billowing shapes of harem pants, draped sparkling turbans, embroidered, bejewelled jackets, in a brilliant spectrum of gold, emerald, cobalt blue, turquoise, flame and silver.

An equally extravagant mood springs from the Baroque influence; a cross pollination of gilded, jewel encrusted evening wear inspired by ecclesiastical pomp, the Renaissance, Ottoman Empire and Baroque architecture. Although revived by Paris Couture – at Saint Laurent, Lagerfeld and Lacroix – its opulence can be copied on a cheaper scale. The silhouette is theatrical with hooded cloaks and doublet jackets;

Folklore style (previous spread left) *Fendi's full-skirted coat with Highland wrap and Argyll leggings*

(previous spread, right) *Low profile Mexicana: for rustic summer style*

(opposite) *Kenzo's Cossack style in sweeping brown leathers*

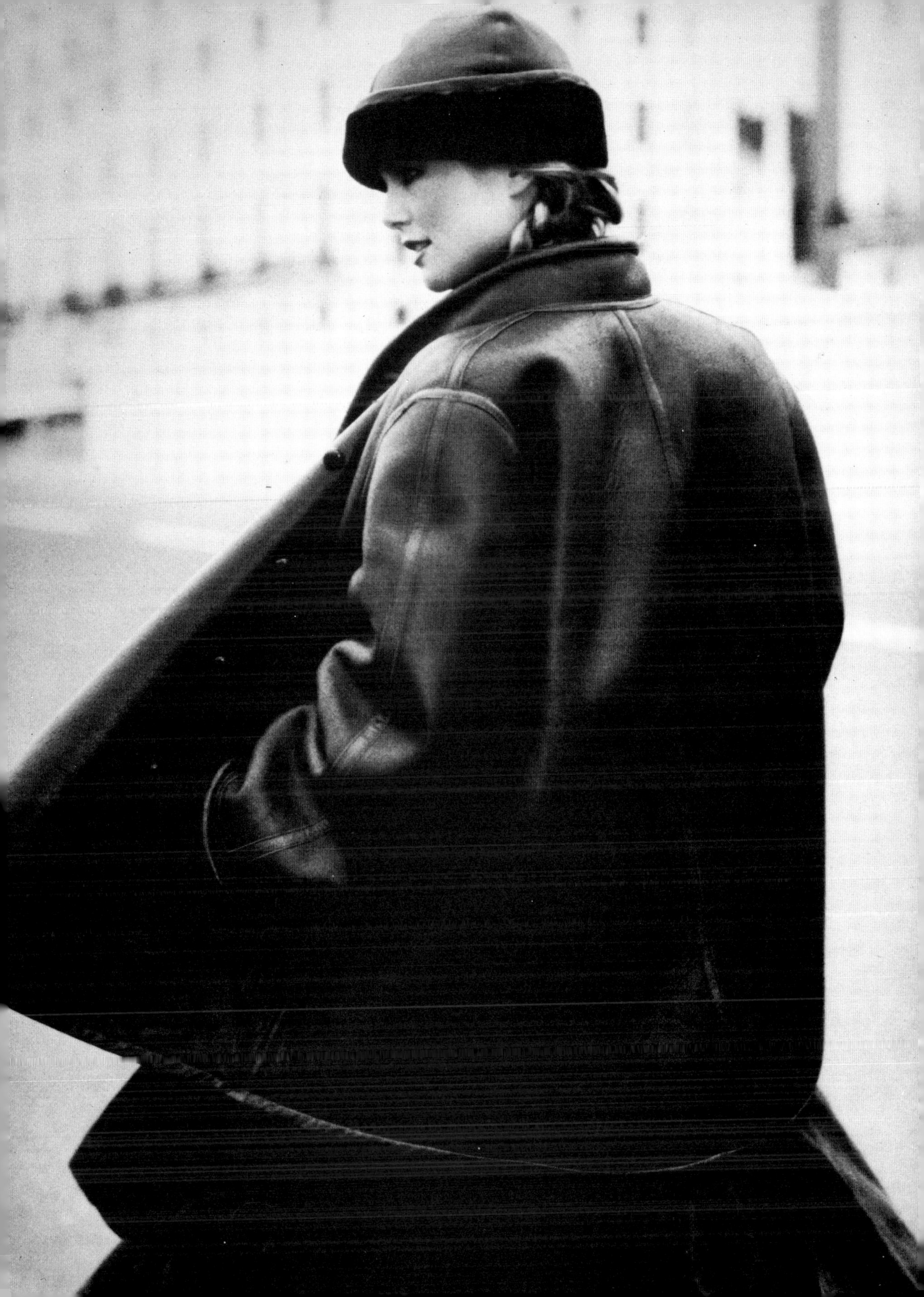

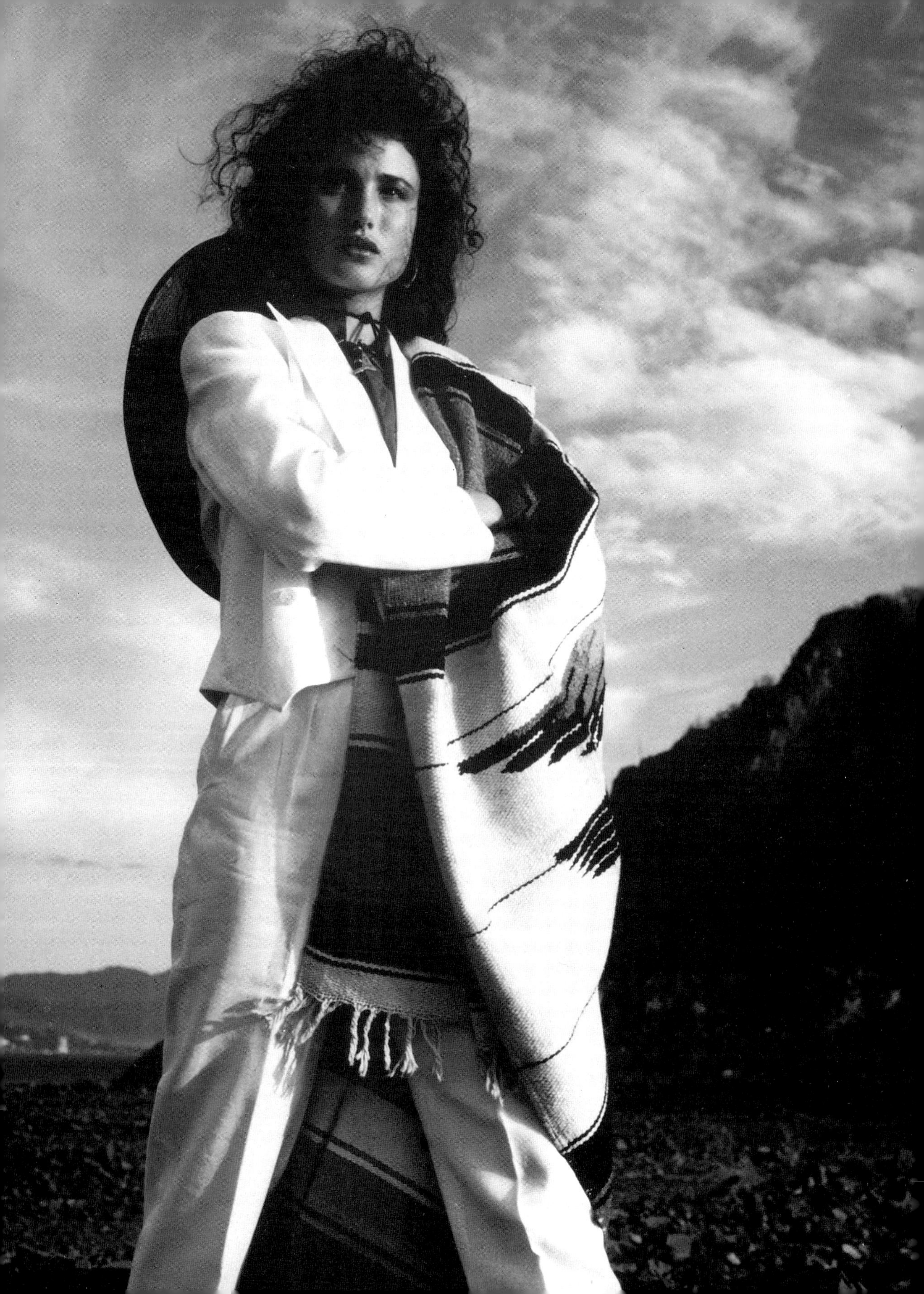

fabrics are velvet, brocade, satin, fringing and embroidery in black, gold, purple and scarlet. Key accessories are rhinestone studded crucifixes, drop earrings, jewelled slippers, gold chains and Baroque pearl brooches.

The jungle look, influenced by dreams of tropical paradise and Crusoe-ish desert islands is a recurrent theme for hot weather dressing, inspiring scanty, mostly cotton clothes, decorated with exotic wild life, birds of paradise, palm trees, tropical fruit, sun, sea, animal markings and tribal prints. Jungle fashion divides into tarzan or white hunter style. The minimal tarzan look is for tanned bodies in high summer or holiday mood. Brief bikinis, swimsuits, one shoulder tops, vest and the essential sarong come in hot coloured cottons. Authentic kangas or kikoies from Indonesia or Africa are most coveted, but a large rectangle can improvise as sundress, skirt, scarf, belt or sunbathing mat. The white hunter look is suitable for cooler climates. Key points are safari, knee-length shorts, a crisp cotton shirt, a very simple safari jacket and white hunter's hat with a mosquito net veil, all in neutral desert tones of sand, buff, khaki, white and eau de nil. Jewellery should be bold and primitively shaped: handmade necklaces, chokers, worry beads, wide carved bangles and earrings made from natural resources like wood, shell, bone or sharks' teeth. The best jungle belts are in tough brown leather, webbing, stretch canvas, or cotton. Footwear should be flat and practical: thonged leather sandals, white gymshoes or plimsolls.

Cowboy clothes are more than an influence, they belong as a part of fashion – practical, knockabout, sexy clothes that look just as good on urban cowgirls as they do back West. The main ingredients are well-worn, straight-leg jeans, mansize wool or cotton check shirts, silver-buckled, tooled leather cowboy belts, cuban-heeled cowboy boots to go under, not over, the jeans. Optional extras: a denim jean jacket, classic sheepskin coat or waistcoat, a jeans skirt, preferably mini, a genuine or toyshop stetson, red and white spotty handkerchiefs to fold into triangular kerchiefs, silver buffalo 'bolo' ties, leather bootlaces to tie in the hair or keep up the sleeves of an eagle-printed shirt. If the whole Western look seems too overpowering, the trick is to soften the cowboy clothes with some surprise feminine touches. Substitute the check shirt for an embroidered silk one, or a pastel Shetland; wear a lace scarf instead of the kerchief; swop regulation cowboy boots for a bright red pair.

The Red Indian tradition has also inspired fashion. Cowboys and Indians are often grouped together, and the influence that should be attributed to Red Indians is often referred to as part of the Western style. The Indian look is characterized by Hiawatha-style headbands, fringed shirts, tunics, trousers and skirts in pale chamois. The accessories are distinctively Indian, especially the silver and turquoise Navajo jewellery, the finely beaded belts and white leather moccasins.

Frontier fashion: crossing Spanish and prairie tradition in linen bolero jacket, matador straw and Navajo blanket

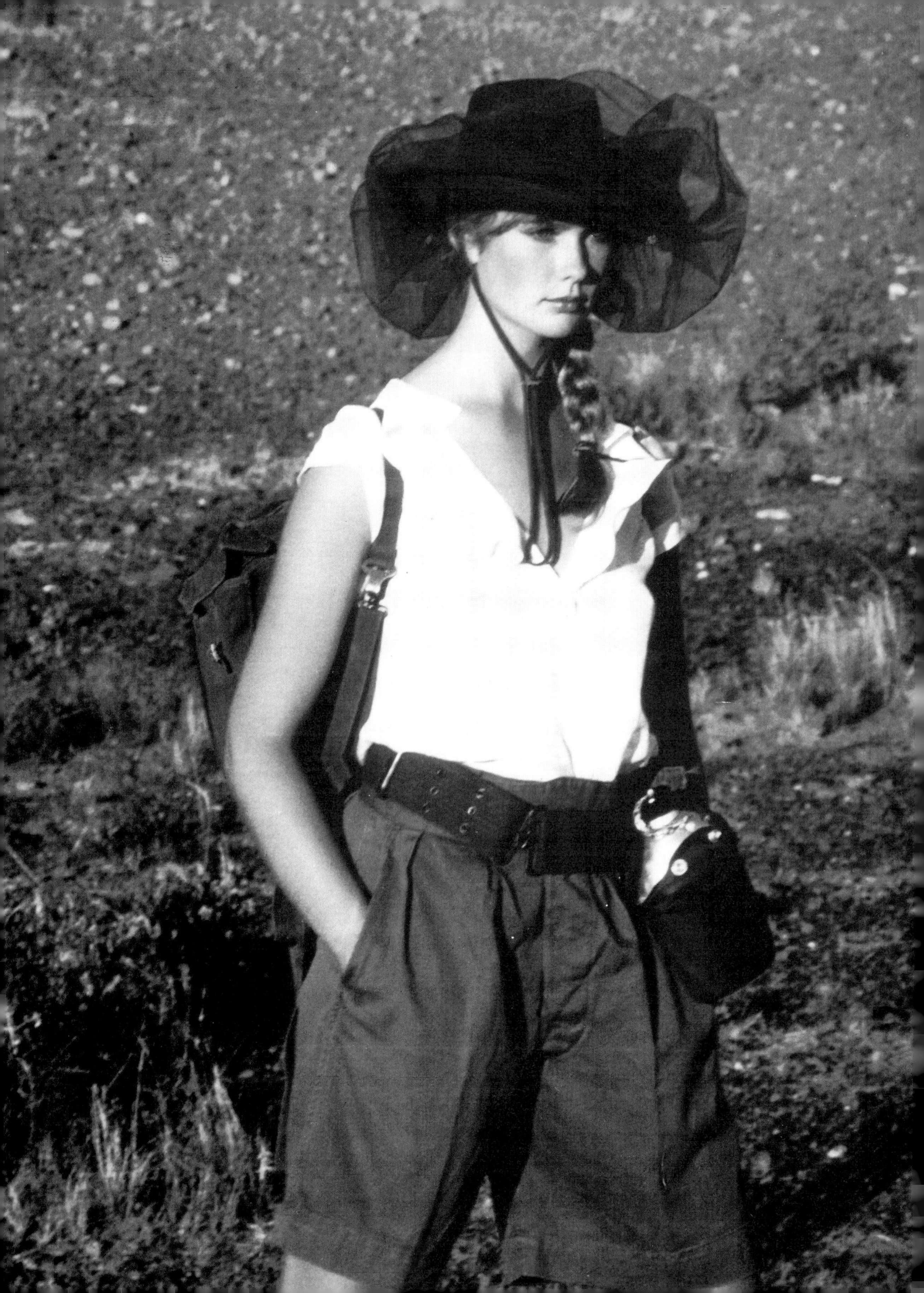

THE ALTERNATIVES

One of the most irritating points about wearing clothes from inexpensive chain stores and boutiques is the chance of meeting someone else dressed identically. Being confronted by a mirror image at a party or in the street can take all the pleasure out of your new clothes. A solution is to find your wardrobe from alternative places: in every town, however quiet it may appear, there is disguised fashion potential. Untapped, original treasures wait to be exploited by an adventurous and imaginative shopper in local jumble sales, thrift shops, antique markets, sports shops, traditional men's outfitters, children's departments and government surplus stores. Finding clothes in these alternative sources is a time-consuming business. You need patience and perseverance to explore every possibility, to scrutinize the shop stock (probably exasperate the proprietor), and try on anything that looks promising. When you do find something to buy, the thrill of an original bargain is immeasurably satisfying. Alternative shopping can become addictive. Like collecting old books or junk china, you develop a craving to check out every shop in each new town you visit, anxious not to bypass any treasure.

To make a success of this style and avoid looking like an over-dressed magpie, you need a well-tuned eye and a talent to sift the genuine finds from the rubbish. How you wear the clothes counts as much as what you wear. You need the skill to make something extraordinary look intended and not like fancy dress, the flair to mix old, new and contrasting styles together – call it 'cross-dressing'. It is a fresh way of seeing clothes requiring elastic economic values. For instance your scarf may cost more than your entire outfit, but it might be just what you need to add polish to the look: you should never overpay for second-hand clothes, especially ones in poor condition, but before you reject your find for being too expensive, it is worth considering how much the modern chain-store equivalent would cost instead. Second-hand (especially men's) clothes

How you wear the clothes counts as much as what you wear; add a flounced linen shirt to soften khaki shorts

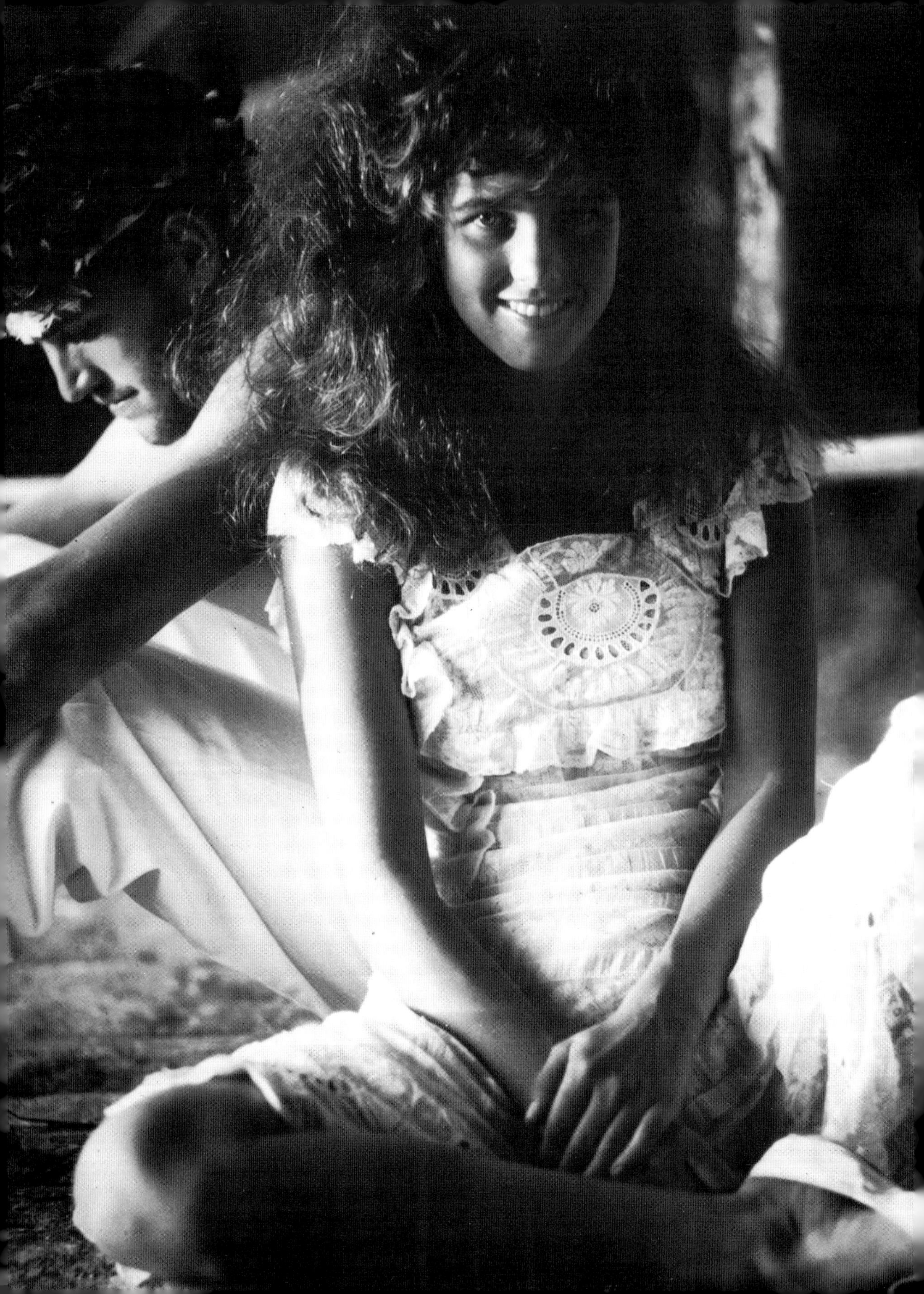

need working at before they start to look good. As well as having them immaculately reconditioned, ironed and starched you need ingenuity to spot new ways of wearing traditional clothes – to turn them back to front and inside out, to hitch men's trousers to skim the ankle or chop them off at the knee. It is essential to treat the style with a sense of humour and spontaneity. The minute you start to take it all too seriously, it becomes pretentious.

BARGAIN TACTICS

Buying second-hand clothes has turned into a cult. As the passion for nostalgia increases, the second-hand market is swamped with a mass of old clothes, many of which are vastly overpriced, tatty and without charm. The quantity of second-hand clothes available, whether in jumble sales, fêtes, bazaars, auctions or markets, is an incentive in itself to track down anything worthwhile. But it is easy to get carried away by the bargain atmosphere: unless you have enough space to keep a private junk shop, it is important to keep ruthlessly high standards.

At the top end of the second-hand clothes market, prices seem to soar out of proportion because the clothes are limited and much in demand. The clearest example is the fashion for Victorian white lace clothes. Each time the antique look is revived, the clothes double or treble in price. The shrewd alternative shopper buys her Victorian lace before the market reacts to the boom. Shops in London and major cities are always quick to realize the potential profits, but as is often the case with old clothes, some wonderful bargains can still be found in towns around the country, away from the pulse of fashion. Shops to head for are the sort that sell a mixture of junk and bric-a-brac and a few clothes suspended from picture hooks, draped over decaying statues, or tucked away negligently in a corner. Country markets often have stalls selling old clothes which are definitely worth investigating. Local house sales occasionally include an assortment of clothes, although anything special seems to be snapped up by eagle-eyed dealers and collectors for a staggering price.

Unless it really *does* only cost twenty pence, it is a mistake to buy anything from a second-hand store in a hurry. Making friends with the shopkeepers can be very rewarding; they may unearth some hidden prize stock for you to see, and respond to a spot of bargaining – which is always worth a try. (Never make remarks about the low prices, they will have doubled by your next visit.) Before you buy, examine every garment in daylight for moth holes, tears, stains and faded patches. If any buttons are missing, see if the shop sells anything similar, otherwise find unobtrusive bone or mother-of-pearl buttons in a haberdashery depart-

Nostalgic treasure: an antique lace petticoat

ment. If they are intact, it is worth resewing them all securely. Be realistic about how much repair is needed before the garment will be wearable. If it has already been mended in several places, the material will be weakened and might not stand up to further work. Even if you cannot sew, it helps to understand alterations; which changes are straightforward, which are more involved and expensive. Replacing zips, mending broken seams and torn linings are fairly simple jobs, and depending on the material and existing hem, most garments can be altered in length or taken in. Removing shoulder pads from coats and jackets can turn into a complicated structural alteration, best left to a professional, as it involves taking out the lining as well. If the lining is not replaced, the garment often loses its original shape and looks droopy.

As a general rule it is not worth buying something second-hand with the idea of totally reshaping it. In most cases you have to take it as it is. But should you find a large-sized bargain coat, jacket or suit in a beautiful, well-preserved material, find an inexpensive tailor to scale it down for you. It is pointless to buy anything badly stained that is too fragile to stand up to washing or dry-cleaning. Fortunately most natural fibres keep their resilience and can be restored. Silk is the weakest natural fibre and there are mixed opinions about cleaning. It is less of a risk to dry-clean delicate silk, providing you check with the cleaners which chemicals they use. Cotton and linen are much tougher and have more chance of being completely reconditioned. White cottons can be boiled up with bleach in a saucepan, or left to soak in a cold water solution. Rust marks spoil the look of white cottons, and can be prevented by removing the hooks, eyes and any other metal fastenings before the cleaning process starts. Existing stains can be rubbed before a wash with the old wives' remedy of half a lemon dipped in salt.

Fortunately there is still a wide selection of Victorian and Edwardian white lace in nearly mint condition, well-preserved in their time under layers of outer garments, hidden from heavy wear and tear. What was originally intended as underwear now adapts beautifully into everyday clothes. The antique cotton and lace petticoats make perfect skirts; when one is too transparent, if you can afford another, wear two together, one longer than the other. A white lace blouse is the most attractive item of antique clothing because it is so extraordinarily versatile. It works with every single style, shape and texture, from a plain Shetland jersey, a tough tweed or thick leather jacket to sequins, velvet, sheepskin, suede or more white lace. Fragile cotton camisoles with little buttons or a ribbon drawstring make pretty summer tops. Antique white cotton nightshirts with ruffled lace collar and cuffs can be worn as dresses or cut off into billowy shirts. White cotton pantaloons make fine summer bloomers, belted with thick leather or a bright scarf. Lace fichus, lace collars and

An antique cotton and lace chemise; once strictly underwear, now a most covetable top layer

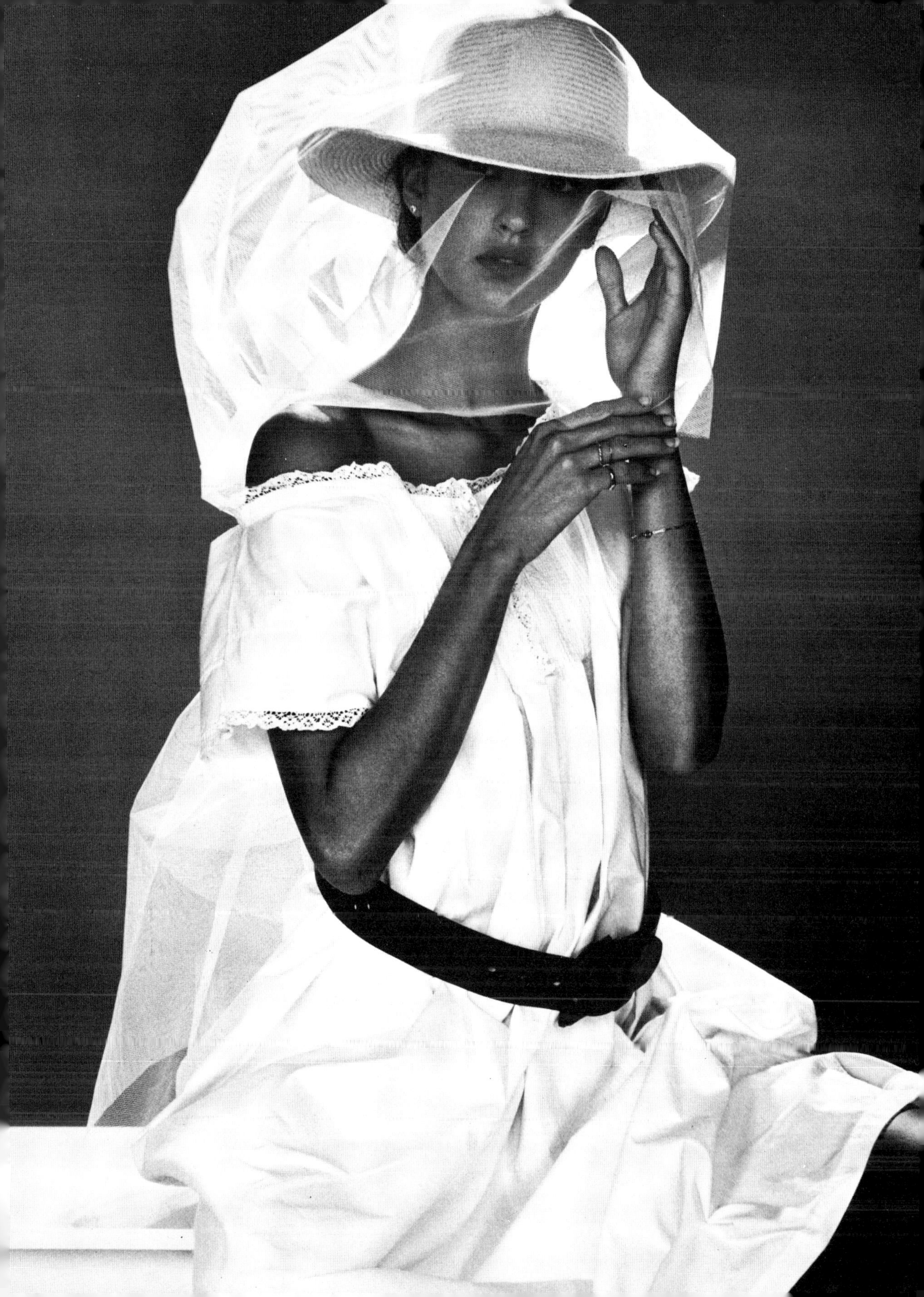

even antique lace runners intended for dressing tables all make exquisite scarves, belts or hair bands. However much of it all you choose to wear, the finish is critical. Everything does need to be well laundered and crisply starched, chipped or missing buttons replaced, frayed ribbons mended or renewed. Of course it doesn't *have* to be white. If the material is stained or blotchy you can dip it in a solution of weak tea to make it a soft biscuit colour.

CLASSIC TREASURES

The charm of old-fashioned classics is their increasing rarity value. Like antiques where demand outstrips supply, nostalgic treasures should be snapped up fast. Original thirties and forties knitwear is prized by collectors. Look out for Fair Isle handknits, fitted lacey sweaters with pearl buttons, men's slipovers, fifties mohair sloppy joes and beaded cardigans which make pretty evening jackets. Antique ethnics like embroidered silks, fringed shawls, paisley stoles, satin kimonos are highly coveted. A floral crepe Granny tea dress conjures the antique market image, particularly the classic waisted style with a trailing skirt, fine lace collar and elbow-length cuffs. Evening finds come in floaty chiffon, bias cut satin, Fortuny style pleats, or embellished with sequins, bugle beading and embroidery. Secondhand fur coats tend to look mangy and rather bulky, but a stole or wrap in good condition could be worn at night when the light is less truthful. Providing they are a classic shape, old tweed coats and jackets still look contemporary. Men's jackets often improve with age once the stiffness has worn into a pliable jacket, soft enough to roll up the sleeves and belt like a cardigan. Antique markets and second-hand shops are a source of well-priced original accessories. Track down fine quality silk and chiffon scarves, delicate lace handkerchiefs, long kid gloves, old fashioned tortoiseshell or gold-framed spectacles to adapt into sunglasses. Period straw hats have an eccentric charm – particularly straw panamas, sunhats, boaters, felt cloches and berets. Look out for silk roses, ostrich feathers and jewelled hat pins to decorate them. Luggage and handbags in classic shape and good condition are worth attention. You may discover a tapestried carpet or leather Gladstone bag, a beaded velvet or sequinned satin evening purse. It is rare to find shoes that fit, but worth hunting for button or buckled pairs in fine kid or suede. Antique costume jewellery is satisfyingly indeterminate as no one knows if it is a fake, or a real family heirloom. Accessible finds are imitation or real black jet, coloured glass beads, rings, pearls, chandelier drop earrings, diamanté paste brooches, necklaces, bracelets, buckles, tiaras, cameos and stick pins.

SURPLUS STYLE

Another great source of bargains is the government surplus store. But the style does need careful treatment to step out of the uniform mould and be feminized. Treat surplus clothes as separates; isolate individual garments and mix them with contrasting, particularly feminine things. Although khaki is not flattering against pale skin, it looks marvellous with plenty of other colours; anything pastel, primrose, lilac, pale blue, cream, white. The trick is to avoid other drab colours, or shades too close to a khaki tone. And a pair of army shorts somehow looks far more glamorous than their £1 price tag implies if you wear them with your best belt and a good shirt.

One of the quandaries of buying surplus clothes is not knowing which size to take. It is impossible to make rules, as so much depends on how you look in a particular garment; whether you want to flaunt your figure in tight shorts or boilersuit, or camouflage it under folds of material. But clothes that are too enormous will swamp you, which is not the point of wearing the clothes. You do not actually want to look as if you belong in the army or work as a plumber's mate. You wear the clothes because they are cheap, but also because they are simple enough to be transformed into an individual style.

Army surplus classics are knee-length white or khaki cotton drill shorts which look good with a white tee shirt, or even a white lace shirt, bare legs and flat tan sandals. Mansize shorts are fine as long as you define the waist with a belt and keep your top half fitted. If the shorts are too long, try rolling the legs up to mid-thigh level. Depending on the stock in your surplus store, you may find thick, cotton, padded combat jackets. They are waterproof, windproof and make great everyday jackets. The US Army issue comes in an attractive buff colour, which makes a change from khaki. Woollen army shirts are a perfect classic shape, with small pointed collars, breast pockets and long shirt tails but they are often too prickly to wear next to the skin, so can be turned into light-weight jackets to go over tee shirts or thin sweaters. The standard white or service blue collarless shirts make surprise mini-dresses, or useful nightshirts, especially as they are often the cheapest things in the store. The accessories are worth exploring — amongst the first aid kits and torches, hunt for knitted pull-on beenie hats, leather-edged berets, towelling or wool comforter scarves, canvas satchel bags, webbing belts and woolly socks.

Each time the nautical look is fashionable, bargain hunters dive to the nearest surplus store for the real thing. If you can find them, white and navy sailor tops look best worn like short smocks, over white drill sailor trousers. The thinner, white cotton naval jackets are more successfully

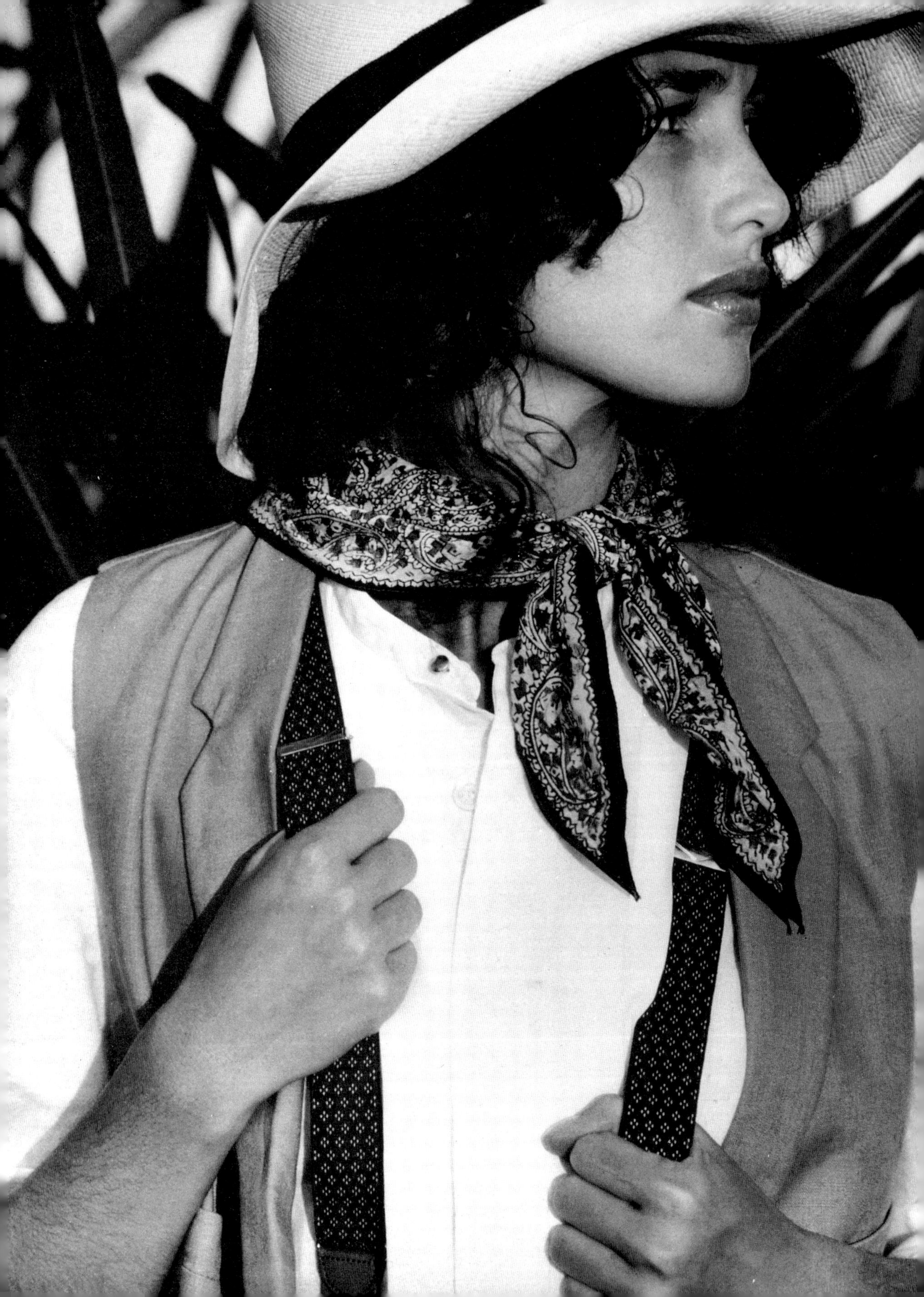

Safari style in the best tradition: mixing breeches, braces, panama, paisley, linen and khaki

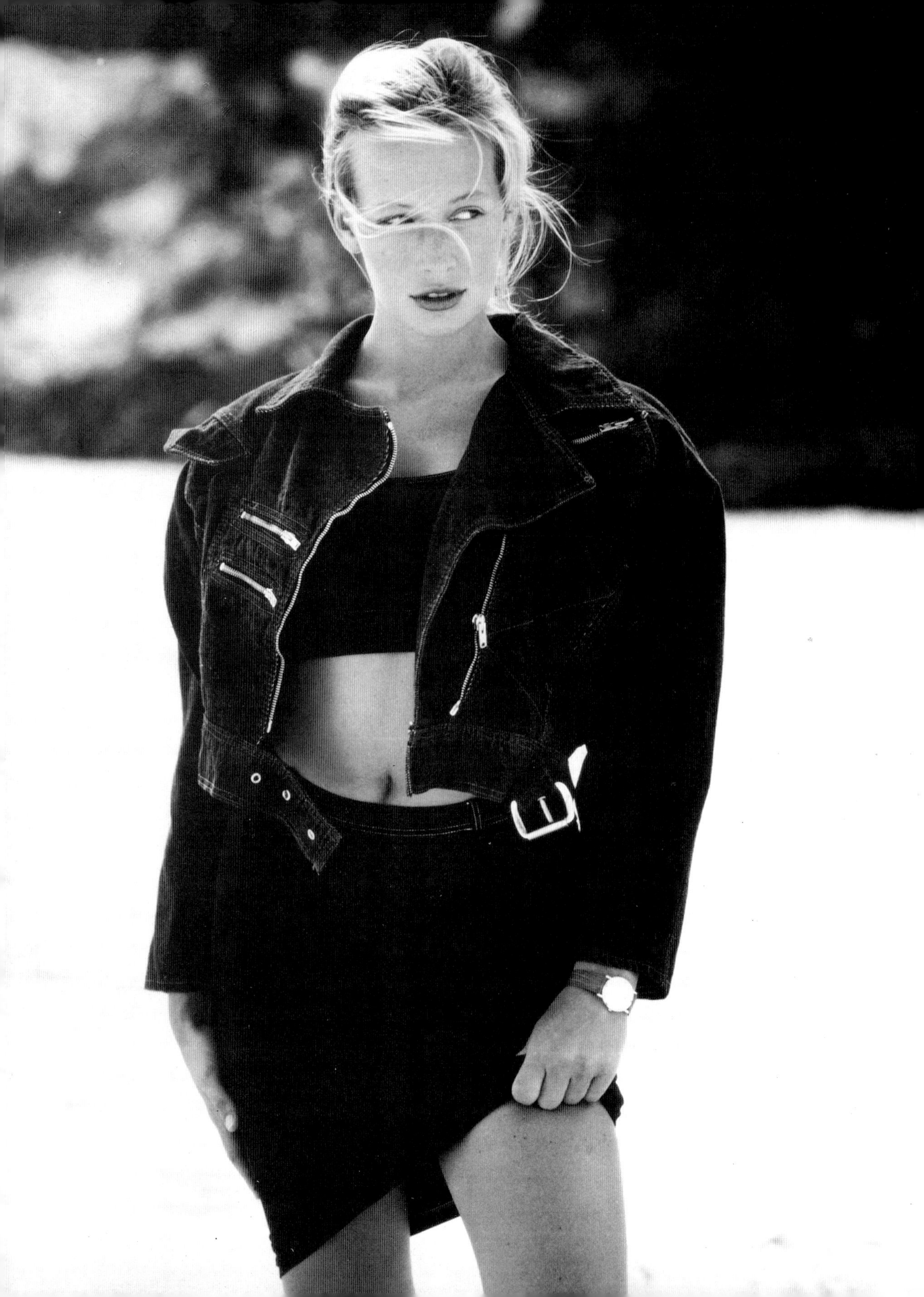

The Alternatives 97

adapted than winter issue navy blue ones which tend to look too theatrical. Navy sailor boat-neck sweaters are incredibly warm and partially waterproof – they look less bulky than Guernseys at a fraction of the price. Rifle through collections of old buttons and trimmings; if a shirt or jacket is going cheap, it may be worth it just for these. Other sea-faring bargains can be found in sailing shops. Amongst the compasses and logbooks there is a store of proper nautical fashion. Look for traditional yellow oilskins and sou'westers, white and blue matelot tee shirts, Breton sailing jerseys, in striped or plain navy, red and cream, always with the characteristic three buttons down the shoulder. There are thick, oiled sweaters in warm tweedy wool, smarter navy knitted cardigan jackets (meant for the yacht club, but perfect with jeans). The best shops are filled with random extras which make great accessories; polka-dot handkerchiefs, silver whistles on chains, bright parachute nylon holdalls, thick socks, woolly hats, peaked captain's caps in navy felt or white cotton.

Not all uniform clothing comes from the armed services. There is a wealth of surplus bargains intended for waiters, chefs, plumbers and workmen that can be bought brand new from civil service or trade stores. All the clothes are wonderfully cheap, but as function is a more important criterion than style, they usually need to be dressed up imaginatively. Uniforms to investigate are white cotton drill boilersuits, to wear belted with the sleeves and legs rolled up; white or navy cotton drill dungarees, worn large and belted over a tee shirt or sweatshirt; button-fly blue and white check cotton chefs' trousers, to wear long, or cut off as Bermuda shorts; white cotton waiters' jackets with slim lapels or a curved shawl collar, which can be dyed to a bright colour; and for winter, navy wool workmen's jackets – the best have leather patches across the shoulders.

STYLE IN THE BEST TRADITION

School uniform departments are worth browsing through. Boys' tweed jackets or unlined flannel blazers in grey, navy or bottle green are inexpensive and completely classic buys (if you don't object to buttoning on the boy's side). Sports jerseys are often original and good value especially pure wool, cream, cable cricket sweaters and slipovers, or thick football sweaters with little collars. Regulation school knitwear can also be a classic find; look out for plain, ribbed V-necks with the school stripe around the neck and cuffs. Several designers have rediscovered divided games skirts, so economize with the genuine article; the winter netball flannels with bright warm tights and flat shoes, the navy cottons with bare legs, gymshoes or flat sandals. The most covetable school

A well zipped biker's jacket supplies alternative summer cover

Jackets that owe their style to the comfort and practicalities of menswear: (above) the multi-pocketed safari jacket translates into linen, cotton or chamois; (right) single-breasted whipcord, cut long and curved in dandy tradition

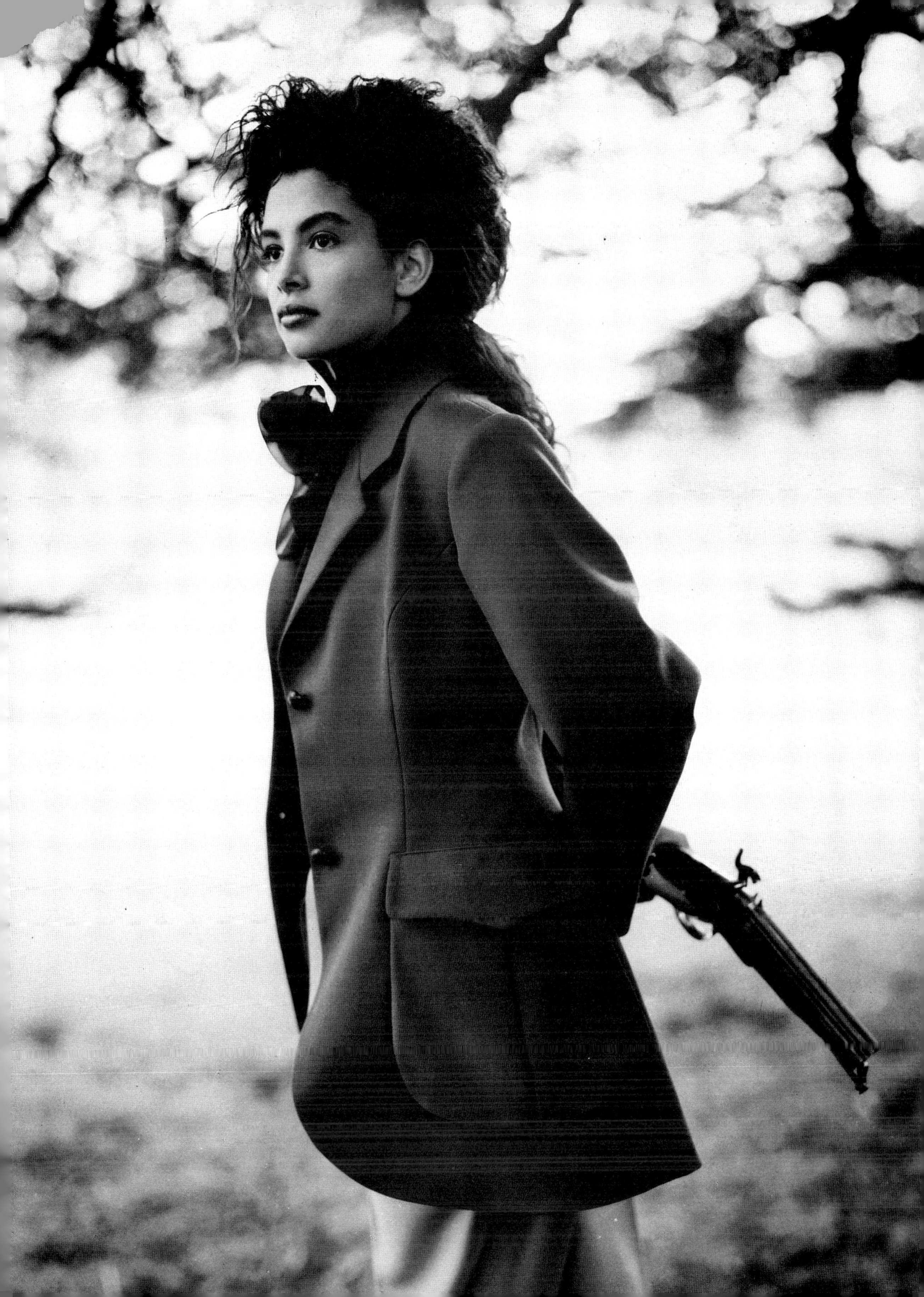

Borrowed traditions: (below) Boy's Own style in collarless shirt, braces and men's trousers

(opposite) Alternative evening dress in white tie and piqué waistcoat

accessories are stretchy boys' snake belts and brown leather or canvas satchels, which make extremely practical handbags.

Men's departments, or the traditional male outfitters, can be havens of alternative fashion. Top priority is to charm the salesmen. Gentlemen's shops are still bastions of masculinity and may not welcome or see the funny side of a tiresomely thorough female shopper. You may have to accept rather condescending service, but don't be deterred. Some of the more desirable articles of men's clothing are the most conservative classics: quietly checked viyella shirts, discreet, striped Oxford cottons with button-down collars, the collarless striped shirts that go with stiff collars, pie-frilled or pintucked white cotton dress shirts, collarless if possible. Traditional waistcoats should not be bypassed. Consider silk-backed white piqué for evening, pinstripe, felt or leather for day worn over a plain white or chambray shirt. Providing it is free from fashion detail or fancy stitching, mens knitwear is a wise investment. The simplest cardigans, sweaters and waistcoats are often cheaper and more generously shaped than feminine counterparts.

Trousers are never quite so straightforward; success hangs on the size range and shapes. The sort with the most potential are the most old-fashioned; the thick corduroys with button flies, brace loops and a high waist to keep farmers' kidneys warm, in country shades of olive green and donkey brown.

Men's leather jackets are often more of a classic buy than the female kind. The shape to go for is a simple tough leather or suede blouson, like a motorbike jacket. (Avoid any knitted collar, cuffs or hem, which don't last with the leather.) It is well worth looking for a second-hand one, which will have had some character knocked into it for you. Most jackets come in brown or black, but a good source for brighter red, green, white or blue leathers is a motorbike equipment shop. They are certainly not cheap, but definitely count as investment buys.

For alternative evening dress, try the legendary black tuxedo; a classic black jacket, which looks more striking if it is not too oversized, with curved satin lapels, and narrow trousers with satin side stripes. Dinner suits, or tuxedos, are expensive to buy, so you can hire one for special occasions, or look for a second-hand one from dress-hire shops. The sharp lines need feminizing with soft ruffles, a bright cummerbund, a lace or spotted handkerchief and elegant courts. If you prefer lower heels, and can find a pair to fit, men's black patent dancing pumps with gros grain bows make original alternative shoes to wear day or night. Men's classic felt trilbies or straw panamas are much the easiest and most relaxed kind of hat to wear. Buy them large so they sit well down on the head, or if you have a small head, you could go back to the school uniform department to investigate the straw boaters or winter felt hats.

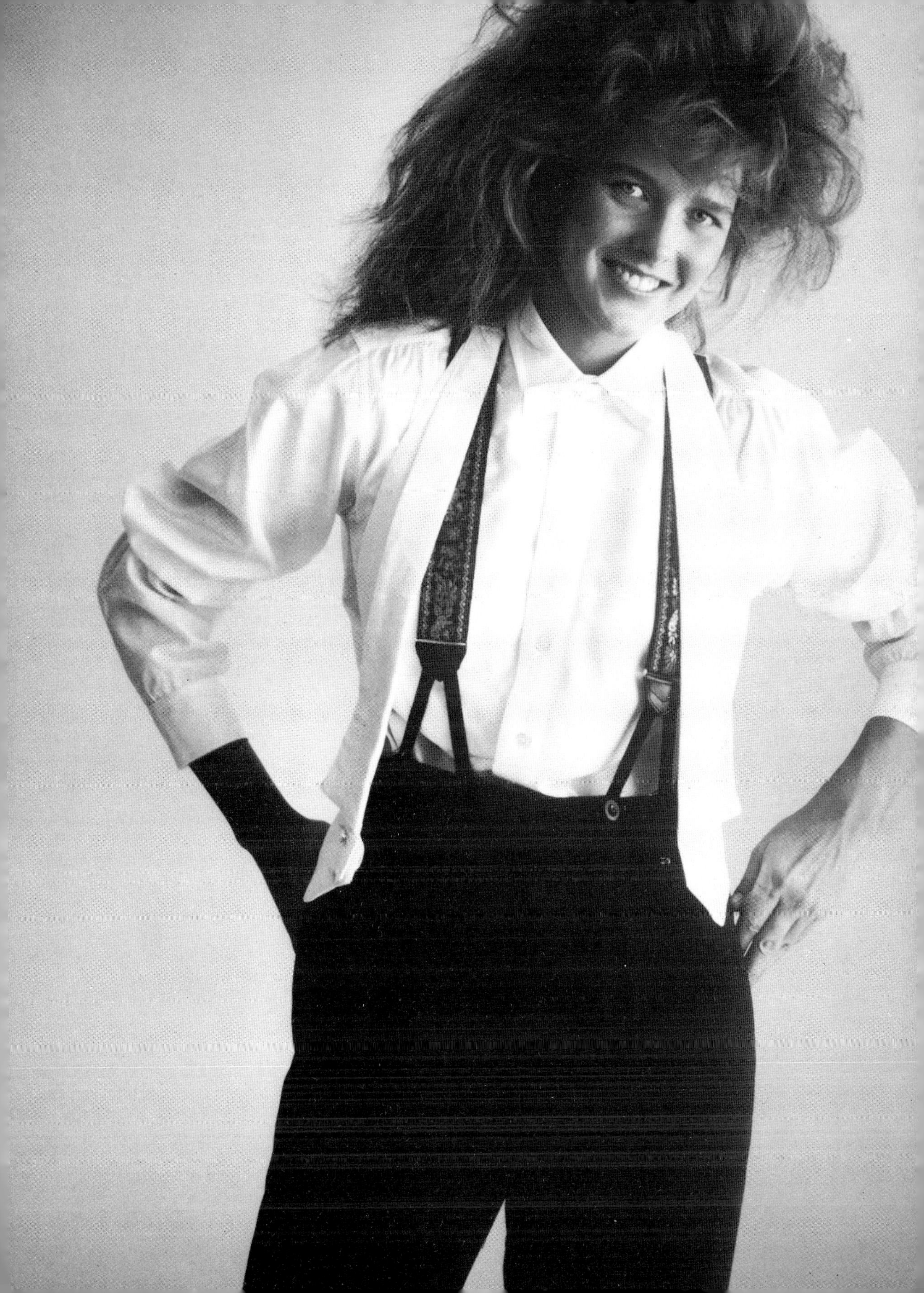

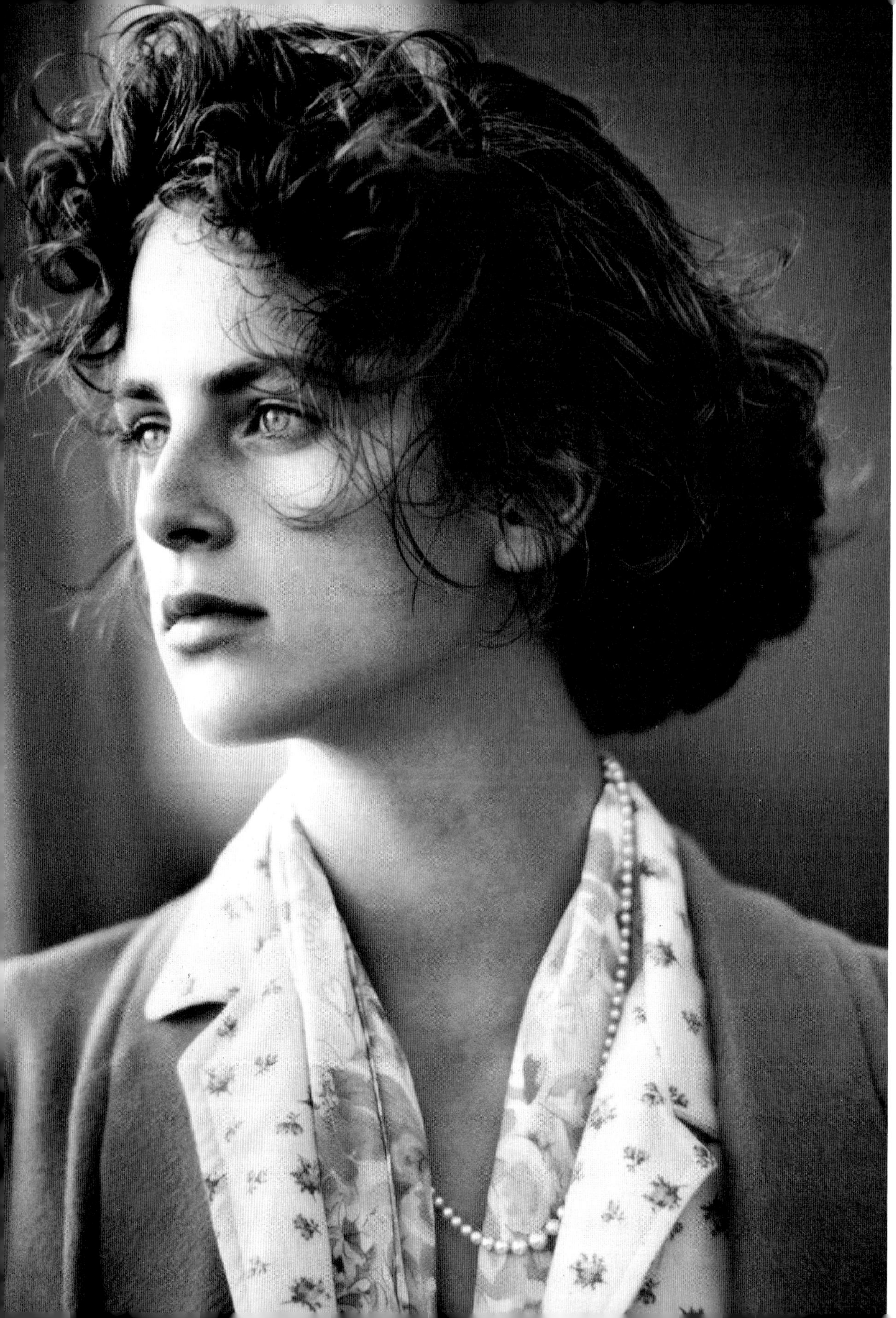

(left) *A sprigged viyella pyjama top doubles as a shirt*

(right) *Try men's piped pyjamas for original summerwear*

The male underwear and nightwear counters have hidden potential. Plain cotton pyjama tops can turn into unexpected shirts, particularly the quality brands with contrast piping. Look for delicious combinations of pale pink and white, or white with red, blue, black or yellow. Pyjama tops can be worn buttoned up to the neck, or like an open shirt with the collar turned up or down, and the bottom halves can be transformed into drawstring summer trousers. Traditional wool dressing gowns in unbedroomy, deep coloured plaids, can adapt into light, winter wrap coats. They look less like a dressing gown, although there is nothing wrong with that, if they are not too long, and the cord is changed for a wider leather belt. It is probably wiser not to wear your pyjama shirt under a dressing gown coat, or you will be irritated by remarks about forgetting to get dressed!

Men's white cotton singlet vests make bargain summer tee shirts, but inspect them first for their depth of armhole as most of them require a low-sided bra underneath. Extra long sizes can be turned into white summer minis. Long and short-sleeved Grandpa vests, with a three-button front, in cream wool or cotton are another alternative top. And if

Distinctions between under and outerwear need not apply in high summer

(opposite) *In the pink in crisp cotton pyjamas*

(next spread, left) *Enwrapped in a jumble of treasure: patchwork heirlooms, well-worn cotton smocks and pinafores*

(next spread, right) *Nostalgic cottons – antique lace blouse, bloomers and bobbly cotton knit*

you can find a supply, men's combinations have definite possibilities – as a cuddly boilersuit with sleeves and legs rolled up, or as a warm exercise suit. Leave them cream, or dye them pale pink or blue. Woolly bloomers and long johns also make useful winter leggings. Cotton or silk boxer shorts can be adapted into brief summer shorts, best in a bright stripe or check that isn't obviously an underwear pattern.

The female underwear department also has concealed promise. In spite of its sensible image, thermal underwear can be surprisingly pretty. A white lacey cotton, fine wool or knitted silk vest is appealing enough to be worn under an open shirt, a deep V-neck sweater or alone, in place of a tee shirt. For an alternative evening wrap you could try the bedjacket counter – there might possibly be a Hollywood-style angora jacket trimmed with maribou.

The overlap between lingerie and evening wear can be an economical advantage. Silk camisoles, pyjamas, kimonos and satin slippers from the lingerie department can easily pass as informal evening wear.

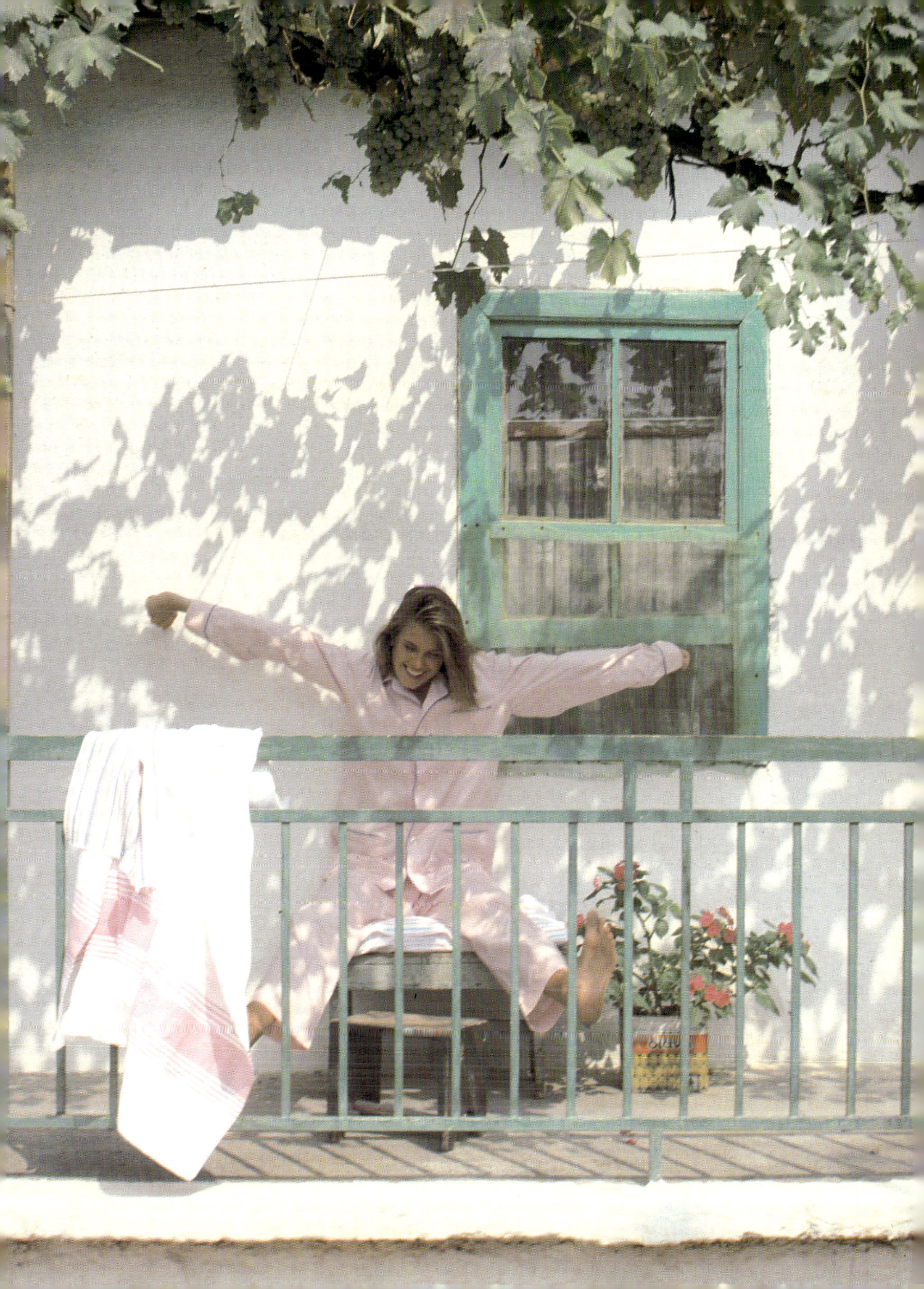

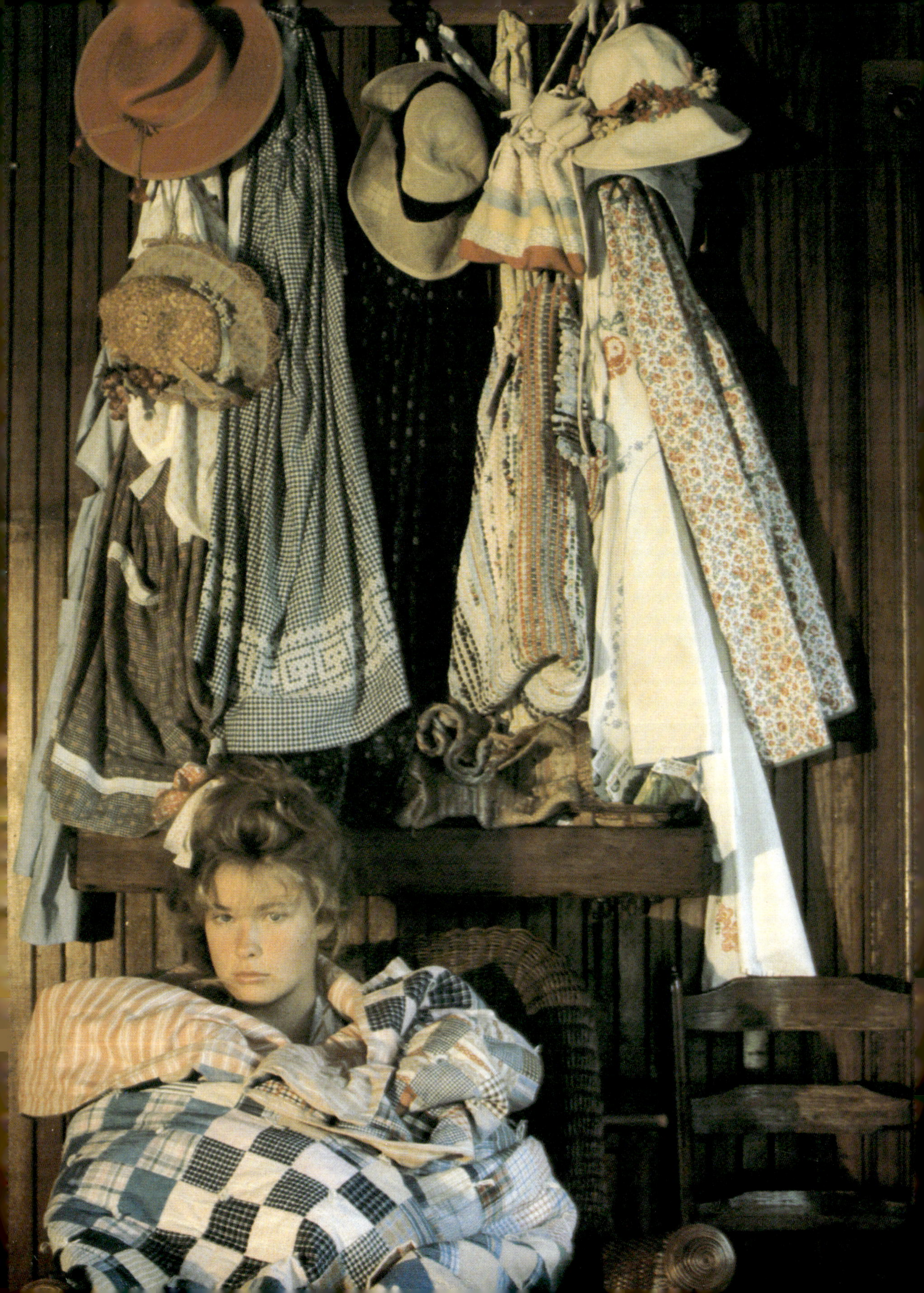

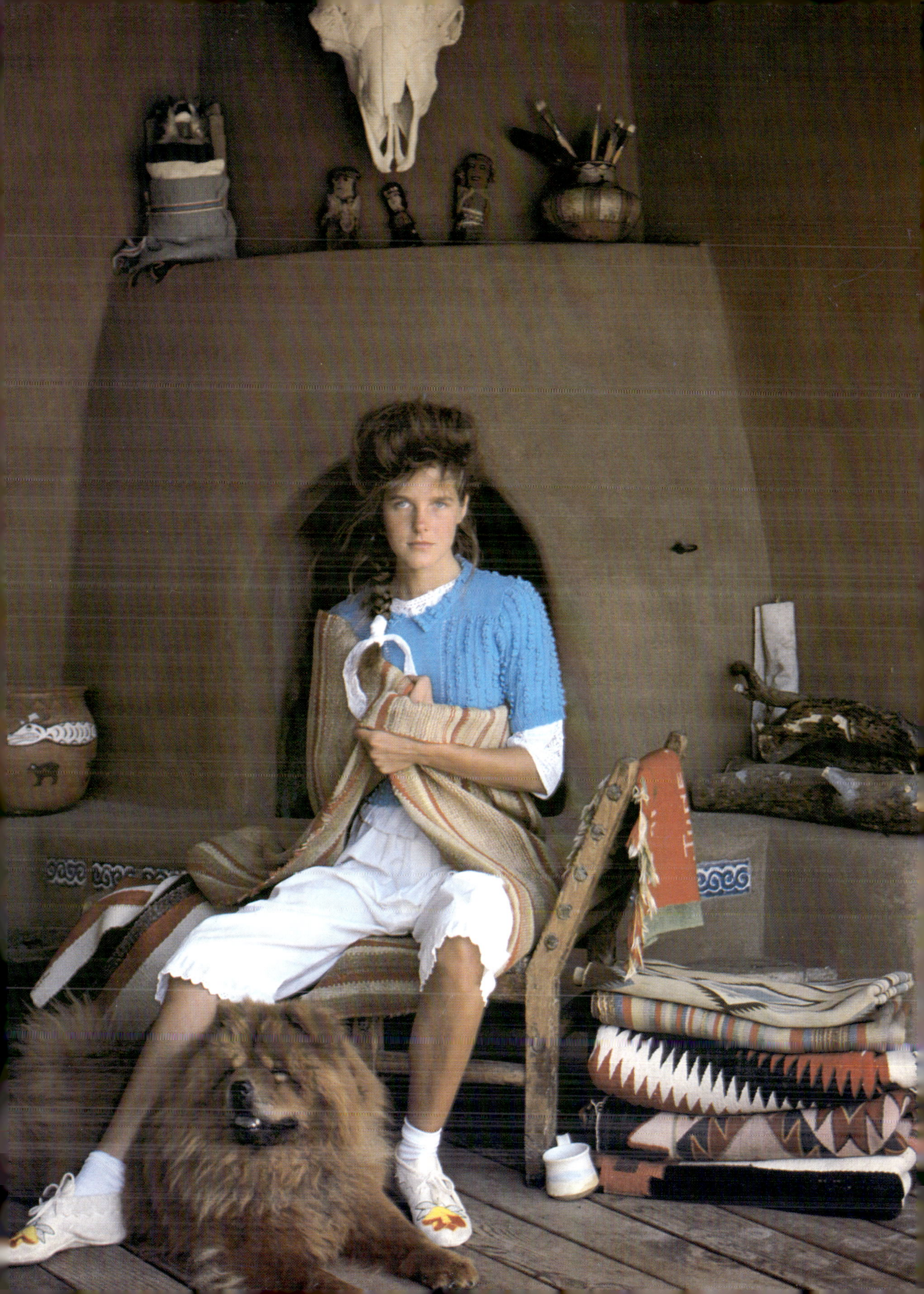

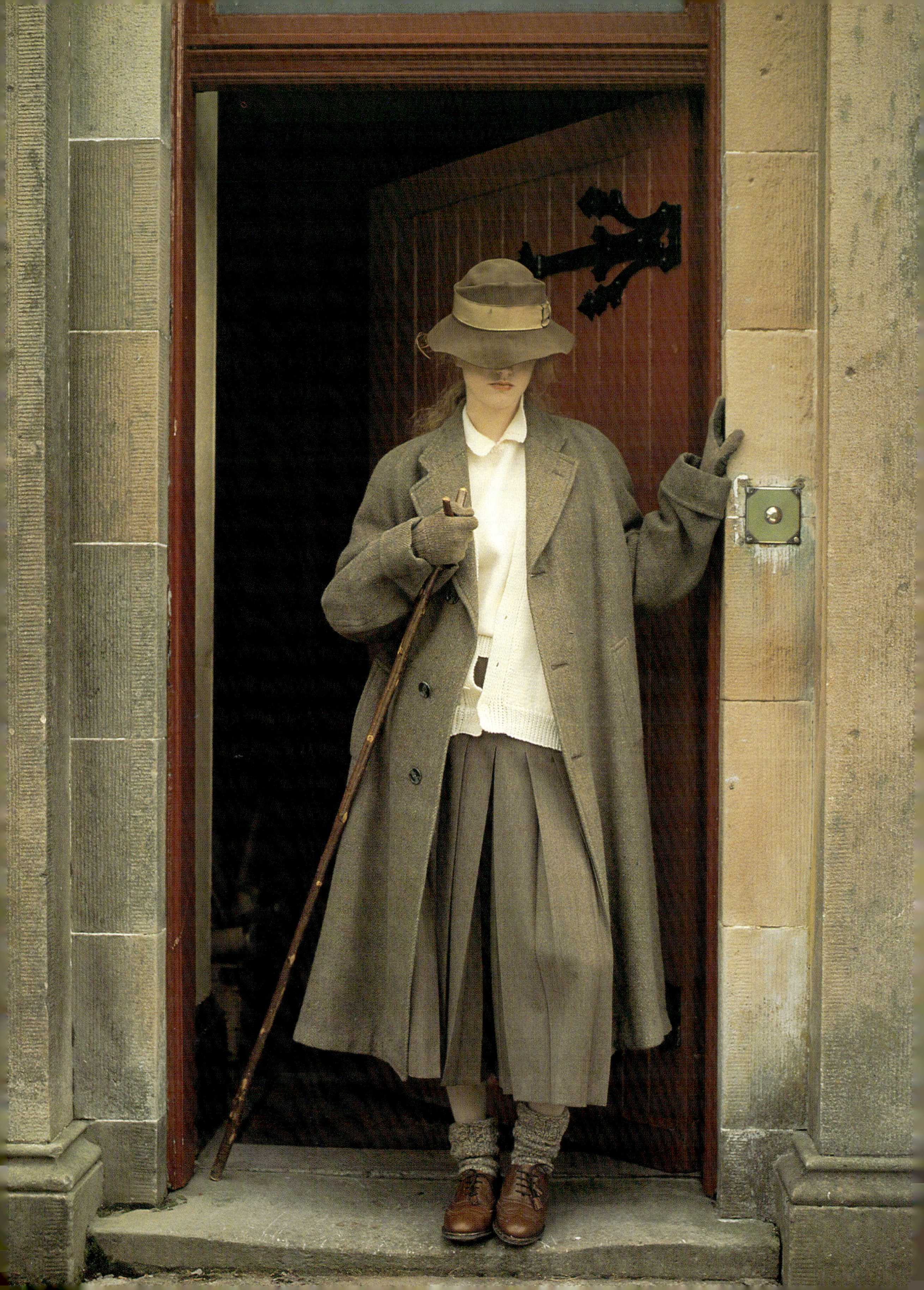

SPORTING FINDS

Next stop on the alternative shopping expedition is the sports store: shops that specialize in clothes for country pursuits – fishing, riding, shooting, camping and hiking. The coats and jackets are the most versatile buys. Oiled, thornproof, green jackets with check linings are typical of the best country look, but providing they are not mud splattered, they are classic enough to go anywhere. When hacking jackets become an essential in every fashion-conscious wardrobe, the craftiest shoppers buy genuine tweed riding jackets. Others choose boys' tweed sports coats, but the real hacking jackets are a slimmer, more flattering shape, usually in a finer tweed with smart velvet collars. Duffel coats are great value and look good anywhere. The familiar cut of a duffel ranks as a classic coat shape, one that reappears regularly in fashion collections. The best are regulation navy blue with wooden toggles, deep pockets and red tartan lining, worn as a three-quarter coat. The reefer and donkey jacket are more grown-up versions. Both are traditionally navy blue; the reefer is boxy, double breasted with silver buttons; the donkey jacket is more casual, single breasted and tent shaped. Country trouser possibilities are tweedy, corduroy or moleskin (thick brushed cotton) knee breeches or baggier plus fours, to wear with thick, ribbed socks, green gumboots or punched leather lace-ups. Stretch jodhpurs are a sporting answer to leggings. Or, if you prefer a baggier style, look in a surplus store for a landgirl corduroy issue with buckled waistband and laced calves – an increasing rarity that should be snapped up.

If you don't feel happy wearing alternative clothes, genuine country accessories should not be overlooked. They are often better made than the fashion equivalent, and certainly better value for money. Sporting bags and baggages come in various sizes and materials, and convert into excellent roomy handbags. Look for canvas fishermen's satchels with strong webbing straps and leather reinforcements, wicker fishing baskets, shooters' cartridge bags and belts, tweed flat caps, equestrian, primrose-yellow string gloves, tough leather hiking shoes or genuine, shiny leather riding boots – expensive, but unbeatable craftsmanship.

From the more active sports wardrobes, cricket clothes can have enormous style. Those attractive cream sweaters, if unobtainable from the school uniform department, can be tracked down, along with cream flannel trousers, striped cricket blazer and peaked cap, in sports outfitters. The best pickings from a golfer's wardrobe are the knitwear. In reality the concept of golfing clothes is based on the thirties-style gentleman golfer, more than today's natty check-trouser pros. The best traditional golfer would wear a diamond-knit cardigan or slipover, tweed plus fours, Argyll knee socks with fringed correspondent brogues.

Proofed against the elements in sensible country clothes: herringbone coat, warm knits, trilby, thick socks and brogues

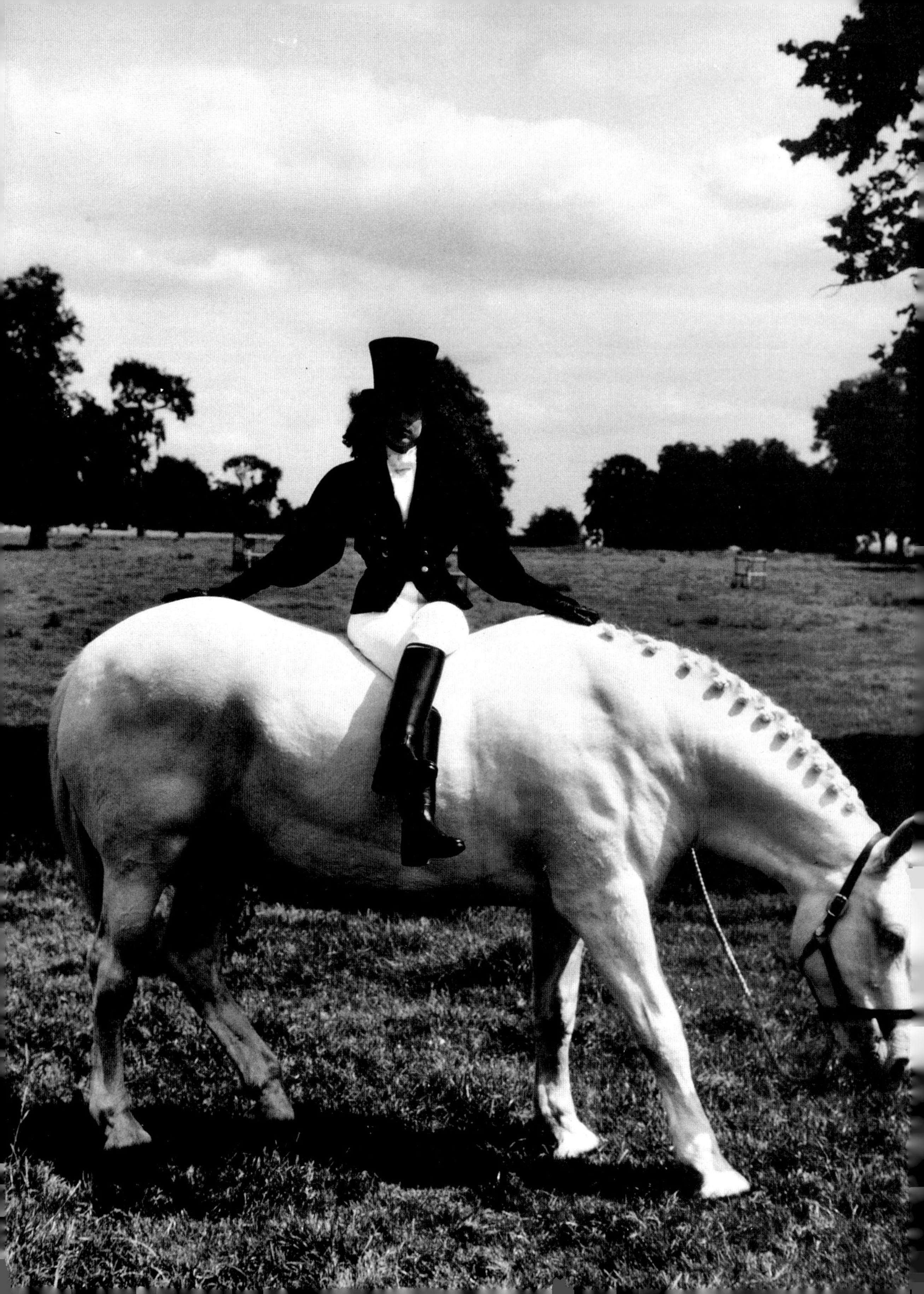

(right) Mid-winter cover:
enveloped in tweedy layers,
schoolgirl sweaters, sporting skirt
and lace-ups

Equestrienne style (left): the well
groomed habit of jodhpurs, riding
coat and boots

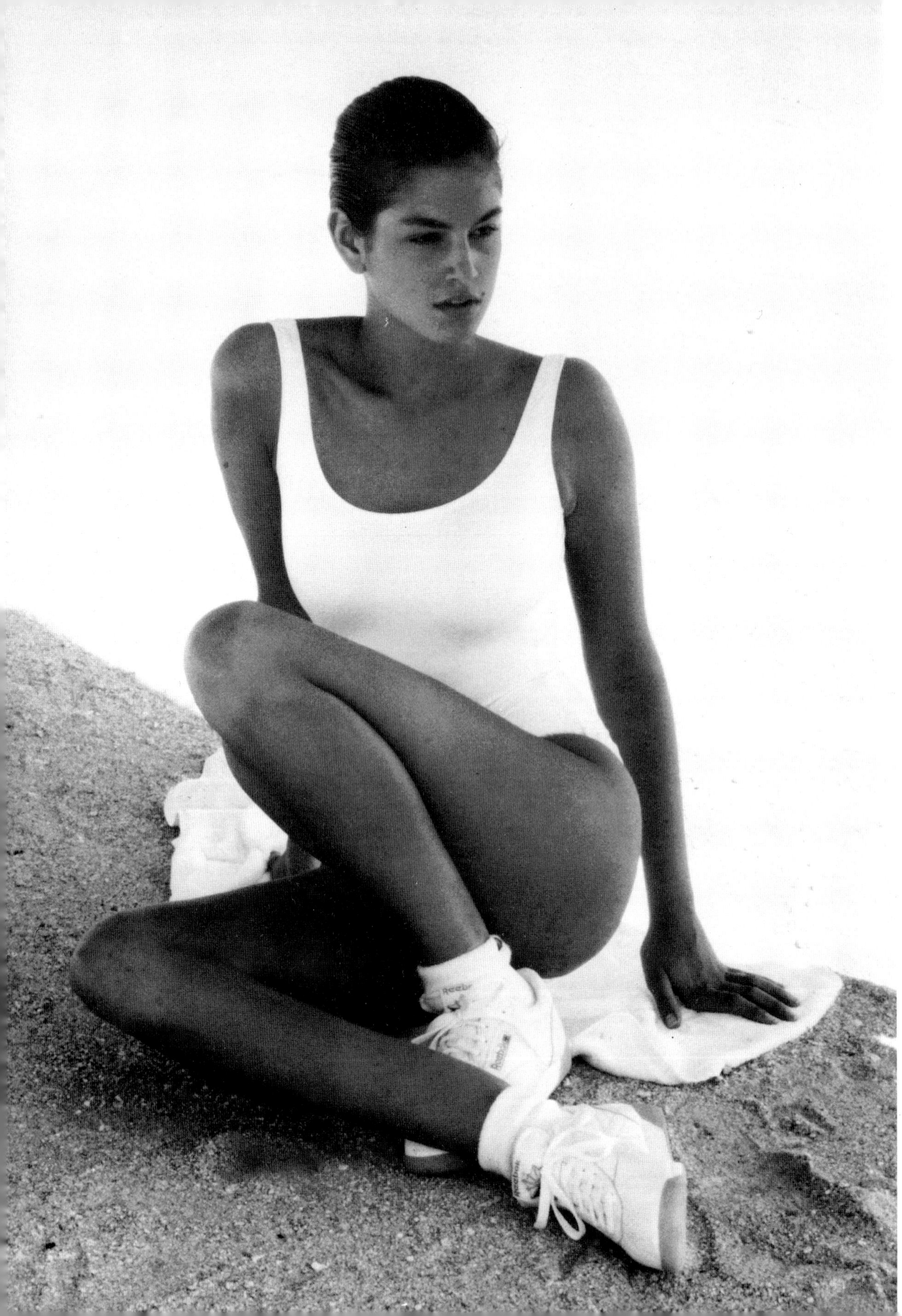

The Alternatives

The bonding of fitness to fashion has raised the design standards and versatility of exercise clothes. Now leotards, swimsuits, leggings and sweatshirts double for day wear and workout. It makes sense to buy the basics from sports suppliers, dance bars, chain stores, even supermarkets, rather than high fashion sources where prices are bound to be higher. Less body conscious shapes still count as sporting classics. A plain cotton tracksuit with a crew neck sweatshirt and generous cuffed pants is a comfortable alternative to second skin separates. The original Fred Perry polo shirt has become a casual summer staple to collect in white, primary and pastel cottons – avoiding any loud logos or motifs. Aerobic shoes have a high fashion profile, worn for exercise, comfort and cult kudos, particularly in America. Plain white tennis shoes are a cheaper option to cushioned leather trainers, but they lack the spring in the step. Beside the practical equipment in sporting stores – divers' watches, sweatbands, sports socks, luggage – why not invest in a hooded boxer's towelling robe as a dressing gown? A black or brilliant leotard with a deep scooped neckline can be the starting point for evening, worn under a layered net skirt or skinny lycra tube. Or use a brief body suit as

Fitness clothes (left) *add a new dimension to the wardrobe: and occasional cult kudos*

On the right track: (right) *flounced leotard, footless tights, satin ballet slippers;* (far right) *perfectly plain tracksuit – an alternative to second skin exercise wear*

*An alternative party frock –
a frothy pink tutu*

the under layer of a sheer chiffon dance dress.

If you can find a shop specializing in dancing clothes, look for ballet practice, knitted leg-warmers, baby wool 'cross-over' cardigans which tie into a bow at the back or front, and black or pastel pink, opaque exercise tights. Satin ballet shoes make beautiful and inexpensive evening slippers in white, shell pink, scarlet or black. In summer try the

The Alternatives

leather ballet pumps or white lace-up jazz shoes as alternative footwear. If you have secret longings to be a ballerina, you could answer them with a tutu party frock in white, pink or black tulle from the same source. It is pure fancy dress, but can look enchanting if you have the figure and sense of fun to carry it off.

HOME-MADE STYLE

As a more down-to-earth last word, it is unfair to ignore home dressmaking. It is an alternative source of fashion with a guaranteed bonus that everything you make will be an original, and one that is extremely economical. In spite of these incentives, home-made clothes still have a sadly second-rate image – probably because the disastrous efforts stand out as obviously home sewn, and the successes pass effortlessly as shop buys. Providing you aren't over ambitious with a complicated pattern, follow every instruction to the letter and never cut any corners, there is no reason for home-made clothes to look amateurish. Sewing does require patience and skill, and you do need to enjoy it. There are pitfalls to beware of; make sure that the material and pattern you choose are right for each other. Consider the shape of the design and the way the material falls – thick corduroy won't behave like crepe de Chine. For a professional result is is essential to buy thread, buttons and zips that match the material exactly, and to iron each part as you go along. Once finished, pressing by a dry-cleaner can make all the difference in lifting the home-made stamp. If you are not enthralled by the choice of dressmaking materials, investigate other sources which are often cheaper and more original. Furnishing fabrics are the best alternative, particularly linen union, toile de jouy, ticking, calico, muslin or flower-printed chintzes.

One of the let-downs of home dressmaking can be the limiting choice of paper patterns. It is frustrating to have an idea of what you want to make and not be able to find a corresponding simple pattern. Unless you are a real expert, the experiments where you cut out and sew from a picture or inspiration too often end up in the dustbin. If you want a designer look, it is worth paying a little extra for a fashion name pattern, and making your own Ralph Lauren or Christian Lacroix, which will after all work out at a fraction of its shop equivalent. Or if you prefer something more original, scour jumble sales, attics and junk shops for job lots of old paper patterns. Sewing straight from an authentic forties, fifties or sixties design is the surest way to genuine alternative fashions.

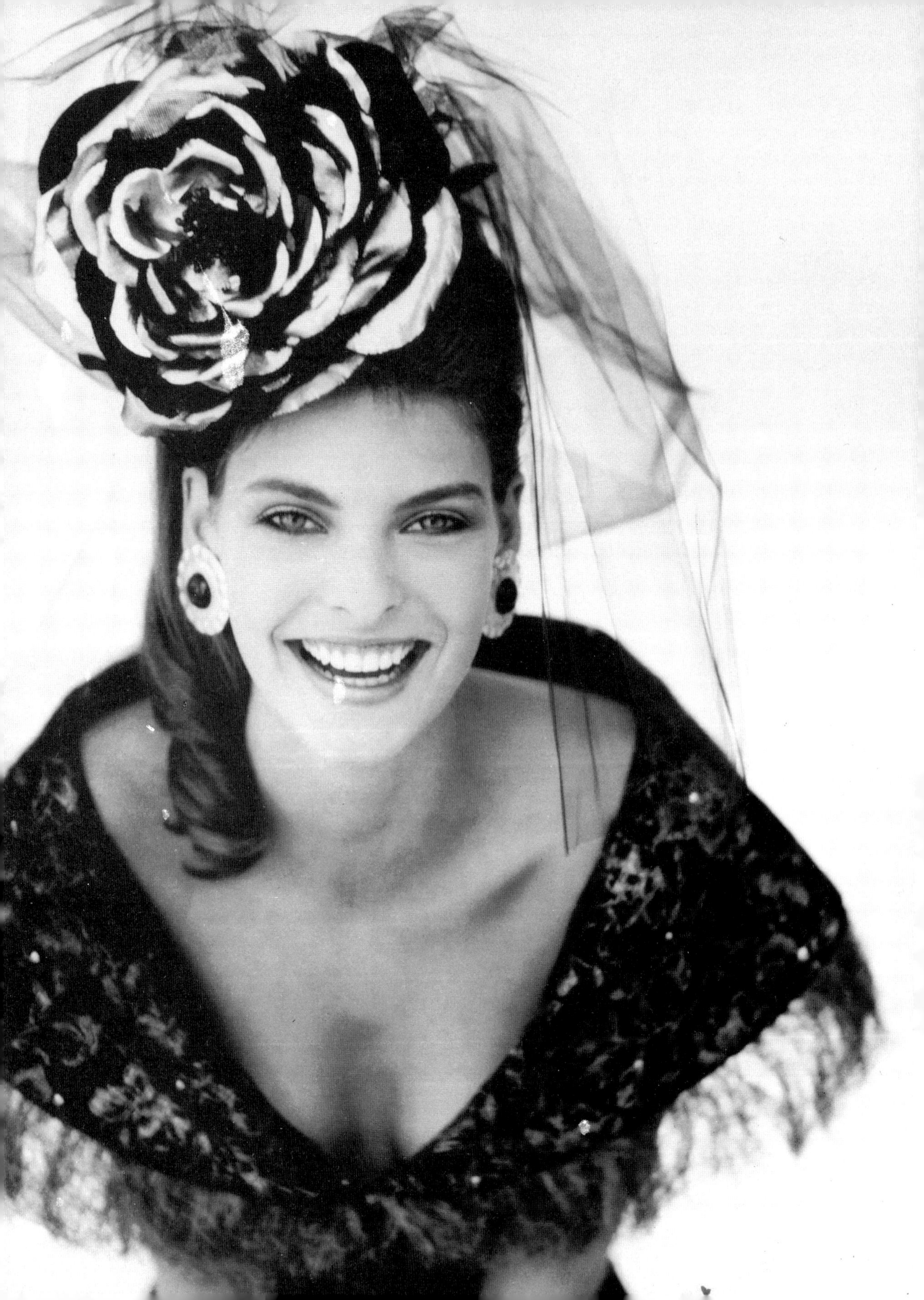

READING FASHION

A fashion magazine can be a valuable source of inspiration for individual style, but how much you get out of it depends on how and why you read it. Some readers treat glossy magazines as an escape from reality into a never-never land where people are beautiful, have perfect figures and live in a tropical paradise or cool white rooms. These readers go into a trance and forget their own lifestyle and budget, and luxuriate in private fantasies of wealth, beauty and stardom. When the pages come to an end they bump back to earth feeling dissatisfied and fed up that magazines never show clothes for ordinary people.

The opposite approach is the magazine addict reader who devours each page like the gospel, accepting everything as the last word on fashion. Unfortunately she often forgets to stop and consider whether the clothes would suit her style, or if she actually likes them. One of my most disillusioning moments while working at *Vogue* was spotting one of these readers who had copied a look slavishly from head to toe. The result was disastrous. She had taken the message literally: lifting it from the page on to herself, detail for detail, colour for colour. Any trace of her own style was swamped by the fashion statement.

The selective reader has a more rational approach. She never loses sight of her image and often buys a magazine because she identifies with the girl on the cover and expects to find corresponding fashion ideas inside. The independent reader has the most relaxed attitude. She is never a slave to magazines and usually flicks backwards through the pages, stopping for a second look at the clothes she likes. Certain ideas sink into her subconscious which may influence her decisions next time she goes shopping.

But whatever the type of reader, most people are too impulsive when they look at a magazine, too quick to dismiss the fashion as ridiculous, unrealistic, exorbitant, or intended for somebody else. These irrational, sweeping decisions make you disgruntled and blind to the point of the

Keep magazine fashion in perspective, treating it as a source for your own style

The image a model projects is an essential part of a fashion photograph. Whether her look is (clockwise) high energy, streetwise, sultry or innocent English Rose, it must be in keeping with the clothes she wears

fashion in the pictures. The important thing about reading a magazine is balance; between seeing it all as pure wishful thinking, a load of rubbish, or the extreme of following each direction with blind obedience. The point of fashion in a magazine is to tell each reader about as many different options of style and price as possible, and to offer ideas and suggestions. It is not a manifesto that dictates what must be worn each season, but a source of inspiration to help you decide how you would like to look.

It is difficult not to be prejudiced for or against the clothes by the girl inside them. If you identify with the model, or long to look like her, you automatically take more notice of what she is wearing. If you dislike the model, or hate her hairstyle or expression, you are prompted to dismiss the fashion and turn the page. To be entirely neutral the clothes would have to be photographed on coat hangers, but that would remove a lot of their character. The person inside is just as important as the clothes themselves. Even for fashion photographs, it is essential to find a model whose image suits the style of the clothes. If you put glamorous, sophisticated evening dresses on a young, outdoor girl, the moods clash and the picture fails. The image of the model has a powerful effect on the fashion. Unlike the sixties when Twiggy was a household name, models today rarely become individual stars, but their type of hairstyle, make-up and figure can spark off a new look – whether athletic, elegantly polished, nostalgic, countrified or vampish.

What you see in a photograph is a fashion editor and photographer's interpretation of current fashion. The clothes that are featured and the way they are put together are bound to be a subjective choice. There are no definite rules as to what sort of clothes should be shown. One magazine may be showing cowboys, another smart city clothes or ethnic dressing. It does not mean one is behind the other, it is up to the reader to be discerning and choose for herself. Magazines have the power to promote a particular look and equal power to mix clothes and create separate fashions within a fashion. They can invent strange combinations, mixing designer clothes with traditional classics, antiques and sportswear – ideas for the reader to interpret and improvise on herself, without obligation to buy the actual clothes featured.

BEHIND A PHOTOGRAPH

A fashion story starts with a basic idea, usually a theme that focuses on a colour, new proportions, textures, patterns, or clothes for specific occasions. The fashion editor scans the market for appropriate clothes to tell the story. In cheap fashion features, you seldom see an outfit put

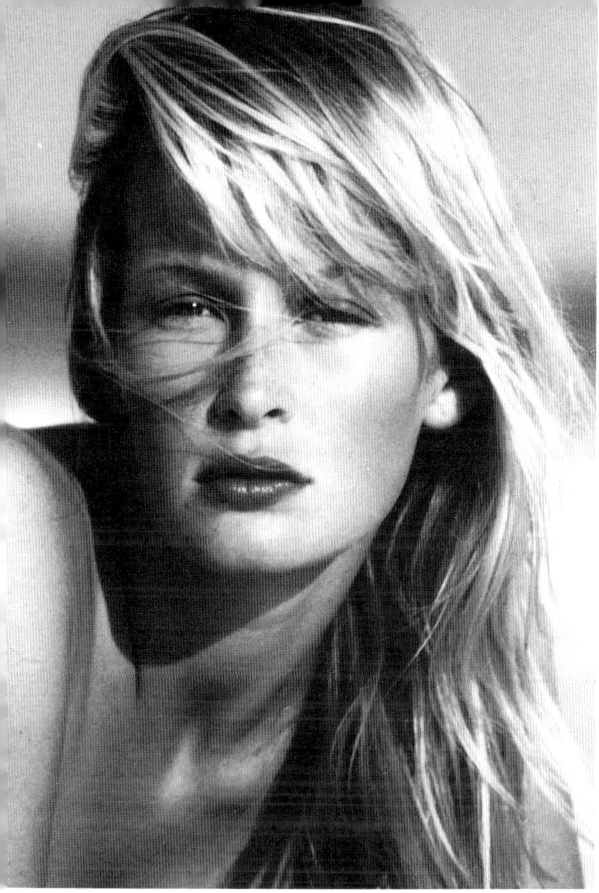
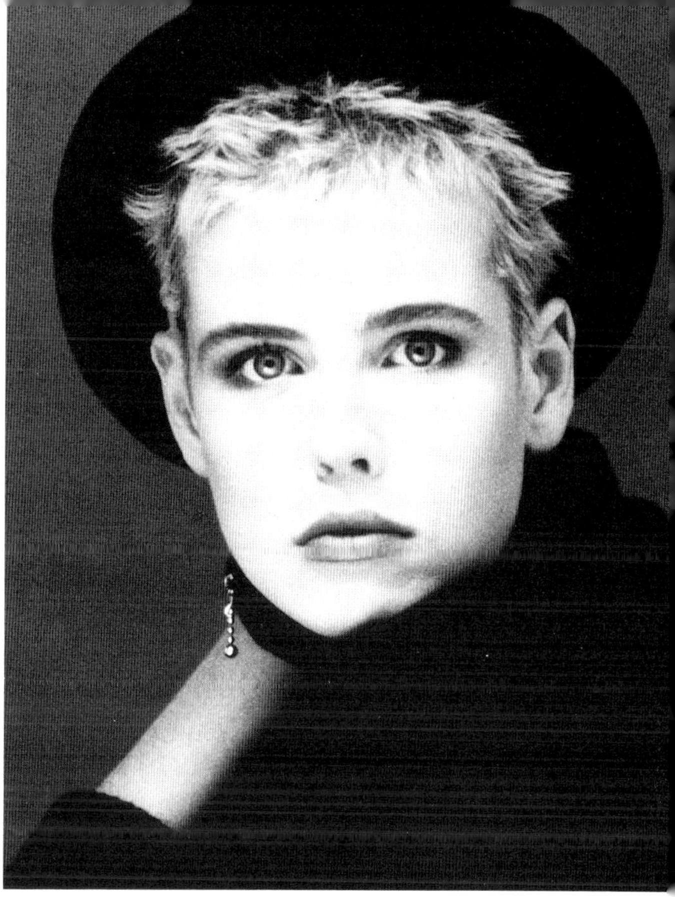
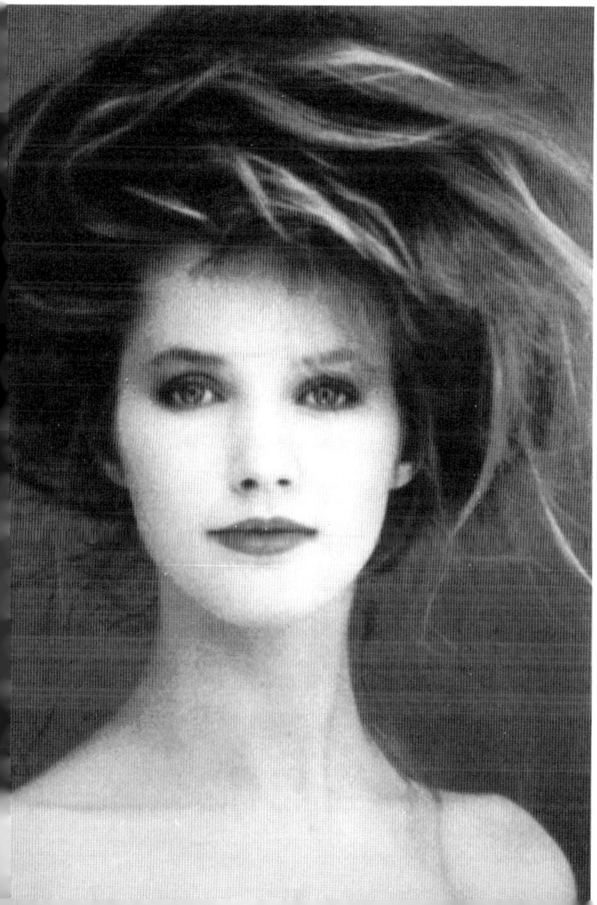
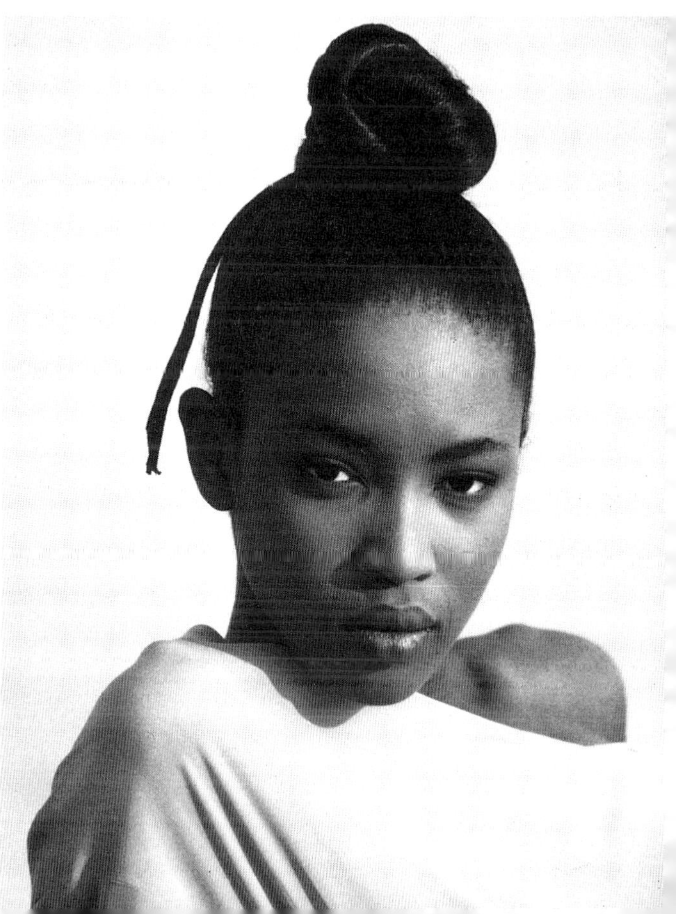

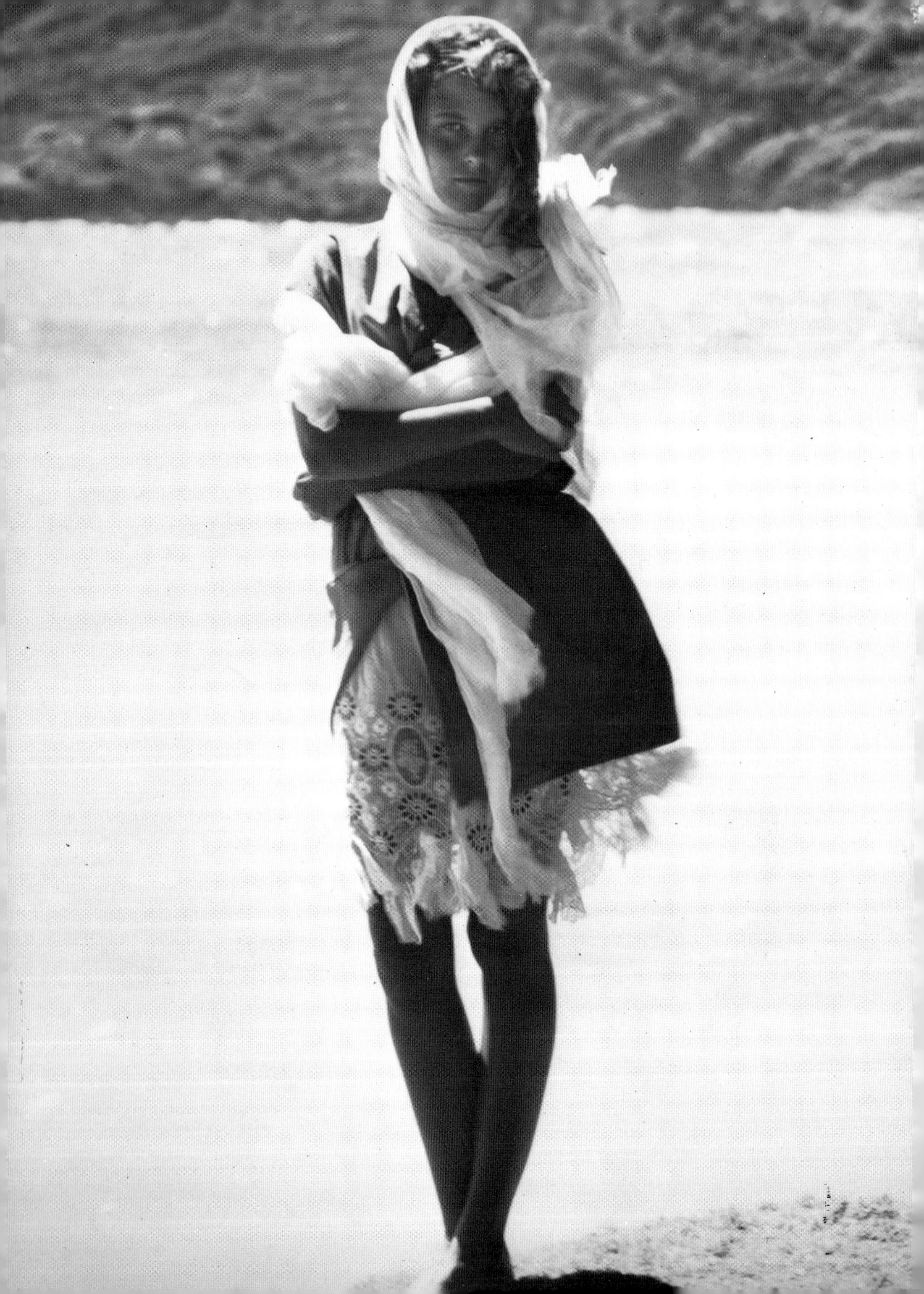

together exclusively from one label. Making original looks involves a mix of garments – and adding something unexpected provides extra dash. Luckily fashion editors have the freedom to juggle tops and bottoms to create the right effect. (Fashion advertisements often lack originality and style because they are bound by the confines of selling one brand name.) The outfits that emerge from the selection process are then ready for photography. Once on location, whether in a studio, a house, the countryside, on the street or a tropical beach, the clothes start to live.

But just like real-life dressing, a combination that looked good on a hanger may look uninspiring on the model, and may need some working on. It is time to experiment with different shoes, belts, jewellery, scarves, taking things off and on and off again until it all fits together. Besides the clothes, the hair and make-up are vital ingredients in the final image. Both have to be in keeping with the mood of the clothes and location. Even if they are performed by experts, the most successful fashion pictures give the impression that the face and hair were done by the girl in the picture. A model lolling on a windswept beach with an intricate hair-do and full make-up looks ridiculously artificial.

The most critical ingredient is the photographer. Like top models, the best photographers have a distinctive style which may be more compatible with rugged outdoor fashion than glossy evening dresses, or vice versa. The success of the feature depends strongly on the affinity between the photographer, the model and the fashion itself. The aim is to create a picture that is both artistic and informative. A picture that tells the reader as much as possible about the clothes; the cut, the shape, the texture, the colours, and how to wear them. It can be irritating when art takes over and the clothes are photographed from behind or scrunched up on the floor, or the feet are cropped out of the page, so you have to read about them in the caption instead. But there is a positive angle to these 'mood' pictures. If you like what you see of the clothes, you are forced by necessity to use your imagination and build up the look for yourself.

With most fashion photographs there is a degree of spontaneous invention. Sessions can never be planned like military operations. No one can forecast an exact result until the team joins together, then things that may not occur to the reader can influence the final picture. The size and shape of the model can alter the way the clothes are worn. The pair of shoes that appears on every page could be the only pair that fits her large feet. That ingenious way of wearing a sweater with the V at the back is a successful accident – it looked better back to front so it stayed put. A resourceful hairdresser may devise a new style of fastening a ponytail with a brooch because his last elastic band snapped, or use a tie from a leather sandal to make a headband because it is longer than his ribbon.

Fashion editors can create their own impromptu combinations; mixing designer's clothes with antique lace and lengths of inexpensive materials – ideas to interpret and improvise on

When you realize it is not a cut-and-dried procedure, but one where a strong element of trial and error counts, it makes sense to treat fashion photographs as a springboard for information and ideas. Too often when a particular garment is featured, the buying public have a distinct imagination failure and rush off to find a duplicate, preferably in the same colour. Not surprisingly shops cash in on publicity and encourage you to buy the duplicate jacket or skirt just because it has appeared in a magazine. That does not make it better than everything else in the shop; there may be similar shapes and colours that will suit you more. (When the garment was photographed, it may only have been available in one sample colour, and not necessarily the prettiest.) It is worth remembering that in black and white photography, the clothes featured are often very pale or white, or very dark colours, because they photograph more sharply than medium colours like mid-blue, red and green.

THE SEASONAL FACTOR

The annoying part of buying high-fashion clothes from magazine features is that by the time they arrive in the shops, which usually coincides with the magazine publication, they are, as far as the fashion experts are concerned, on the wane. The trade latches on to spring and summer fashion in October, and autumn and winter fashion in March, and there is nothing to stop you doing the same. Twice a year the collections in London, Paris, Milan and New York are given wide press coverage. As magazines work three or four months in advance, newspapers supply the instant fashion report. The trouble is that it is hard to feel enthusiasm and interest for clothes relevant to a season we have just been through. But it is well worth studying the reports and digesting the new details, themes and colours which, with skill, can be used ahead of time. What you buy for summer can be influenced by your knowledge of the winter collections. It is a really useful idea to cut out and keep pictures of the styles you like, and use them as a guideline. If you are not a regular magazine buyer, the most informative issues to read are those with a summary of the coming season's fashion – issues which usually coincide with new stock in the shops. If you can find them, foreign fashion magazines, especially the French, Italian and American ones are worth looking at. The fashion stories offer a different viewpoint, and because the price and stockists are irrelevant, you take more notice of the clothes, colours, and the way everything goes together.

The most habitual complaints from magazine readers are that most of the clothes featured are too expensive. Magazines do not set out to torture their readers with unrealistic prices. The fact that the most striking fashion features consist of expensive clothes is often hard to avoid. Very often they are the only ones of their kind in existence, and have to be used to tell the story. Probably by the time the magazine appears on the bookstalls there are similar versions at lower prices. Magazines also have a duty to provide fashion information. Given the choice between a beautifully made pair of dark navy trousers in fine wool gaberdine and a badly cut, royal navy pair in polyester gaberdine, they will select the expensive version as an example of the best of a kind. Careful photography with cheap clothes can be disillusioning; they can look terrific in the picture, but tatty in a shop. Not necessarily because they have been photographed through a misty lens, but because they have been worn imaginatively and mixed with original, more expensive accessories. The usual fault with cheap fashion is the skimpiness of cut, something which can be disguised by putting the model in a size twelve or fourteen instead of a ten. A more generous shape with coats, jackets, shirts and trousers immediately adds more style and improves the look of the clothes.

Reading a magazine is like visiting more than one shop. There are

Use the key details in a photograph as fashion pointers: note the wide portrait collar, high waisted skirt, long gloves and lack of jewellery

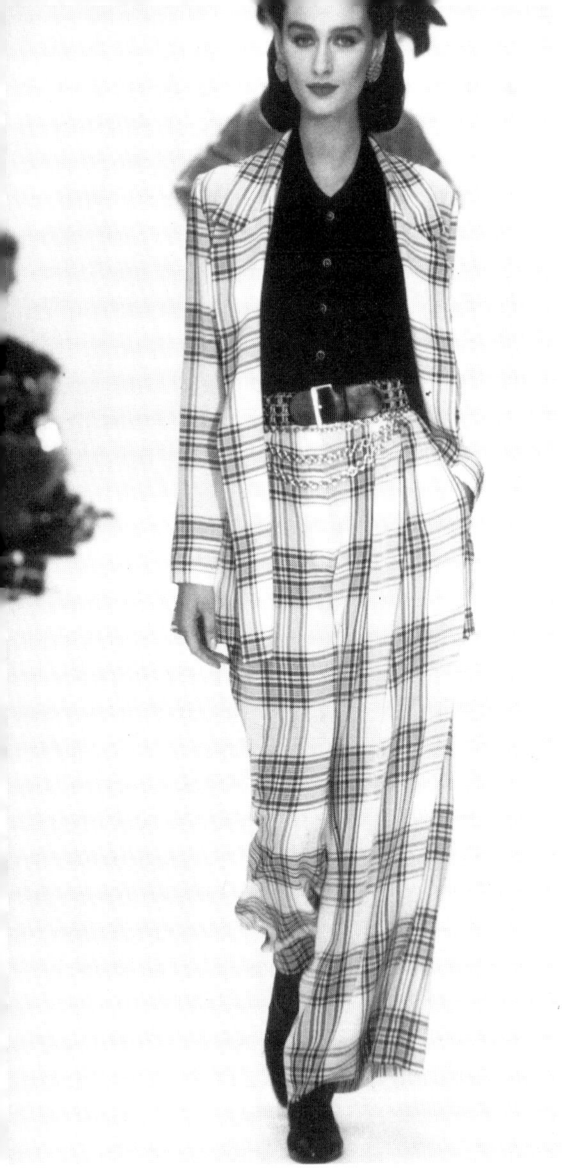
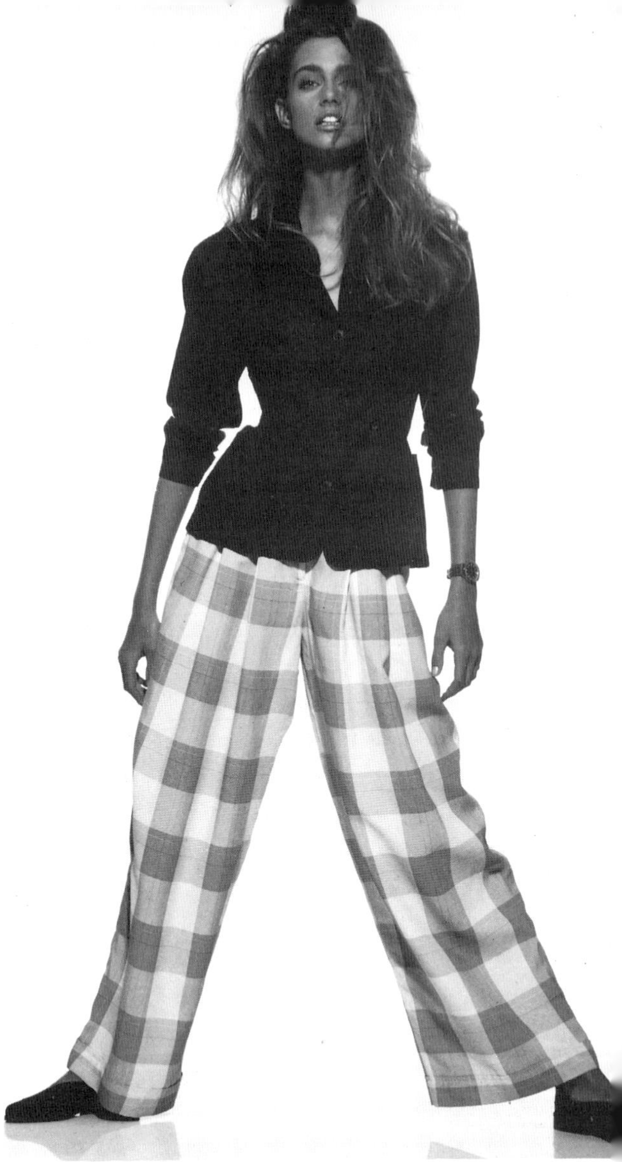
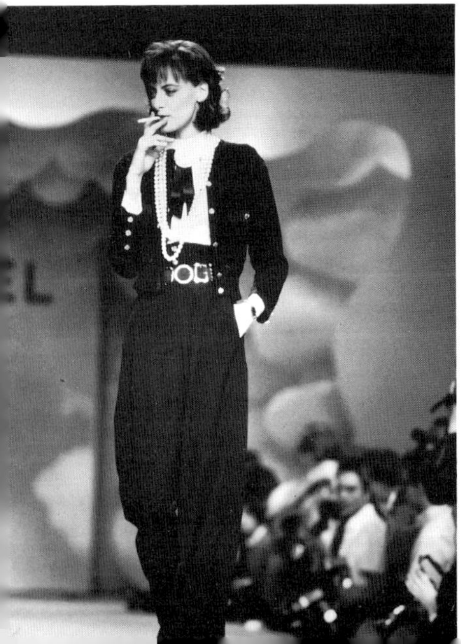
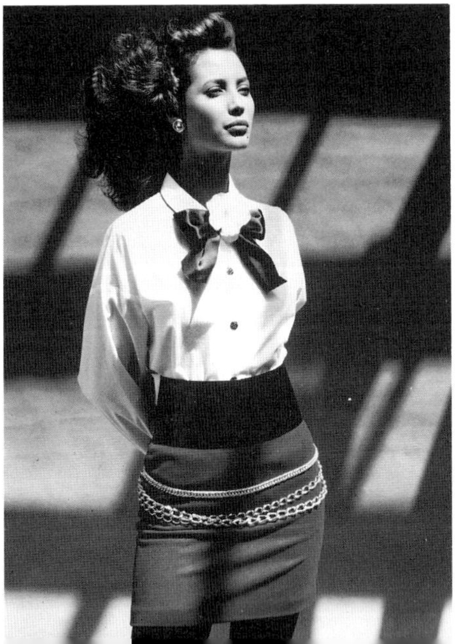
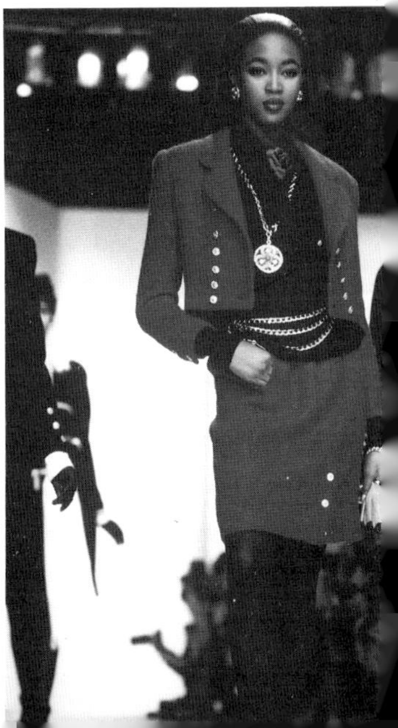

More Dash than Cash Chanel – watch the distinctive hallmarks move from couture to high street: (far left) *Chanel's plaid silk suit, echoed* (right) *in more accessible wide check pants and black jacket*

(below) *Signature gilt chains, pearls, crisp white shirt, black satin bow* (left and right) *reappear* (centre) *at fractional prices*

usually two or three fashion options to consider with different styles and price tags. But being confined to the cheap pages should not stop you benefiting from the expensive pages. If you study them, you start to recognize the handwriting of top designers and notice how their influence filters through to the cheaper market. You are ready to spot a knock-off Azzedine Alaia or Chanel; and a well-made knock-off is the next best thing to the real thing.

KEY DETAILS

Now there are so few overnight sensations, it is often the details of how the clothes are put together that make fashion news. These details, not always immediately obvious, can update what appears at first to be yet another feature about coats or jackets. After the initial browse through a magazine, you need to look back with a more fashion-conscious eye for the key details. Start with the overall shape. Is the silhouette narrow, layered, voluminous or fitted? Then check proportions, scrutinize the lengths and shapes of skirts, trousers, coats, jackets, knitwear and how they measure against each other. Are the skirts longer with loose blazers, shorter with cropped jackets? Do the trousers skim the ankle bone, or fall in folds over the shoes, and are the heels high or low? Where is the strongest focus? Is the eye drawn to square, curved, dropped or exaggerated shoulders? Is the waist accentuated, or is the hip line more noticeable? Do the knees feature at all? How are the clothes structured? Is the look tailored, ruffled, or soft and fluid? Notice how the clothes fit the body; is everything neat and fitted or loosely wrapped?

Then check the finer points. Notice every accessory, storing up ideas you like as you go along, watching the context of the clothes and the way each accessory is used, not just what they look like as individual objects. Is jewellery an important part of the style, or is it unnecessary? Is there emphasis on one thing – a special brooch, long pearls, heavy bangles, spectacular earrings, a blanket shawl, a diver's watch, a hair accessory? Is one recurrent belt the mainstay of a particular look – a wrapped sash, a neat, narrow leather belt that discreetly defines the waist, or a bright cummerbund that is a focal point?

While you check the accessories in each picture, think about what has been left out. An essential side of accessorizing is also what you leave off the clothes. The statement often has more impact by reducing accessories to the minimum. When you see a photograph without any accessories, it is not that the fashion editor forgot to take them with her, but because the clothes do not need any embellishments or distractions.

Shoes, socks, tights or stockings are permanent accessories that

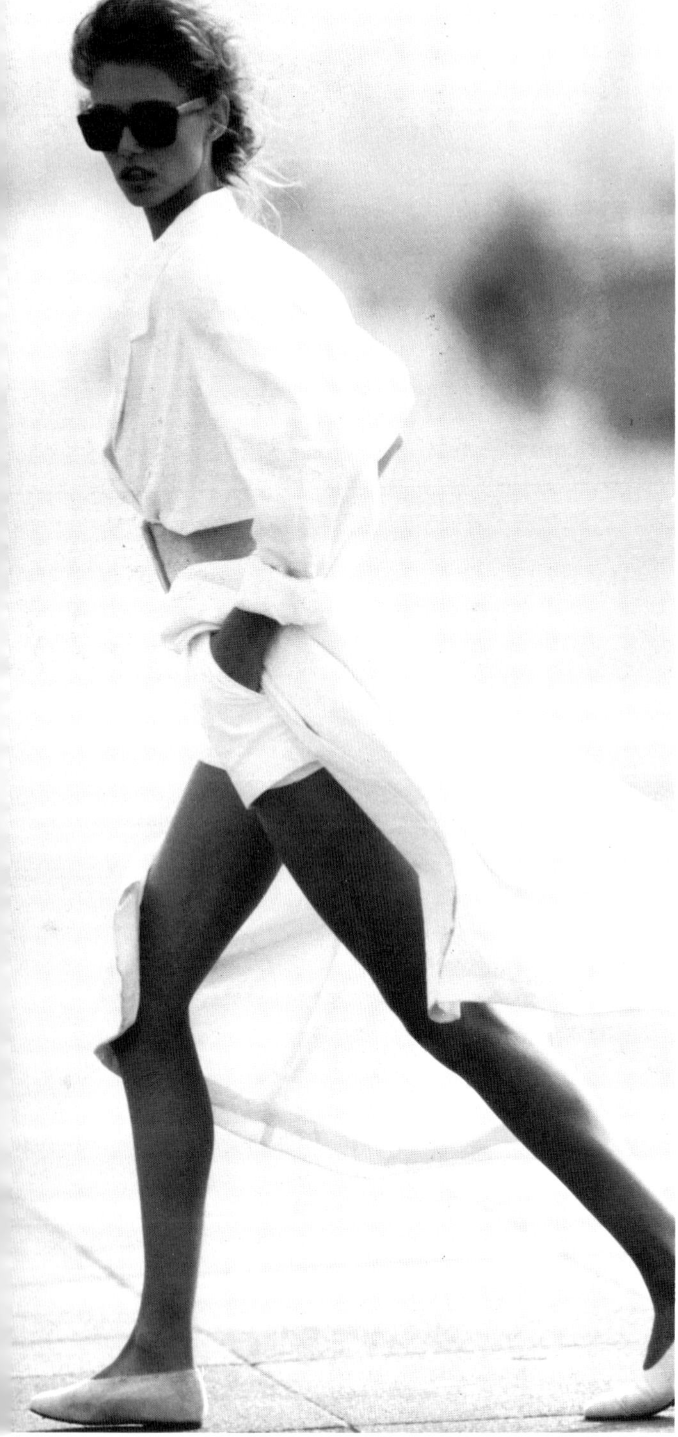
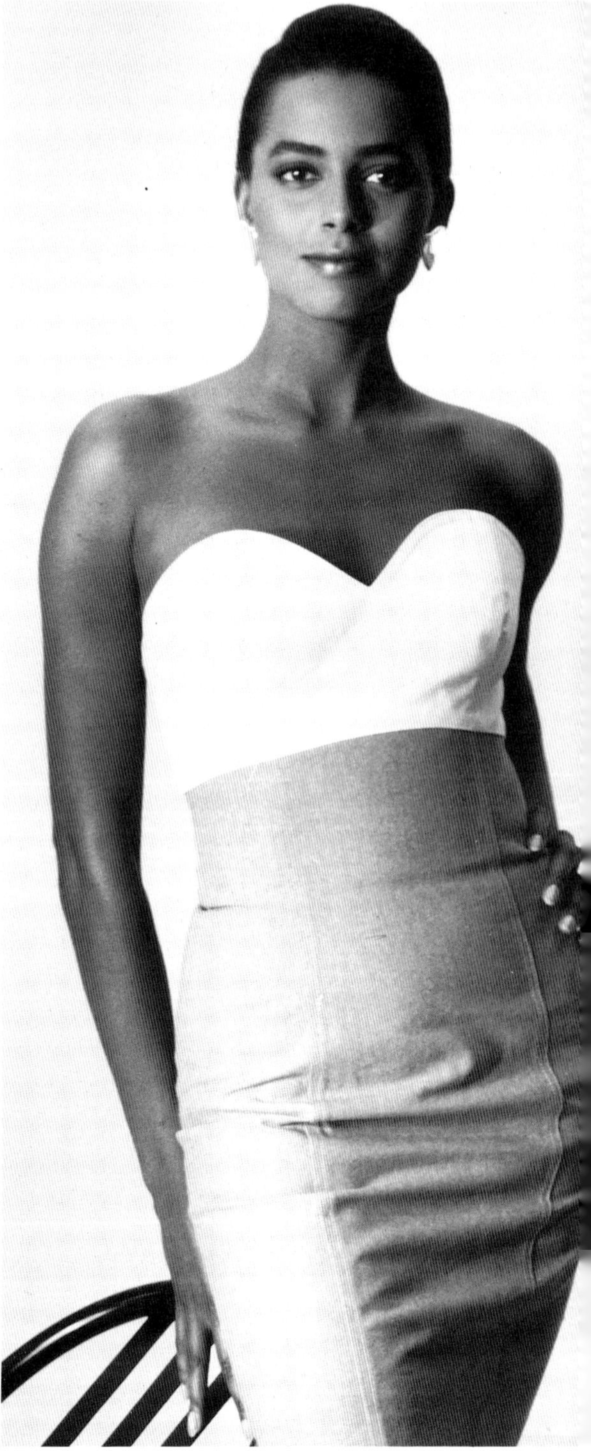

Reading Fashion

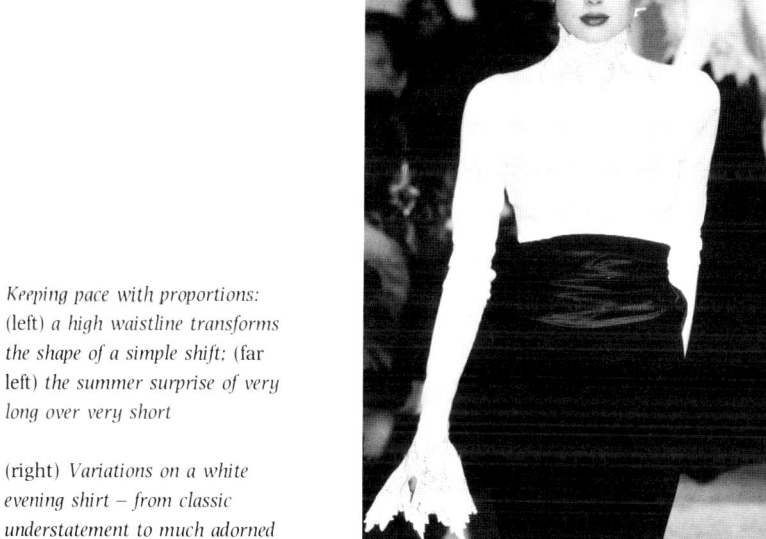

Keeping pace with proportions: (left) *a high waistline transforms the shape of a simple shift;* (far left) *the summer surprise of very long over very short*

(right) *Variations on a white evening shirt – from classic understatement to much adorned opulence*

always indicate a fashion message. New shapes, colour, density and texture immediately update one look into another. Heel heights alter the whole proportions. There are still fixed associations with shoe types: low heels with coloured opaque tights spell relaxed, informal dressing, and elegant high heels with sheer, neutral tights imply smarter, grown-up dressing. But footwear can provide the unexpected twist that updates a classic style into something new. Suddenly putting flat country shoes and thick tights where you expect to find high shoes and ten-denier stockings can be the difference between last year's style and this year's.

When you find a look that you like, besides studying the actual clothes, notice how they are worn. It can be the smallest details that make them stand out. The points to check may sound insignificant, but they are what counts. Little details like whether the sleeves of a shirt, tee shirt or jacket are rolled back; whether a collar is turned up or down; whether a jacket is belted or left unbuttoned; which tops are tucked into skirts or trousers, which are left loose, which ones belted. Whenever a belt features, how is it worn? Is a coat or raincoat belted with a self belt or a different one? How is the scarf tied; like a muffler, a kerchief, a headband? Must it be a square or oblong to work that way?

It is important to disinguish between these subtle finishing touches and shortlived fashion gimmicks; the looks that stand out at the time

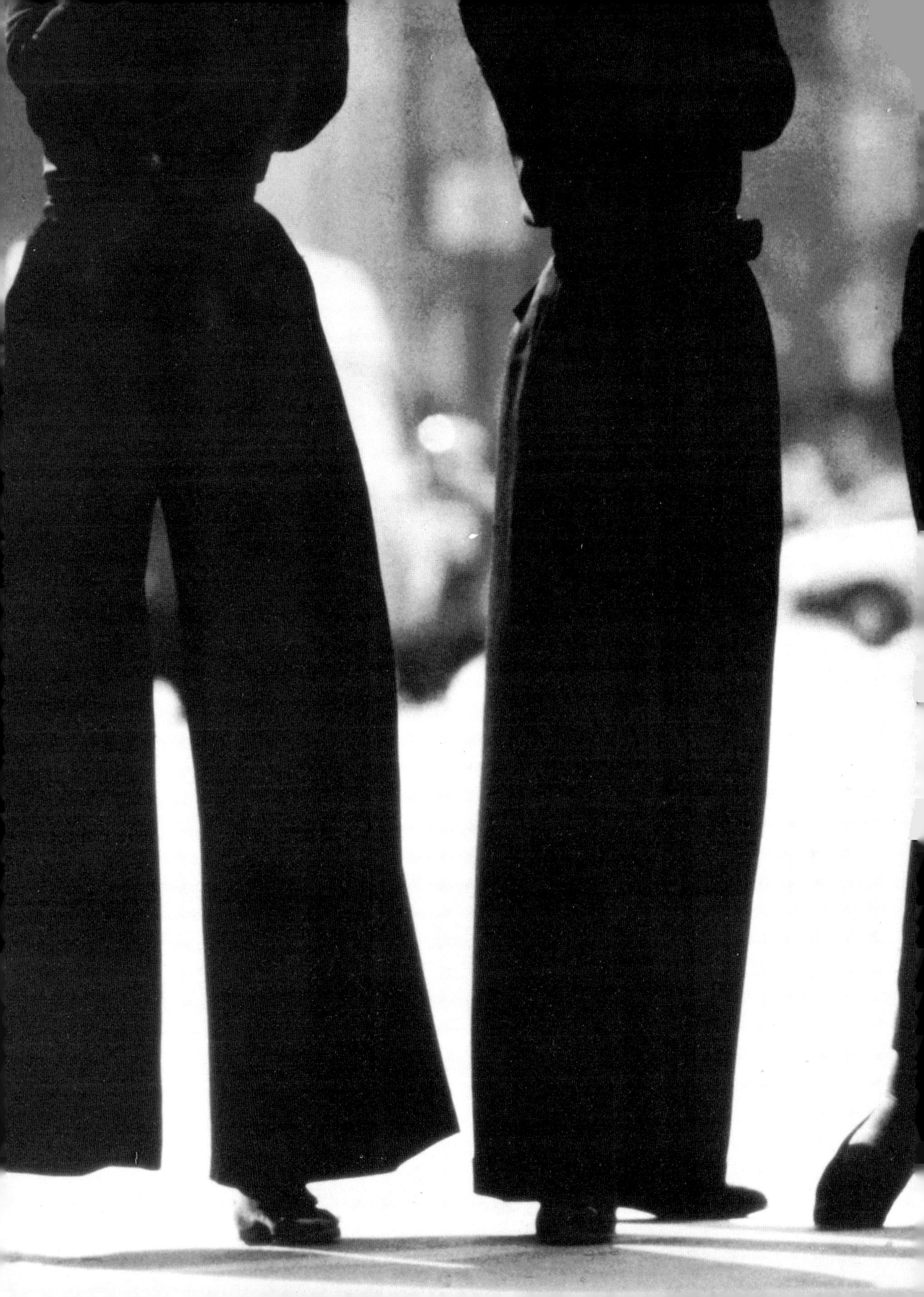

One season's range of conflicting trousers shapes – flared, straight, cropped or jodhpur – emphasise the flexible state of contemporary fashion

Fashion extremes – a lethal exaggeration of styling: mini-coats in 1969 with oversized collars, lapels, pockets and belts

Timeless classics: with contemporary hair and make-up, this 1965 Fair Isle sweater would look quite in keeping today

because they are extremes, but date overnight when the next craze arrives, and feel like history five years later. Anyone can learn to spot a fleeting, but newsworthy look. The key point is an exaggeration of styling – clothes with completely opposite qualities to a classic.

The shoe cycle is an example. Fashions for platform soles, wedges and stilettos occur sporadically and each time round are worn for their novelty value, but when the look reverts to a naturally elegant, thin-soled, fine-heeled shoe, the other styles seem like monstrous, clumpy gimmicks.

See-sawing hemlines are another obvious fashion extreme. looking back at the late sixties and seventies it is almost possible to tell the year by the length of the skirts. Now the shapes and proportions are more telling than hemlines. The critical details to watch – not difficult, as exaggerations tend to hit you in the eye – are overemphasized lapels, oversized collars and cuffs, unnatural shoulder shapes, trouser widths, turn-ups,

(right) *High fashion classics do move with the times; short skirts have been a key direction of the late eighties – a far cry from the 1965 mini (bottom right)*

(bottom left) *Gimmick looks – often a source of confusion while they last. 1984 followed a Japanese mood in asymmetric, cut-out clothes*

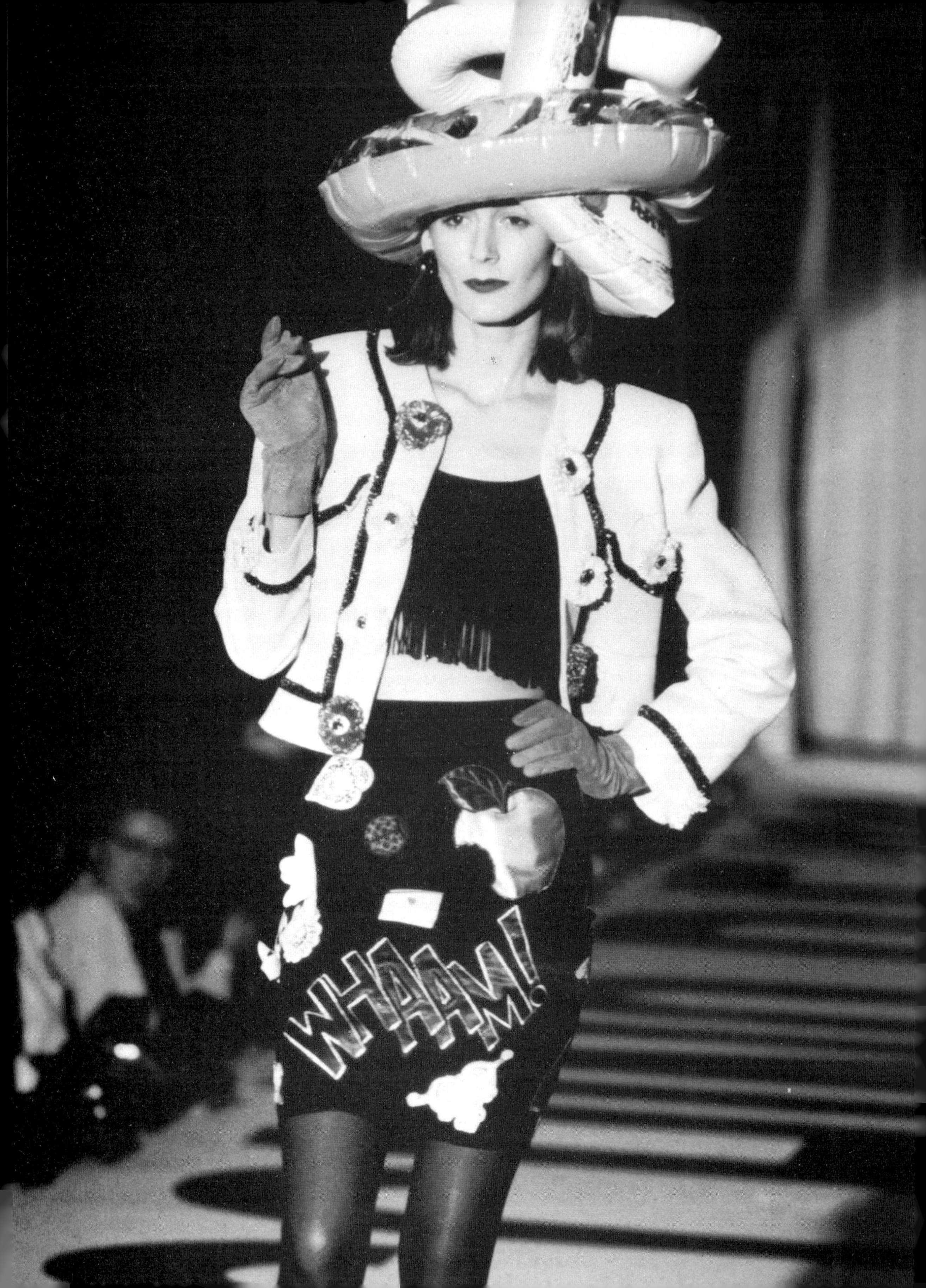
WHAAM!

Catwalk style: (left) *with tongue in cheek, Moschino takes the Milanese fashion victim to extremes*

(above right) *Yves Saint Laurent exaggerates the point of his Cubist collection*

wide waistbands, contrived details like top stitching and excessive trimming. They are all danger spots prone to overdesigning.

The pattern is apparent when you look at back copies of fashion magazines and pick out the most dating aspects of the clothes. With true classics, the only part that dates is the way the fashion is put together, with accessories, hair and make-up typical of that year. Taken out of context and updated, the same clothes – a trench coat, a sweater and shirt, a blazer – can all look quite in keeping today. But the high-fashion extremes just make us laugh and feel amazed that anyone could actually have walked around looking so extraordinary. Gimmicks, which at the time were the key fashion details, show up as ugly, unnatural sensations. There are high fashion classics which reappear in a style to suit the contemporary climate. The sixties mini – a straight shift, pinafore or little suit – re-emerged as the key direction of the late eighties, influencing couture, mass market and street style. It has evolved beyond the sporty mood of leggings and long sweaters into a sophisticated alternative for tailored suits, coats and party dresses.

One thing to remember is that from a magazine viewpoint an extreme fashion with a definite message is a news story which, as an information service, it is their duty to pass on. A photograph illustrating the total look from one designer is a faithful reproduction of how he or she sent the models down the catwalk. A collection is shown as a fashion package, complete with theatrical accessories where needed and larger-than-life hair and make-up. It is often an extreme statement which the designer knows will be diluted and rearranged with other fashion, but one that puts the point of the new collection across.

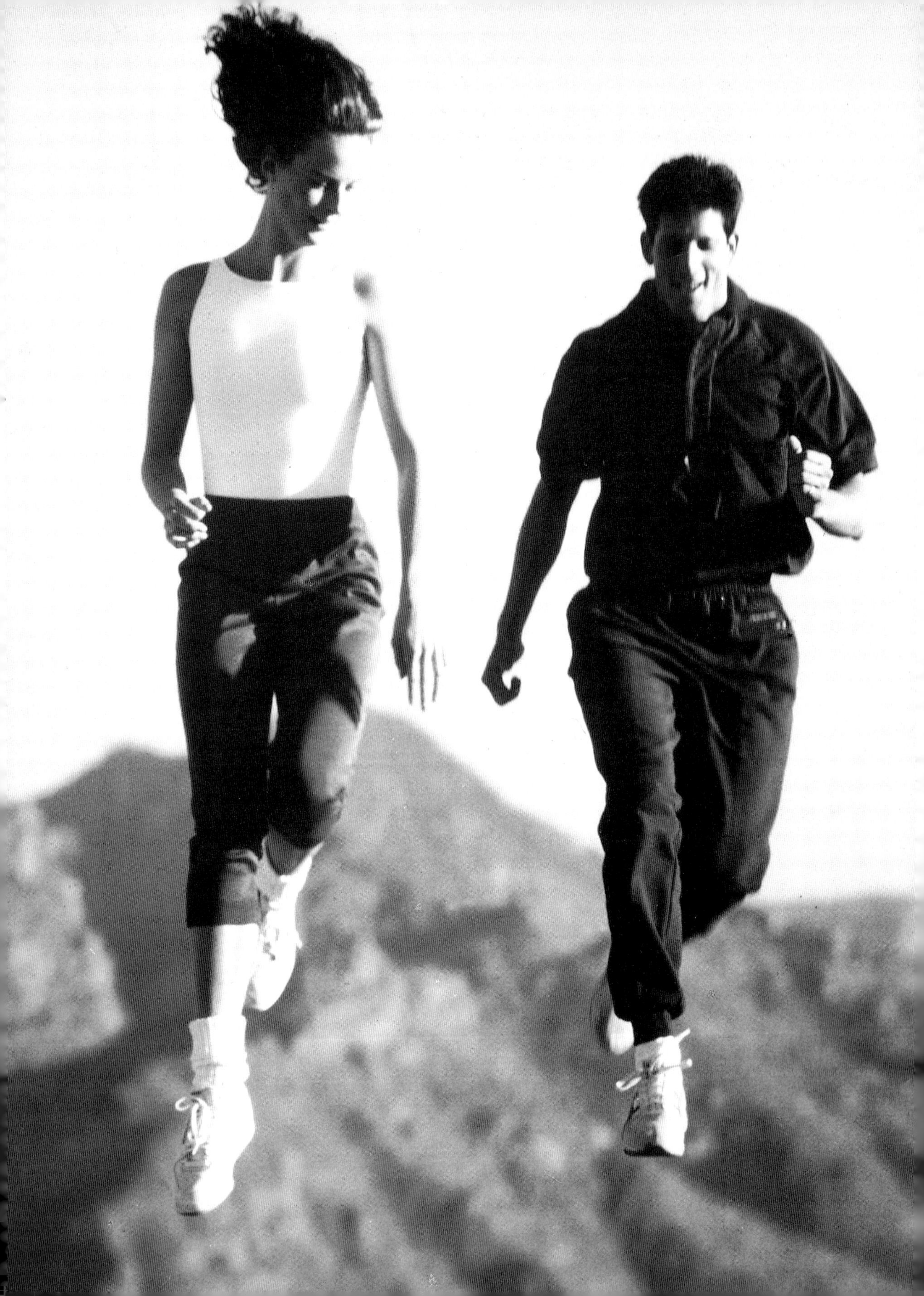

INSIDE STYLE

No clothes, however beautiful, can detract from a neglected physical appearance. An unhealthy body, unkempt skin and hair ruin everything. To look great you have to feel great, and that means looking after yourself, inside and out. You need the natural self-confidence that comes from a state of inner well-being. It all demands the right attitude to yourself, one that banishes any idea that a pre-occupation with health and appearance is self-indulgent. Looking after yourself is the best investment possible, one that requires more time and effort than money. It means incorporating a health and beauty routine into your lifestyle, so that it becomes second nature, but never an obsession. You may have to work out a new balance, like getting up ten minutes earlier to fit in a morning skin-care routine, or to wash your hair or repaint your nails. You need the self-discipline to find time for a proper night's sleep and a healthy breakfast, to keep a dental appointment, to find a bra that fits perfectly, all of which becomes easier if you see them as pleasures rather than chores, and accept that looking good involves consistent effort. Even born beauties have to work at staying beautiful. It is not something to take for granted – 'Il faut souffrir pour être belle,' as French mothers preach to their daughters.

To keep things in perspective, it is important to understand the basic principles of good health: how the body is affected by day to day living; what is good for the system and what is harmful; that it is possible to maintain a healthy state without cranky dieting and anti-social habits. Moderation is sensible – and necessary if you are to keep the constant wave of health hazard revelations in proportion. According to newspapers, magazines and television documentaries, there are dangers lurking in the most basic products – meat, milk, muesli, tap water – but virtually everything in unbalanced quantities is unhealthy, even health foods. If we reacted to every scare, life would be no fun at all.

How much you spend on beauty products is a matter of choice. With

To look your best you have to feel your best – that means looking after your body, inside and out

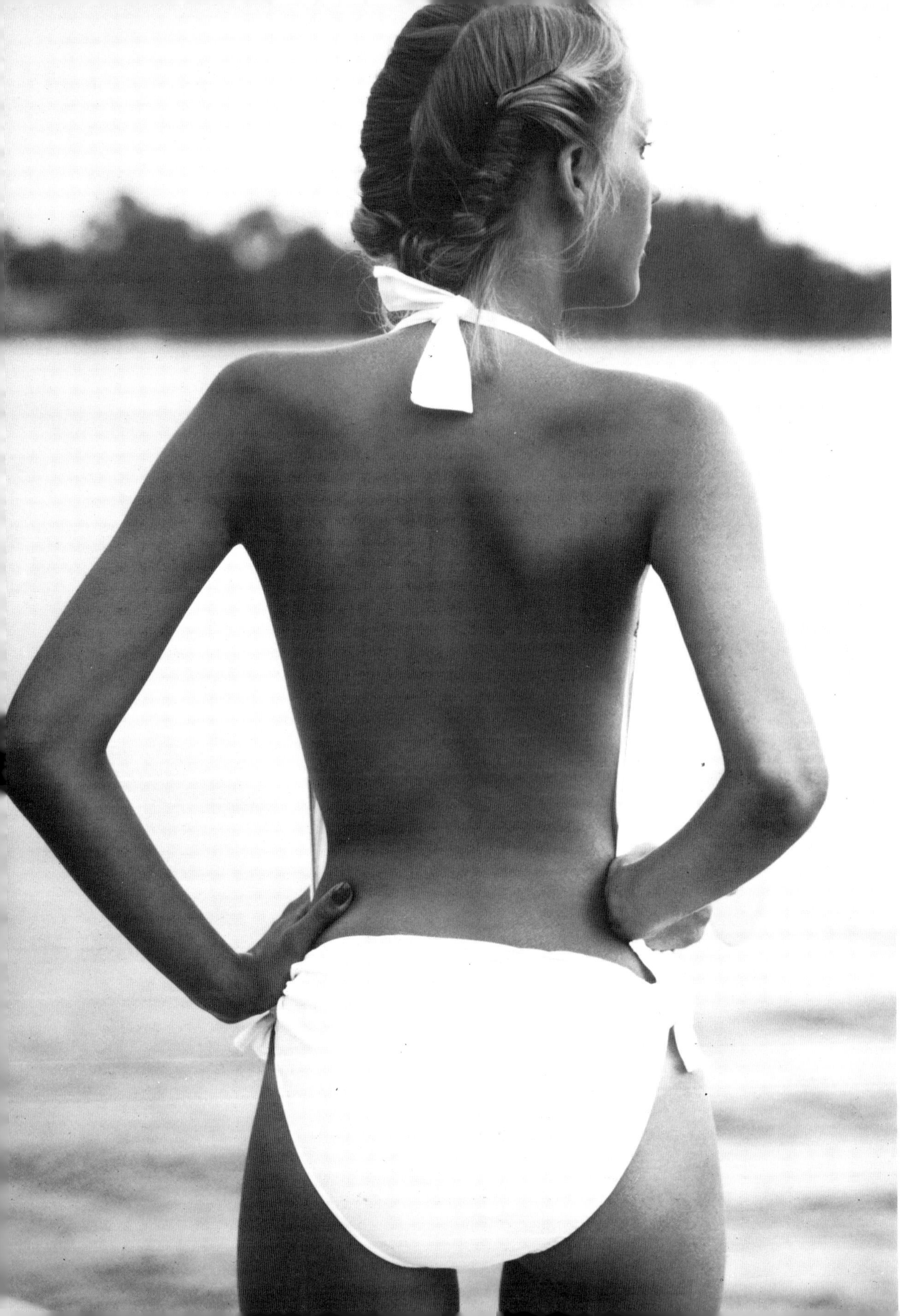

INSIDE STYLE

No clothes, however beautiful, can detract from a neglected physical appearance. An unhealthy body, unkempt skin and hair ruin everything. To look great you have to feel great, and that means looking after yourself, inside and out. You need the natural self-confidence that comes from a state of inner well-being. It all demands the right attitude to yourself, one that banishes any idea that a pre-occupation with health and appearance is self-indulgent. Looking after yourself is the best investment possible, one that requires more time and effort than money. It means incorporating a health and beauty routine into your lifestyle, so that it becomes second nature, but never an obsession. You may have to work out a new balance, like getting up ten minutes earlier to fit in a morning skin-care routine, or to wash your hair or repaint your nails. You need the self-discipline to find time for a proper night's sleep and a healthy breakfast, to keep a dental appointment, to find a bra that fits perfectly, all of which becomes easier if you see them as pleasures rather than chores, and accept that looking good involves consistent effort. Even born beauties have to work at staying beautiful. It is not something to take for granted – 'Il faut souffrir pour être belle,' as French mothers preach to their daughters.

To keep things in perspective, it is important to understand the basic principles of good health: how the body is affected by day to day living; what is good for the system and what is harmful; that it is possible to maintain a healthy state without cranky dieting and anti-social habits. Moderation is sensible – and necessary if you are to keep the constant wave of health hazard revelations in proportion. According to newspapers, magazines and television documentaries, there are dangers lurking in the most basic products – meat, milk, muesli, tap water – but virtually everything in unbalanced quantities is unhealthy, even health foods. If we reacted to every scare, life would be no fun at all.

How much you spend on beauty products is a matter of choice. With

To look your best you have to feel your best – that means looking after your body, inside and out

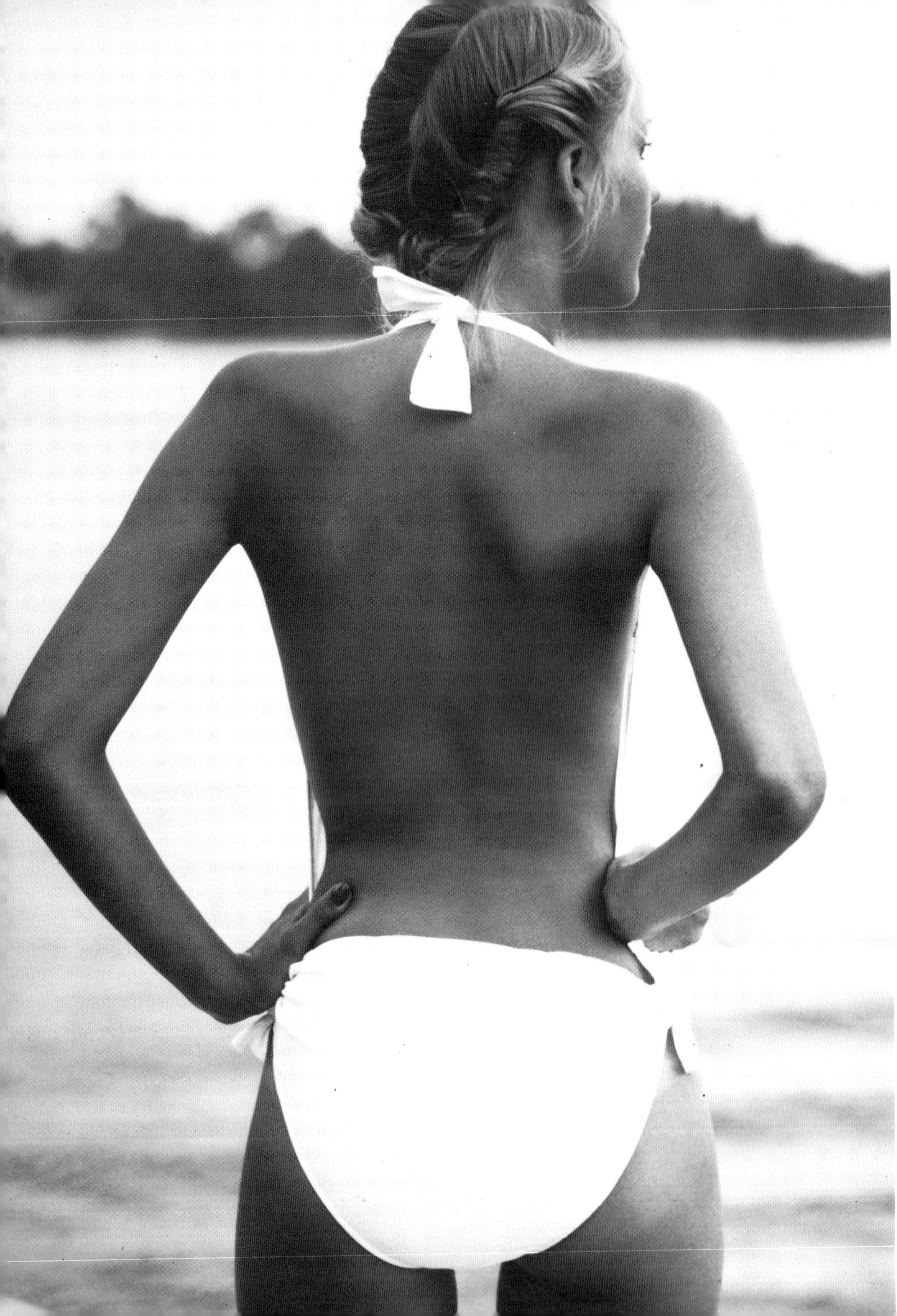

clothes you know immediately what you are paying for. You choose the colour and the shape, you can tell what a particular garment does for you. When you choose beauty products, whether skin care, hair care, cosmetics, or sun products, the price and the advertising are the only guidelines. It is tempting to be seduced by the glamorous image that comes with high-priced products. When you treat yourself to expensive brands, you feel rather special. The effect can be more psychological than directly beneficial to your skin or hair. High-priced products are not automatically superior to cheaper ones; you may be paying extra for advertising, smart packaging and a prestige name. How much more efficient expensive brands are is a controversial point. Basically the various types of product perform the same function; some higher priced ones *may* be more sophisticated and scientifically advanced, and therefore some people would say superior. But if you like the performance and texture of an inexpensive brand, so much the better. The key point is to find a range that works for you and then stay with it. In any event go for the pure, non-scented types – baby products are unbeatable for economy and purity. Whatever your budget, it is essential to portion it carefully across all your demands. But if you have one problem area, be it skin or hair, it obviously qualifies for special attention, especially if the problem affects your self-confidence.

SKIN

Skin is the first area that reacts against poor treatment. Its condition is a giveaway to our state of well-being. Facial skin is the most vulnerable, and its sensitivity varies with everyone, but most faces are affected by certain external and internal conditions – harsh temperatures, cold or hot sun, strong winds, drying atmosphere from central heating, air conditioning, long contact with water or strong detergents. From inside, it is affected by diet, smoking, alcohol, stress, fatigue, illness, hormone balance and erratic sleep patterns.

Whatever your skin type, a consistent **skin care programme** is crucial. It should be as automatic as brushing teeth, twice a day. Vital stages are cleansing, toning, and moisturizing. All faces, however dry they seem, have a T zone of oilier skin across the forehead and down the nose and chin. This area is the most prone to spots and disorders because it has the highest density of sebaceous glands. Unless skin in the zone is kept scrupulously clean, oily secretions from the glands can block the pores and encourage spots and blackheads. Trouble can be aggravated, and even caused, by absentminded habits of holding and touching the chin.

Cleansing can be done in two stages; the first with a cream or lotion

Every inch of skin on the face and body deserves consistent care

that dissolves make-up, the second with mild acid-balanced soap which is the most efficient and underrated method of removing stubborn grime and the left-over greasiness of the cleanser. The soap must be specifically for the face as ordinary soap has a high alkaline content which strips the natural protective moisture from the skin.

Toning stimulates the circulation, closes the pores and helps to prevent a build-up of dead flaky skin. Dry or sensitive skins should avoid astringent toners with an alcohol content, or any product that stings. All toners are too strong for the eye area.

Moisturizing is the essential protective stage. It helps prevent water loss from the skin by sealing in the natural moisture and keeping the surface smooth. Rough, dry skin is a sign of dehydration. Moisturizer is an essential guard against the external enemies and should be applied before the skin is subjected to extreme environments, or sudden changes from one temperature to another. It is wise to carry a tube around with you and use it whenever your skin feels dry or tight, but always in small quantities. Overloading your face with moisturizer leaves it feeling puffy and can block the pores, especially last thing at night. The eye area is particularly vulnerable and needs delicate cleansing with a specific eye make-up remover, and moisturizing with a tiny amount of eye cream. Lips need permanent protection against chapping with a lipsalve, which in summer should contain a sunscreen. The neck is too often neglected but qualifies for the same regular treatment as your face.

Long baths are wonderfully relaxing, but soaking in water draws natural moisture from the skin – the hotter the water, the harsher the action. **Bath oil** and body lotion help to counteract the drying process. Showers are kinder to the skin than hot baths. There is no time for any skin damage, and the force of the water braces the circulation. Whenever you wash the body, use products that match the skin's chemistry. Skin is covered with a protective layer called an acid mantle; a delicate barrier which has to be kept intact by maintaining its correct pH balance. (The pH scale runs from 0, acid, to 14, alkaline.) Most mantles contain an equal, or slightly acid biased, balance producing a pH between 4 and 5 – which is broken down by high pH alkaline detergents – the kinds of soap and bubble baths that lather profusely and leave the skin feeling taut and itchy. Once destroyed, the mantle takes twelve hours to replace itself but during that vulnerable time skin needs extra protective moisturizing and care. Skin renewal is a constant process, too often indicated by dry, scaly patches on the body – areas of dead skin ready to be sloughed away with a loofah, scrubbing brush or exfoliating soap.

The cumulative dangers of **sunbathing** have taken some of the cachet away from a suntan. Now instead of feeling unattractive and lily-white, you can justify a pale skin with the proven argument that you intend to

Baring all in summer calls for year round body maintenance

Inside Style

stay looking young with soft, wrinkle-free skin. But providing you treat your skin like a baby's when you do go in the sun, the psychological boost of being brown is undeniable. A suntan, particularly out of season, does make you glow with a feeling of health and self-confidence. It is the best example of how magical proper self-indulgence can be. A suntan does not have to be a dark chocolate brown, it is safer and just as stunning to toast yourself to a pale honey colour.

Whatever shade your tan, the sun is the skin's worst enemy, so to minimize danger it is essential to understand the mechanics of a suntan. Build up a tan gradually with the constant protection of a sunscreen which filters out harmful ultraviolet rays and lets through the ultraviolet tanning rays in small doses. Turning brown is the body's protective reaction to the sun. The brown is actually a pigment in the skin called melanin which is activated by ultraviolet light. The amount of brown pigment varies with each skin type and determines your sensitivity to the sun. Fair skins produce less melanin than dark ones, so they are more susceptible to sunburn and need a correspondingly high degree of protection. If you have very fair or sensitive skin which cannot tolerate sun at all, resign yourself to staying pale, feminine and in no danger of skin damage. Capitalize on a delicate complexion, which was after all the yardstick of beauty for centuries, and shade yourself behind a wide-brimmed straw and cream tulle veiling. Sunburn is a sign of skin damage. Sore red skin is not the natural beginning of a tan, it may turn brown, but will peel fast, especially after a bath or swim. Even when you are not consciously sunbathing, the strength of the sun is the same and attacks any exposed areas of skin. If you are caught unaware, the only answer is to go inside or cover yourself in more clothes. In hot climates the shade can be almost as treacherous as direct sunlight. Constant protection is *essential*, it is never worth taking a risk, even for five minutes.

BODY MAINTENANCE

Like being brown, being fit is pure pleasure. **Fitness** that comes from regular exercise is exhilarating. You feel in control of your body, become more aware of movements, gestures, posture. Exercise is a great stimulation for both body and mind. Inactivity saps energy and makes you feel heavy and lethargic. Fitness breeds energy, making you more alive, more spontaneous, less inclined to laze about and yawn all the time. It is so satisfying to find enough energy to run effortlessly for a bus without gasping for breath, purple in the face. To stay fit, exercise has to be a regular, preferably daily, part of your life, but not an obsession.

Understand the science of sunbathing and build up your tan gradually with constant protection from a sunscreen

Exercise is a marvellous tonic for mind and body. With regular practice, yoga brings strength, flexibility and peace of mind

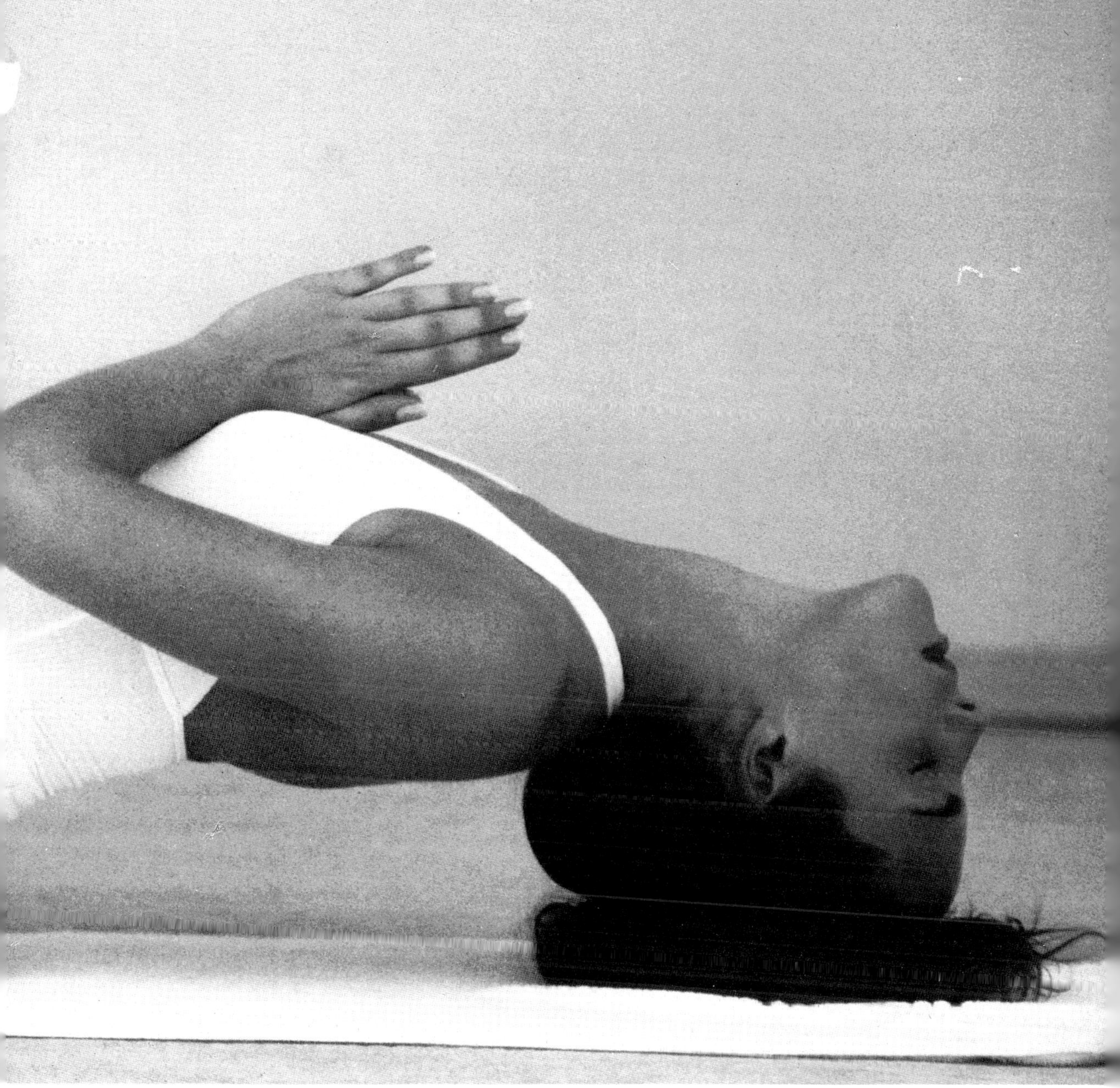

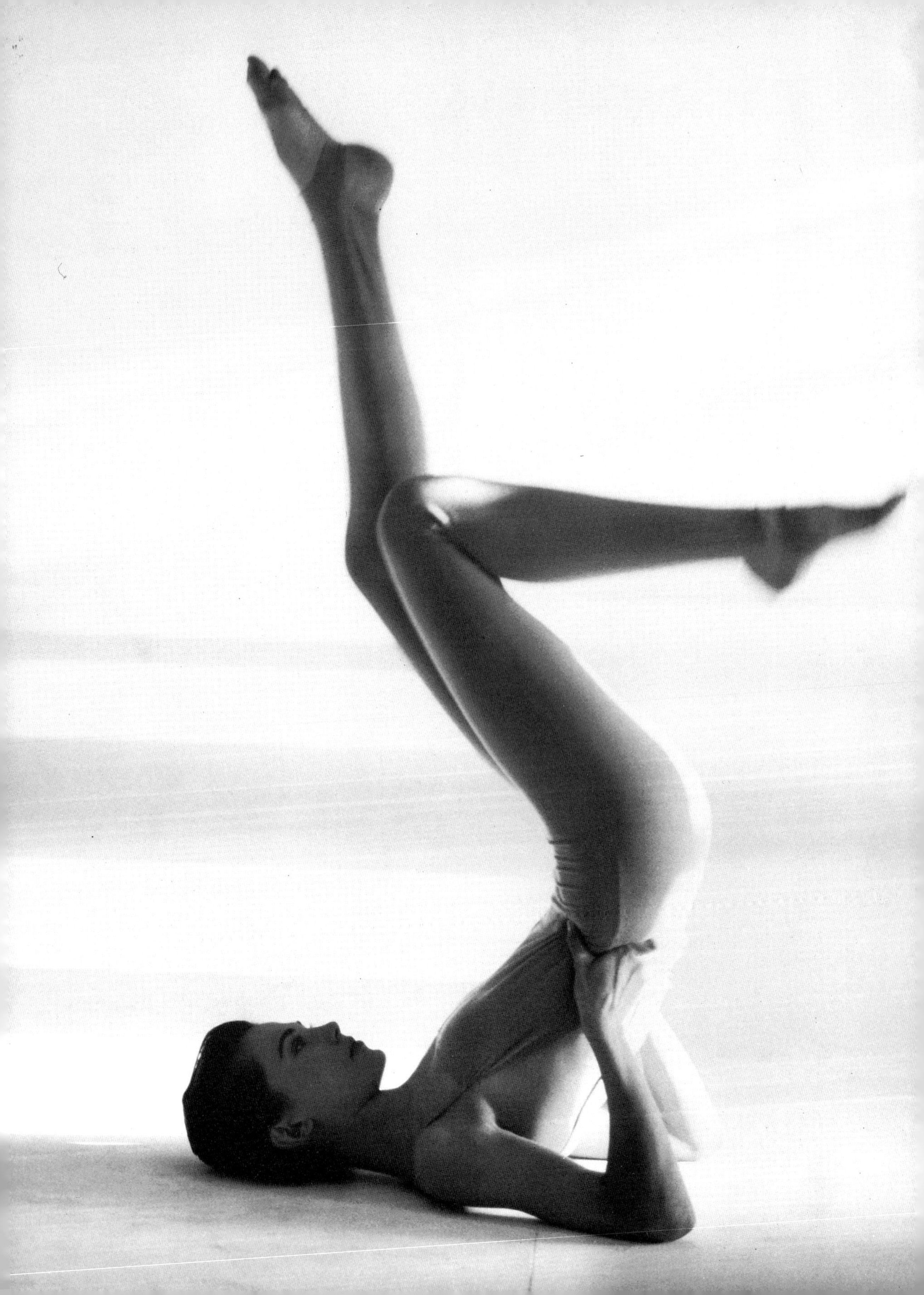

Concentrate on a sport that you enjoy and one that is easily accessible and cheap to practise. If you lead a town life, best options are indoor sports like squash, badminton, swimming, aerobics, gymnastics, dance classes or yoga. With outdoor sports, fresh air helps to boost the sense of well-being; jogging, cycling, swimming, tennis, riding, sailing are all great fitness prompters. At the very least it should be possible to incorporate extra exercise into a normal daily routine, but discipline yourself. Get into the habit of walking everywhere, ignore lifts and use the stairs instead, start to run somewhere every day, even if there is no hurry, or try skipping, or running on the spot for five minutes daily.

Exercise revs the circulation, the essential body process that makes skin glow with health and speeds up the metabolic rate, the process that burns calories. When you stop exercising your metabolism is sill racing and goes on demolishing body fat at a faster than normal rate for up to six hours. It is a myth that exercise alone makes you lose weight. It tones muscle, changes flab into firm body and gives you an incentive to eat healthier food. It is a waste of effort and time to fill a well-conditioned body with stodgy food. A diet combined with an exercise programme is the most logical way to slim – the two processes complement each other. In some people a lack of exercise is more cause for fatness than overeating.

WHAT MAKES A GREAT BODY

It is rare to meet anyone who is content with their size, shape and weight. Statistics tell us that one in three women is on a **diet**. Many base their reasons for dieting on irrational grounds. The most common cause of misery is when you compare yourself with someone the same height, who weighs a stone less than you and takes a smaller size. What gets overlooked is the fundamental build of a body; providing you are in proportion to your frame, measuring or weighing more than the next person is not a sign of being overweight. There is no such thing as the ideal stereotype female. A perfect body may be athletic, petite, curvy, or sticklike. You have to be realistic and accept, to a certain extent, the shape that nature intended for you. It is more attractive to feel positive about the way you are, than struggle on in permanent battle trying to be somebody different. The only judge of your figure is you; if you hate your body and have the willpower to improve it, without damaging your health or personality and without losing friends, then go ahead.

The quickest way to lose weight is to go on a crash diet, but it is a short term solution. The pounds you lose consist of water and body fluids which return when you eat normally again. Most 'miracle' diets are

Exercise combined with good nutrition is the key to a well-toned body

doomed; the mentality of consciously cutting out bad foods for a limited time until the goal weight is achieved is disastrous. The idea that when you are on a diet you eat healthy food, and when you are off a diet you can eat junk food, is schizophrenic. While you diet you feel deprived and plan enormous binges of chocolate cake and lasagne. It turns into an unnecessary battle. Losing weight painlessly needs a different approach. The sensible alternative is to follow a well-balanced diet all the time. The constant preoccupation with health and diet has turned nutrition into a rather fashionable science – once you start being aware of what you eat, it is dangerously easy to become fanatical about your diet. A balanced diet should not be cranky or extreme. There is room for a little of everything. Food is something to enjoy, and eating sensibly does not automatically rule out all treats. When you understand the nutritional and calorific values of different foods it is simple enough to eat healthily and lose weight if necessary by consuming fewer calories. Diets may vary, but the basic principle of losing weight never does. If you take in more than you burn off as energy, you will put on weight.

A **healthy diet** should provide essential vitamins and minerals and include a balance of protein (meat, fish, eggs, cheese), fresh fruit and vegetables, cereals (wholemeal bread, muesli, brown rice, bran), and a small amount of fats (butter, vegetable oil, low-fat cheese). Fresh fruit and vegetables are a great low-calorie source of energy. The healthiest way to eat them is raw, as cooking removes some valuable vitamins and minerals. Raw fruit and vegetables are perfect for dieters because their high water content (much of which is lost in the cooking) makes them very filling.

Healthy eating means training yourself into good habits. It makes sense to eat a proper breakfast as you are bound to burn up the calories during the day. Three equal meals is a better balance than one great binge, but ideally your lightest meal should be at night. The metabolic rate slows down while you sleep, and any excess food, particularly carbohydrates like bread and pudding, is quickly stored as fat.

One habit to get into is drinking as much water as possible, at least a pint a day. It is the healthiest drink there is, calorie free and essential for energy and clear skin. Alcohol in moderation is not unhealthy, but it is astonishingly high in calories. White sugar contains no goodness at all and should be cut out of a diet. Honey is a better substitute. Even chocolate has some useful proteins and can be eaten occasionally without too much guilt.

Nutritional value is affected by the cooking methods. Grilling, boiling or steaming is healthier than frying in oil or butter. Too much fried food is bad for the skin, particularly if it is naturally oily. The connection between skin condition and diet affects some people much more than

A well balanced diet is the best foundation for good health and energy

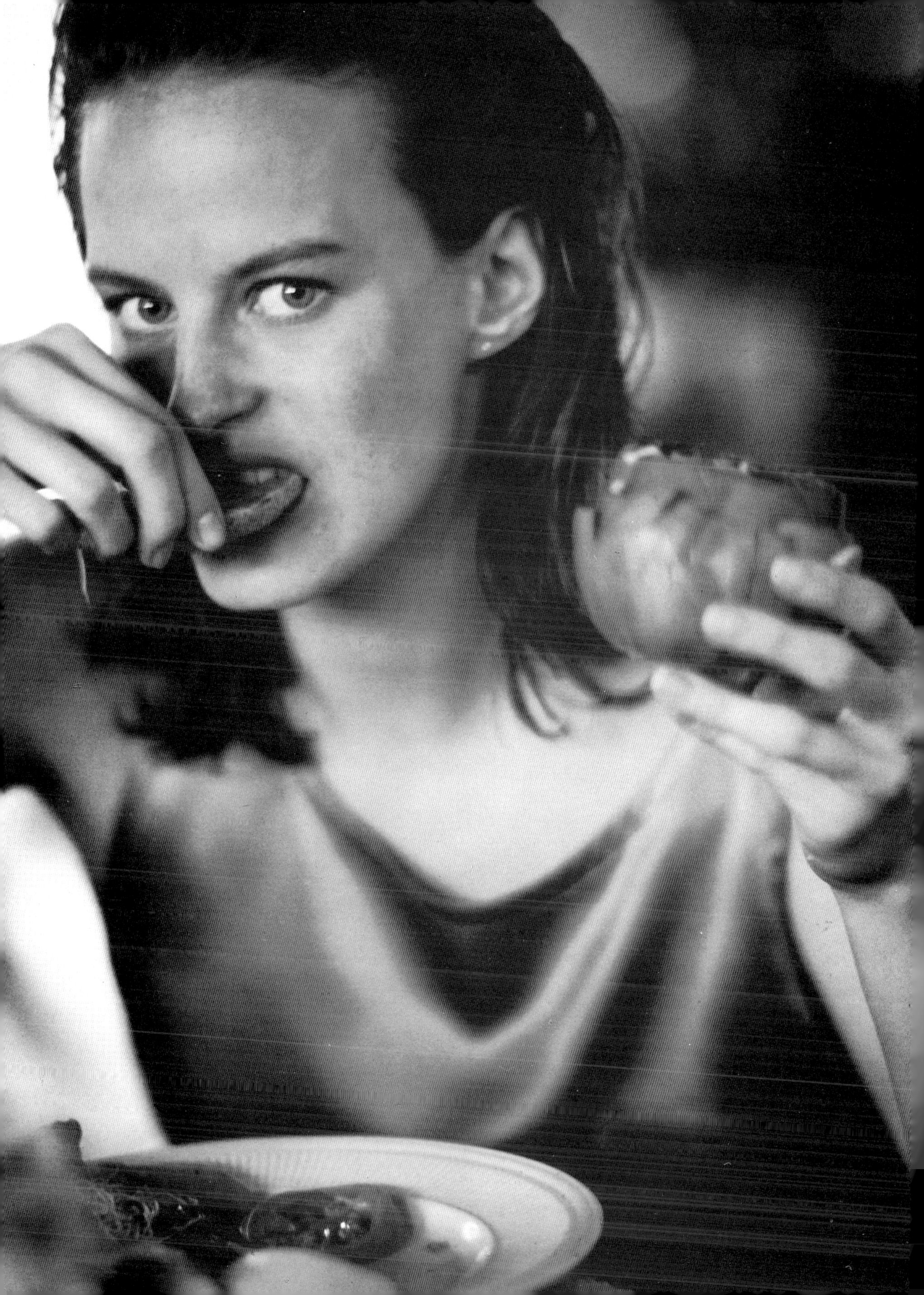

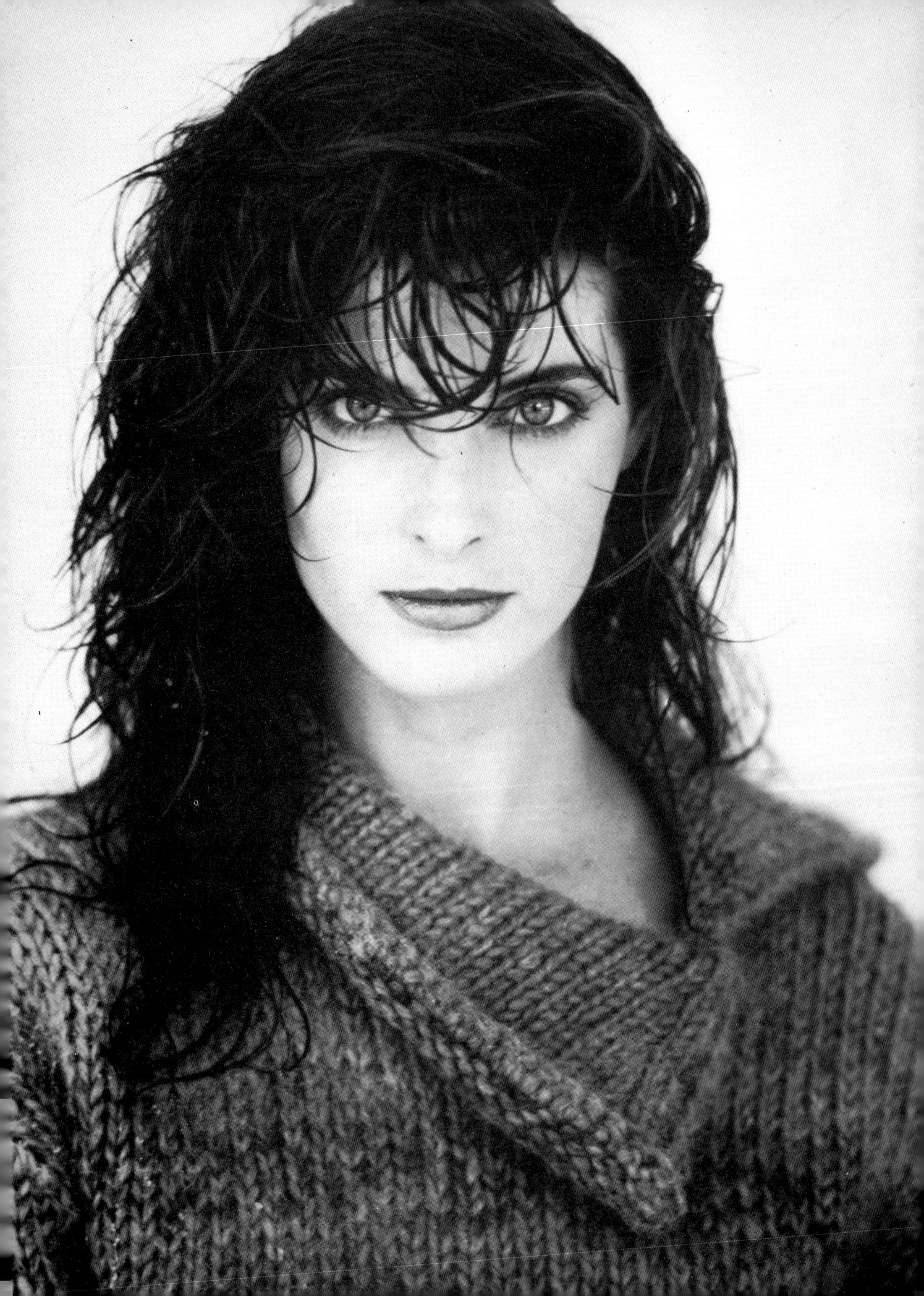

others. There is no doubt that skin thrives on a steady intake of vitamins and minerals from fresh, natural foods and can be disturbed by stimulants like strong coffee, hot spicy foods, too much alcohol, sugar or nicotine. Food allergies are unpredictable and idiosyncratic, but often a skin disorder can be traced to a deficiency or excess in the diet. Because everyone is different, it is impossible to make rules about these allergies – specialists are still arguing over the link between chocolate and pimples.

HAIR

Hair needs as much consistent attention as skin. Like skin, the state of your hair is a sign of your well-being. Hair responds to the right diet, regular sleep, well-charged circulation and scrupulous cleansing and care. Hair needs to be treated with the same respect as your face, never antagonized with fierce equipment and whatever product comes to hand. It needs protection from its worst enemies: from the sun with a hat, scarf or special sun-filtering conditioner; from salt water and chlorine by rinsing after swimming in fresh water; from hot rollers, heated tongs and hot blasts of air from hairdryers. Hair is at its most fragile when wet, and should never be brushed, but untangled with a wide-toothed comb. Long hair is more vulnerable than short hair simply because it is in the way, and slept upon, fiddled with, pulled at much more than short hair can be.

Your hair type determines how often you need to shampoo. Daily washing is quite safe providing the shampoo is mild. One soaping with a small quantity of shampoo is enough. Conditioner helps to add shine by smoothing the scales on the hair shaft, making hair smoother and better behaved. Dry, brittle, split or damaged ends benefit from a deeper treatment which penetrates the hair shaft and helps restore its condition. It is essential to rinse off the conditioner thoroughly which, in soft water, can be a long process, otherwise hair goes limp and greasy almost immediately.

Hair can only look good if it is well kept. The emphasis has now moved away from sculptured 'hair-dos' to a natural look which relies on hair health. It is *the* foundation, however you wear your hair. The mood of fashion and hair are inseparable, hair has to be part of a total look. The most crucial point is for hair to suit your personality, never to take over as a fashion statement. It must fit in with you, but not as a permanent fixture. You can rethink your hair as often as you change your clothes or make-up; often a switch of hairstyle is all that's needed to change the pace of your look. Hair should never be a burden. The attitude must be easy care, style with minimum maintenance, a shape that doesn't need hours of upkeep with damaging rollers or fixing with hairspray. You

Hair deserves the same careful treatment and protection as your skin

need a style that can be out in the wind and the rain; that you can wash on the spur of the moment and shake dry; a style that boosts your confidence about your whole appearance.

The vital guideline is to know how your hair performs; how much the texture and condition dictate the final appearance. If your hair is naturally straight, forget about curling it; if it is frizzy, then let it frizz. Choose a style compatible with your hair type as well as your character. Beware of being blinded by fashion, or inspired by a cut that looks marvellous on someone else. If long, glossy hair is your great pride, don't let yourself be swept along on a wave of boyish cuts; you may regret it – especially as average hair grows only six inches a year. There *may* come a time when after years of experimenting with different shapes and lengths, you find the look that is absolutely perfect for you – one that makes you feel terrific, sexy and self-confident enough to like your face without any help from make-up. When and if this does happen to you, it makes sense to hold on to the style and experiment no further.

Thick straight hair is the most versatile, as it can look good worn any length or style. Long, thick, curly hair looks wonderful worn full like a Pre-Raphaelite, or piled loosely into a tousled knot on top. Very bushy hair is more controllable cut shorter and softly layered. Medium-textured hair is also full of possibilities: if straight, a layered cut adds fullness; if curly, layering helps to bring out the curl, or keeping it one length plays it down. Fine hair tends to be limp and flyaway; straight fine hair looks prettiest in a chin-length blunt cut, or in a wispy short crop. Fine curly hair looks fuller if it is cut in slightly ragged layers.

Hair should not be treated as a means to alter the shape of a face. The suggested corrective style may conflict with the natural tendency of the hair texture, your personality or facial features and you end up with an unsatisfactory compromise. Whatever the shape of the face, it is an important characteristic, and not something to camouflage. But there are some routine guidelines to balance a hairstyle with different face shapes and features – most of which are based on logic. It makes sense not to swamp a small face and delicate features with an overpowering mass of hair; a neater shape swept away from the face works well. Square and round faces need balancing with some extra height on top, and softening with wispy, all-over volume. A wide jaw can be minimized by a style that falls in layers round the face and a shaggy fringe to draw the eyes upwards. A thin face can be softened with extra width at the sides.

Promoting your best features also makes sense; a side parting emphasizes the eyes, and a centre parting emphasizes the nose and mouth. Short hair is easier to look after than long; it is quicker to wash and dry, but it does need to be kept in good shape with a trim every four to six weeks. The cut itself is critical. A precise, clipped cut looks severe and

Providing hair is in good shape and condition, it can change shape with the help of mousse, gel, setting lotion and extravagant accessories

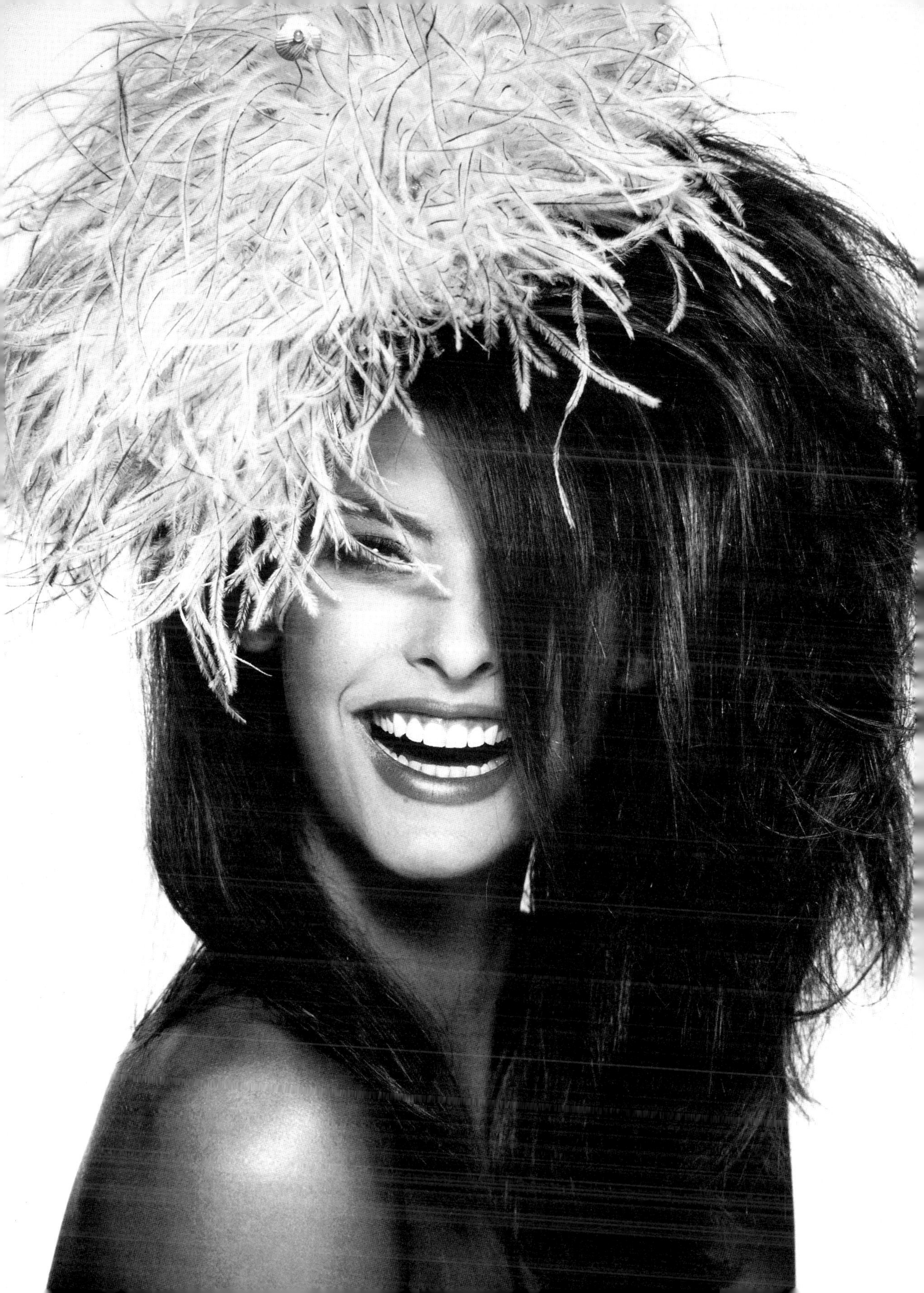

Experiment with long hair – sweeping it up into a casual top knot

too neat. The best haircut doesn't look too obvious, it is left soft and wispy enough to avoid a fresh-from-the-barber look. Layered hair demands more upkeep than one-length shapes. Even if you decide to grow out a layered cut, the only way to carry it off is with regular trims to keep the lengths close together. The longest straggly bits are best cut off, as they look out of proportion and messy otherwise. When hair is left to look natural, there has to be a definite difference between a wayward, tousled head and a matted bird's nest.

Drying hair in different ways can alter the appearance as well. Straightforward blow drying and brushing with a good bristle brush (once the hair is nearly dry) gives a smooth, glossy finish. For a more mane-like effect with a hairdryer, you should bend at the waist and blow the roots from underneath which fluffs up the hair and adds extra volume. Another tip for fullness is to spray the roots with mousse or setting lotion which adds extra body and makes the hair stand away from the head. Finger drying, a technique your hairdresser should teach you, is the most natural and gentle way to dry. Start with a towel to squeeze out surface moisture, then let your fingers take over.

Although the actual process of hair colour is highly scientific (unless you choose henna) the result, if done by an expert, can be beautifully natural. The best kind of hair colouring is one which is not too striking, one which uses subtle streaks or lowlights (less obvious than highlights) that enhance your original colour. It is wise to base any change on a colour close to your natural hair colour. A dramatic change can look artificial and you suffer from noticeable regrowth. Tinted hair needs extra special care and conditioning, but professionally applied colour does not do any damage, it can even thicken the texture of fine hair, making it more manageable. When you have colour on your hair, it is sensitive to certain chemicals and can react curiously against further tinting, perming, or even strong sunlight.

The condition of your hair is controlled by you, but its shape is left in the hands of the hairdresser. Success with your hair is much more likely if you go regularly to the same person. He or she gets to know you and your hair and understand what you like. A small friendly salon is usually less intimidating than a large, impersonal place (even if it does have a grand name) where you may be treated like a number to be processed on your first few visits.

The greatest cause of post-haircut misery is a lack of communication. Hairdressers are not mindreaders. It is essential to explain exactly what you want and how much you want cut off, before it is too late. Whenever possible, discuss the style with the hairdresser before you are shampooed, so he sees how your hair looks and falls when dry. If you are thinking of a new haircut it is a good idea to take a picture with you, as long as you

A fringed boyish crop leaves space for accessory impact

don't expect to emerge looking identical. Your hair type may not suit the shape, but it is a good starting point to work from, especially if you find explaining difficult. When you try a new salon it is worth finding out the price before you make an appointment. Watch out for extras like conditioning treatments and special rinses, which can be done just as effectively at home for a fraction of the salon price using similar products from a chemist, not the expensive salon brands. Some salons run special nights when their juniors practise on the clients. If you need a simple

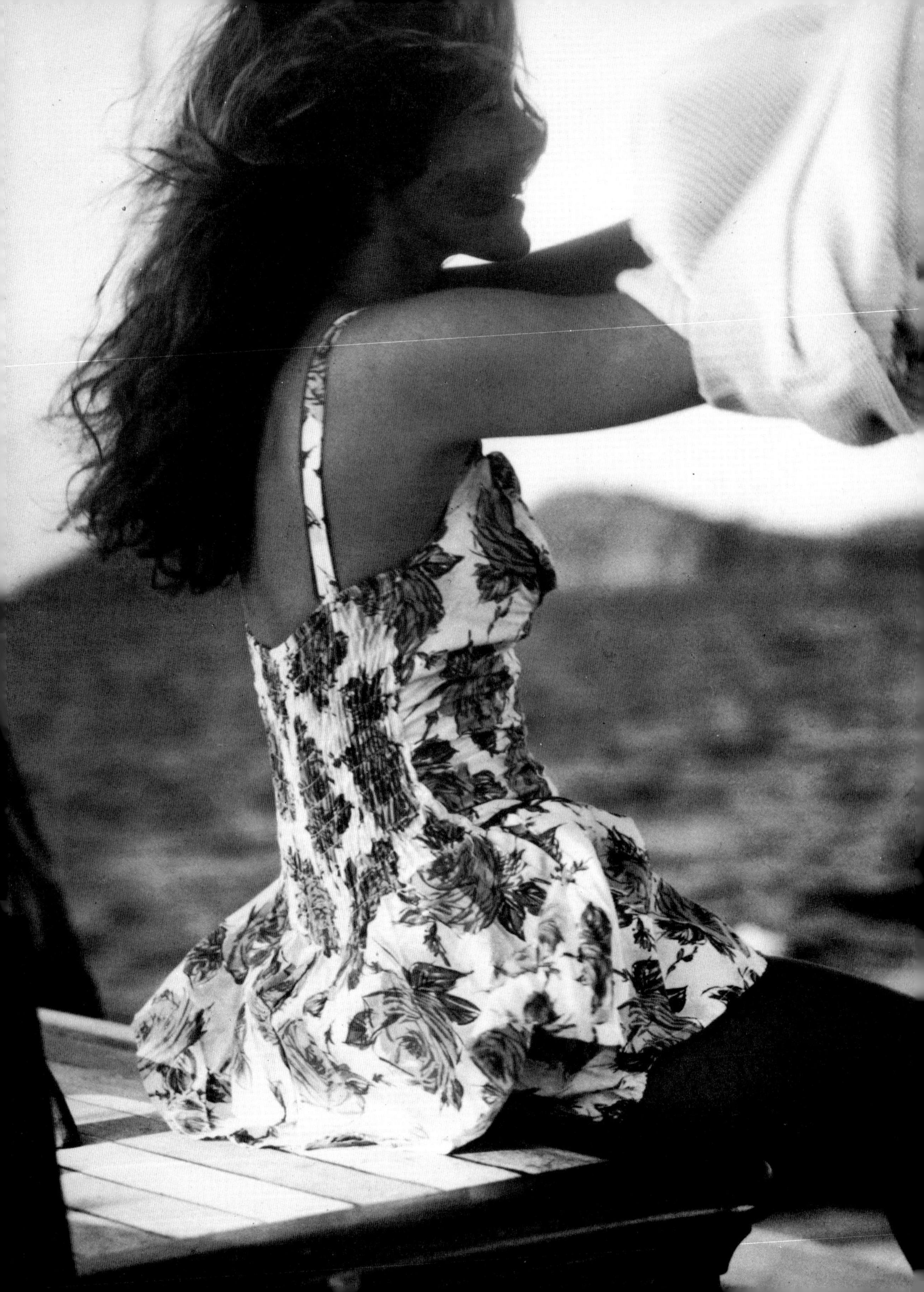

trim it is a good way to have a cheap haircut. The juniors are usually closely supervised by the experts, who take over in an emergency. Be wary about letting yourself be a guinea pig for any creative colouring or styling. Mistakes *can* happen.

Once you have the basis of a good cut and condition, hair can perform as a versatile accessory. A simple rethink like altering or losing a parting gives a new look. Experiment with a plait or chignon at the nape of the neck. Try a ponytail – possible with surprisingly short hair – in fifties mood or groomed into a Chanel style with a gros grain or velvet bow. Or pile your hair into a top knot or French pleat. Avoid a headful of pins and lacquer by using gel to control stray hairs. Short cuts provide just as much scope. Let mousse add volume and a hint of colour for a soft, natural look. Or change the mood at night by slicking it back behind the ears with gel or wax. Accessories add emphasis to your style, or make useful diversions when your hair feels a mess. Try sweeping back a fringe with a leather, fur or tortoiseshell band, using antique combs and slides or tartan ribbons, and bandannas. Evening accessories can look as dramatic as jewellery, but don't let them compete with overpowering earrings or chokers. Satin rosettes, snoods, diamanté combs, tiaras, pearls and fresh flowers add glamorous impact. Be inventive with materials: plait satin ribbons into a hairband, tie a spangled tulle party bow; wind coloured pipe cleaners, nail varnished chop sticks or knitting needles into your hair. Move from the haberdashery to the Christmas decoration department, adapting tinsel, ribbon rosettes, miniature crackers and tree baubles into festive hair ornaments.

COSMETICS

The last stage of self-care concerns **cosmetics**. They cannot disguise unloved skin. Whether you wear full make-up or the faintest trace, a healthy glowing skin is the starting point. The rest is individual choice, one that can be extremely bewildering when you are confronted with an enormous range of temptingly named and packaged cosmetics. Such a selection of products, colours and textures makes it easy to make mistakes and waste money. Knowing how to get the most from make-up is an immeasurable asset. The instant proof is to watch top models. When they arrive on location they are often indistinguishable from anyone else. Fashion editors have been known to mistake the model for a tea girl. But once made up, they look perfect, just like a model in fact. Not because they are caked in theatrical make-up, but because they have acquired the professional expertise to transform an ordinary face into a beautiful one. It is a skill within the reach of everybody who cares

Minimum upkeep – choose a style that doesn't rule your life. You need hair that goes out in the wind and rain without being a worry; that you can wash and shake dry on impulse

enough to make an effort. Few people get the full potential from the cosmetics they use and miss out on the incredible bonus that cleverly applied make-up can give. The essential skill is learning basic techniques; understanding the difference that the actual method makes to the result. Being clever with fancy products is like trying to run before you can walk. What counts most is knowing how to make the best of your face, naturally. Make-up is not a camouflage to be treated like a mask, but an accessory to experiment with and change with different clothes, seasons and environments.

There are times when make-up is unnecessary. It is important not to depend so heavily on it that you feel insecure without any. Make-up should never take over from your natural expression. The point is to make your *face* more striking, not the make-up. Once you have learnt the basics, an open-minded attitude is a must. See the make-up you wear as a way of pulling your whole look together, and adding new dimension to your clothes. Avoid the habit of treating it as a routine. Vary the amount you use, go barefaced when you don't feel like make-up, and don't apologize for your naked face . . .

Buying cosmetics is an indulgence. Few people actually run out of anything, but treat themselves to a new product for the fun of it, and because it is a cheaper self-indulgence than buying clothes. But however much you buy, most good make-ups rely on a few basic products. Like skin care, the final price can be more a reflection of the pretty packaging and prestige name than the actual ingredients of the cosmetic. The performance of different brands varies widely, and if you shop around it is possible to find similar colours and textures in less impressive pots and boxes which do the same job as the expensive versions. It is worth taking time to try the testers. If possible, go to a large department store or chemist that stocks a cross section of brands, so you can compare prices and colours. Salesgirls affiliated to a particular brand name are there to sell you their products, so don't be too easily swayed. Make your own decisions. If you are contemplating an expensive product, it is worth buying a trial size to start with. Some department stores run promotions when they offer a free make-up to anyone brave enough to face the public stare. It can be a humiliating experience, but worth undergoing, because, although the make-up artist usually puts far too much on, you can learn some basic make-up skills. When you get home, try removing one side of the make-up and applying your own products. If you have a free lesson, don't feel obliged to restock with brand-new products. Go through your collection first, as you may already own a similar cosmetic that you can adapt and use instead.

The best investment is the right equipment. The difference between a professional and amateur make-up is how the products are used and

Take care not to overplay your eyes, as a heavy make-up can kill their natural expression. Keep to a palette of subtle, muted colours – well smudged and blended, with no hard lines anywhere

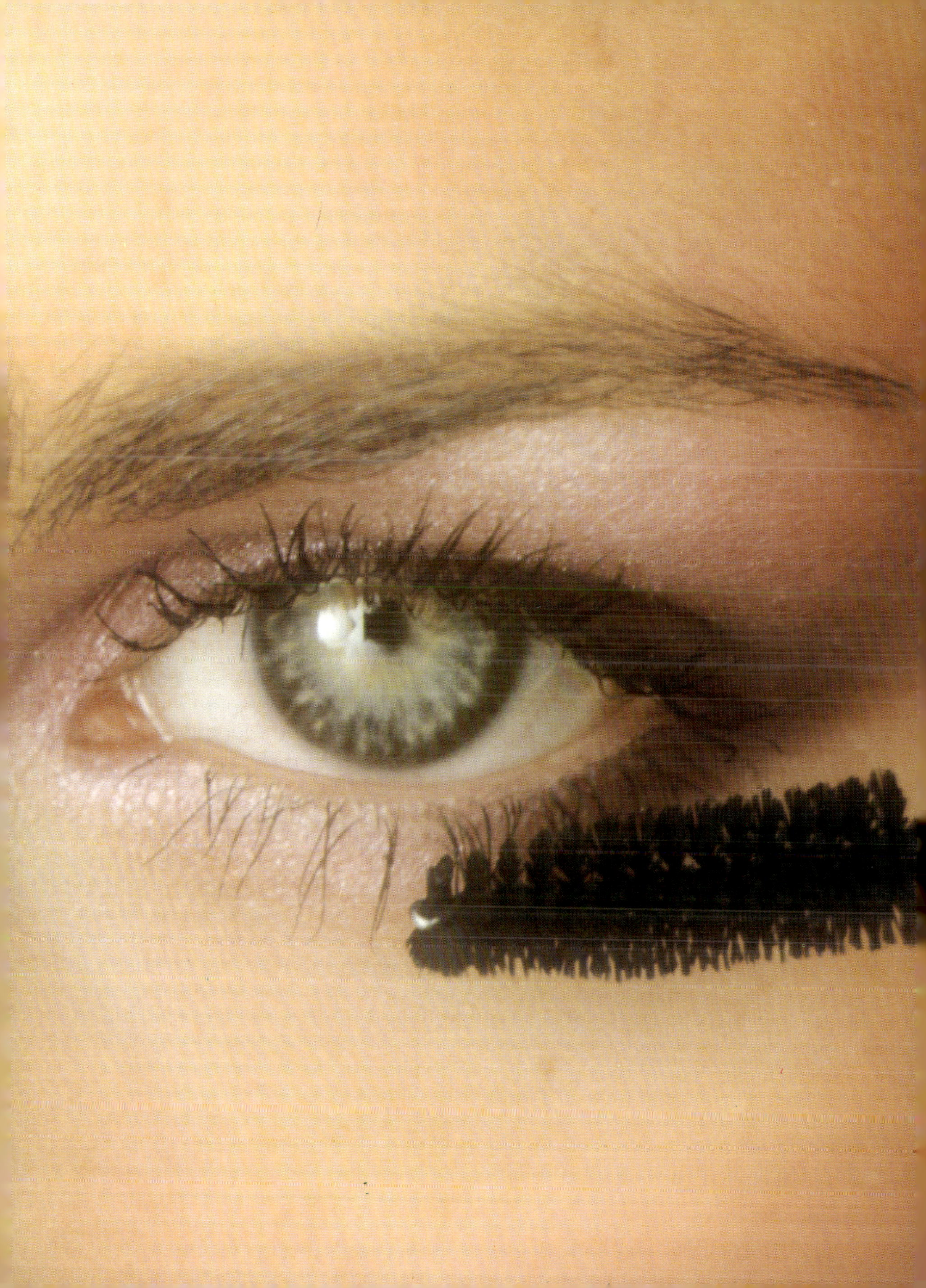

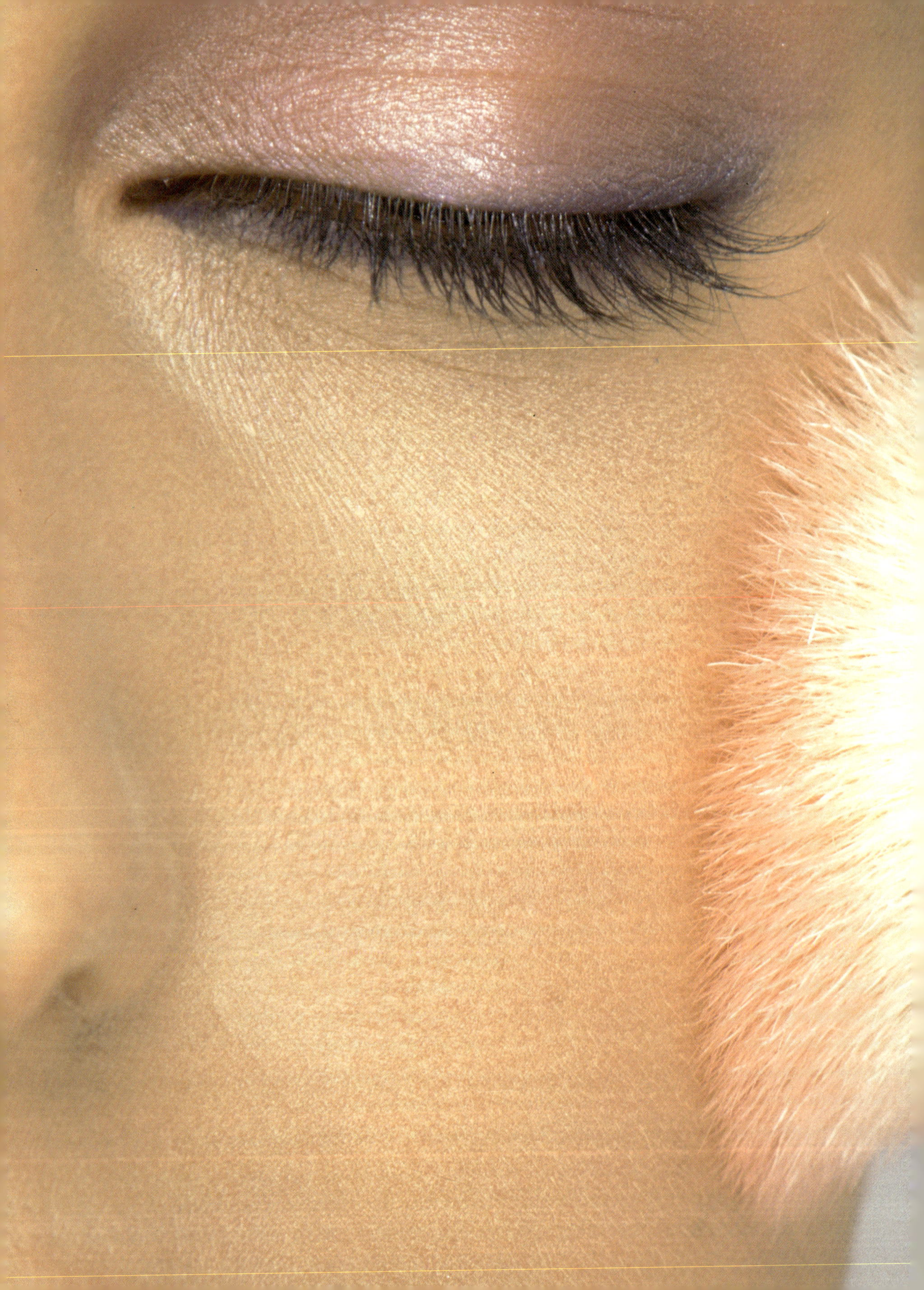

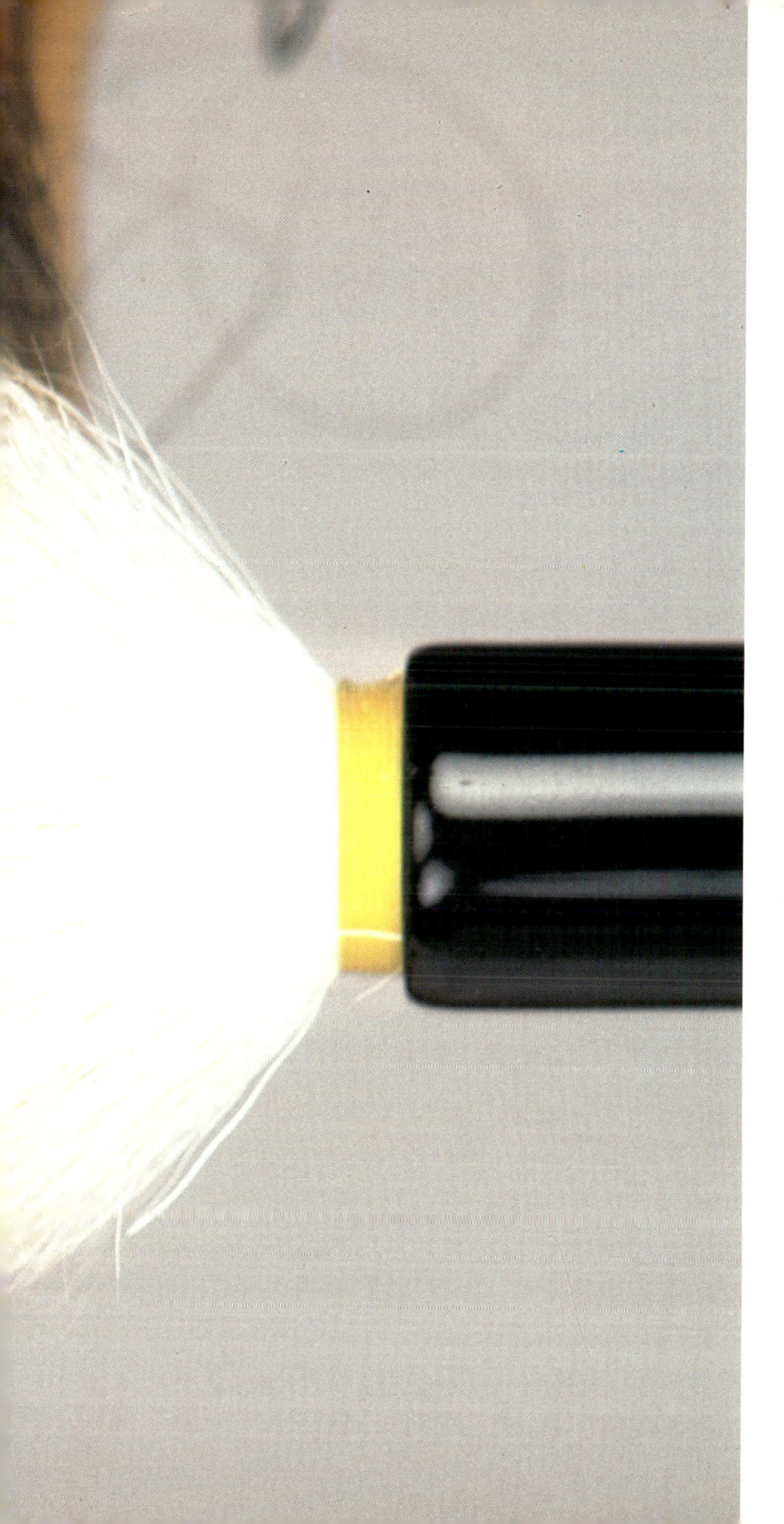

The difference between a professional and amateur make-up is how the products are used, and what they are applied with. Give yourself a headstart with the right equipment and the right approach. You need a well lit, truthful mirror, a set of brushes for eyes, lips, blusher and powder; cosmetic sponges; cotton buds; tissues; a pencil sharpener for your cosmetic crayons; a towelling band or scarf to keep hair off your face; and plenty of time to complete each stage slowly and carefully

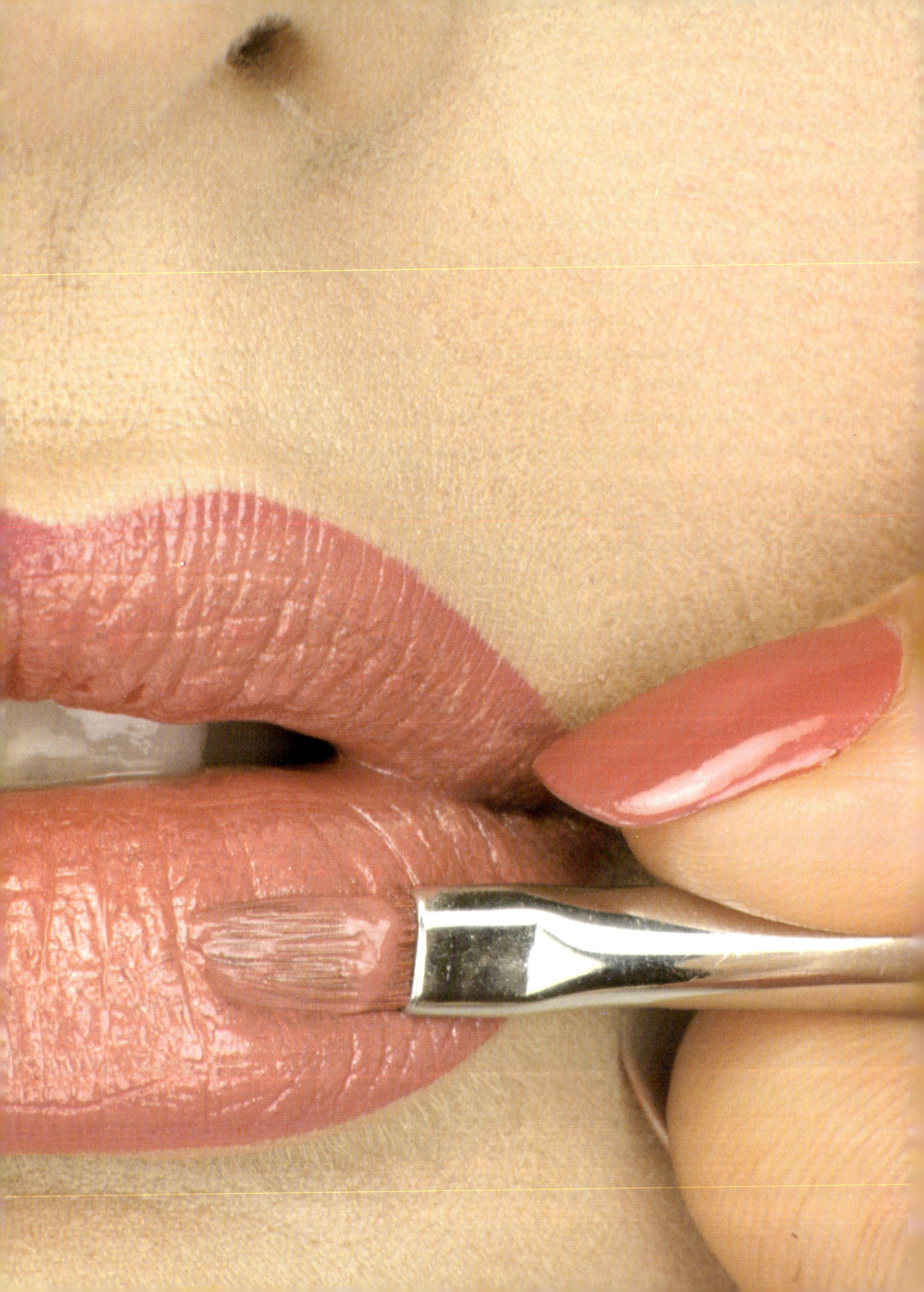

what they are applied with. A model's make-up bag is incomplete without a set of brushes, one for each stage. Sable brushes are expensive, but definitely worth the outlay. If you look after them carefully, they will not wear out, but for an alternative source, investigate paint brushes in an art supply shop. Give yourself a head start by not scrimping on the basic necessities. Besides brushes, you need small, cosmetic sponges, good tweezers, cotton buds, cotton wool and a truthful mirror. A magnifying mirror is a wise investment and invaluable for plucking eyebrows, checking your skin surface and painting lips, but never for a full face make-up.

The light you work in is crucial. The rule is to apply make-up in the light it is intended for. Natural daylight is the easiest to work in, but you may need to make compensations for different environments. Artificial, fluorescent lighting drains colour from the face, so needs balancing with warm tones – shades in the brick, coral, amber, peach family – using stronger colour, but not heavier make-up, to counteract the lighting. Make-up applied in dim lighting can look too hard and bright in daylight, but at night when the light is softer, a stronger make-up does not look exaggerated. A simple test of your technique is to study a photograph of yourself. It shows you, more reliably than a mirror, what your make-up does for you, or what it doesn't do for you. So take action.

MAKE-UP GUIDELINES

Each product you use must be the right one for you. The choice is so large, there is no chance of not being able to find something suitable. Most complexions, except for perfect, flawless skin, are improved with some sort of foundation. The point of a foundation is to even out the skin tone, concealing any blemishes and dark shadows while still looking natural. Panstick days are over, foundation should be undetectable and an exact colour match. The skin on your wrist or back of the hand is not an accurate enough match to the face, so always test the foundation on your face, over clean, unmade-up skin. If you cannot find the exact shade, you can mix your own with the two nearest colours, blending them in the palm of your hand with a touch of moisturizer. It is not extravagant to have different shades of foundation as skin does not stay the same colour all year round. For an especially sheer look, blend liquid foundation (which is less covering than a cream) or fine translucent powder with an equal quantity of moisturizer. For long-lasting coverage, the application is important. Skin must be in the right condition, freshly cleansed, toned and moisturized. When all trace of moisturizer disappears, the most effective method is to use a slightly moist cosmetic

Lip focus: whether you wear bright colours or natural gloss, lips need to be expertly defined with a fine brush or pencil
Matching up your lips and nails is not essential, but it is wiser to keep within the same colour range

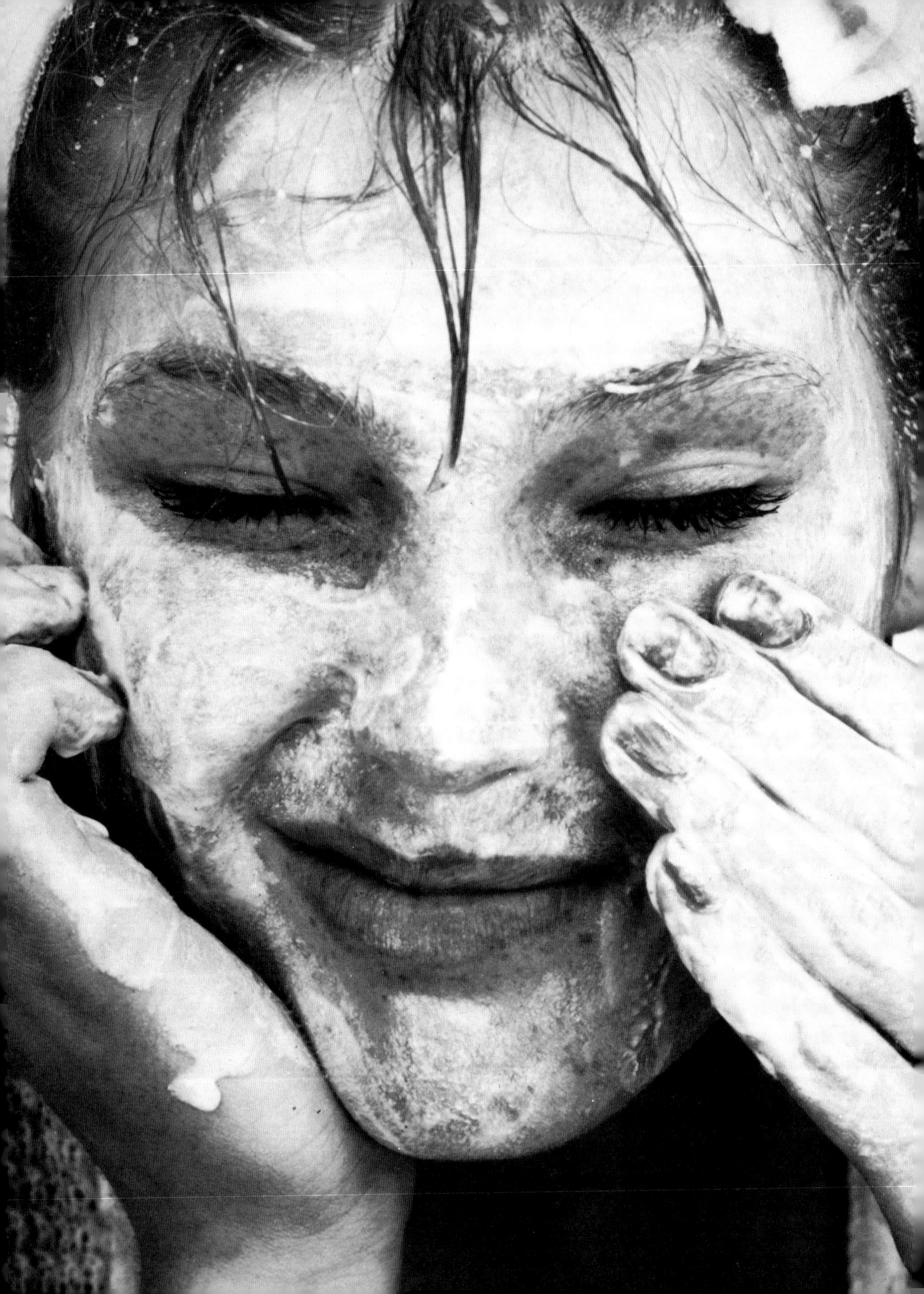

sponge and dab dots of foundation across the forehead, eyelids, nose, cheeks, chin and lips, and smooth it in quickly in that order. Always be careful to blend in the direction that facial hair grows, and to avoid any tidemarks under the chin. Dark shadows under the eyes can be lightened with a paler foundation, applied before the main colour. For a tanned look, a darker foundation is a bad idea, as your white hands and neck are instant giveaways. Instead, try a sheer tan gel smoothed over foundation, and add a subtle glow to the face by putting warm blusher where the sun catches – on temples, across the forehead and a touch on the chin.

Powder still has a rather old-fashioned image, a leftover from the days when girls used to rush off and 'powder their noses'. The product has changed since then into a virtually colourless, mostly translucent protective cover that sets foundation, mops up shine, tones down high colour and provides a base for powder blusher. The best way to apply it is with a brush or cotton wool. Pat a very fine layer softly all over the face, then dust off every excess grain with the brush or clean cotton wool.

Blusher is the make-up stage that too many people miss out, mostly due to an uncertainty of where and how to put it on. Even rosy-cheeked faces need blusher. It does more than add colour; blusher can add shape and contour to a face. It can fine down a round face, soften a long, thin face and emphasize a good bone structure. Blusher comes in powder, cream, pencil or gel form. Powder is the easiest to apply, as it goes on with a brush over translucent powder, and mistakes can be toned down more easily than the other textures. Blusher goes along the cheek bone, brushed in a downward sweep from the top of the cheeks at the hairline to the centre of the cheeks. As a guide, put the index and middle finger vertically against the nose, the edge of the outer finger marks where the blusher should stop. To look completely natural, blusher has to be blended perfectly, with a brush for powder, or a dry sponge for cream, gel or crayons. The colour will be too strong and harder to blend if you put it directly on your face, so use the back of your hand as a palette to measure the colour. When you choose a blusher, pick a shade that works naturally with your complexion. An obvious contrast to your foundation looks more like make-up than a healthy glow.

Eyes are the easiest feature to enhance, but the danger is to overdo it and kill natural expression. The make-up hits you before the eyes do and their impact is lost. Best eye make-up isn't obviously make-up, but simply makes your eyes look beautiful. Avoid hard lines. Every shadow or pencil must be smudged and blended to look a natural part of the eye, and colours should be soft and neutral. The rules of matching your eye shadow to your clothes is a myth, so is the notion that pale blue shadow is the easy answer to eye make-up. Think of subtle muted colours; a

Before any make-up goes on, skin must be freshly cleansed, toned and moisturized

palette of greys, browns, smoky blues, khaki, dusty pinks, rusts, burgundy tones. Don't be confined to matching your shadow to your eyes, a different shade can play up your natural colour more effectively. With green eyes, try sand, grey, smoky blue or brown. Blue eyes need stronger colours to enhance them; try shades of rust, charcoal grey, and a smudge of violet under the eye to add brightness. Most colours work with brown eyes, but experiment with muted pinks, apricots, plum, sludgy greens or different shades of brown. What counts more than the size of eyes is their intensity – bright eyes can be more beautiful than large eyes. A quick trick is to line the inner rim of the lower lid with dark kohl pencil which makes the eyes darker and the whites brighter.

Eyes need shaping. Define the hollow of the socket with a neutral pencil, the darker the pencil, the deeper set the eye becomes. Soften any pencil lines with a matching shadow, brushing under the eye as well, to accentuate the natural shape. Eye make-up is less confusing if you understand how colour behaves. Pale, shiny or frosted shades are colours that come forward, to use where you want emphasis. Darker, matt shadows retreat and create an illusion of depth or a hollow.

Eye make-up is incomplete without mascara – some days mascara alone is enough emphasis, but eye shadow without it looks incomplete. If you hate mascara, and it does take time to apply properly, try having your eyelashes dyed in a beauty salon. (Ask for blue/black, a colour mix to brighten the whites.) Otherwise find an efficient mascara, one product where it can be worth spending a little extra. The aim is to darken, not clog up each lash, so avoid brands that promise to thicken lashes, as they contain tiny filaments that stick to the ends for a while then fall off and smudge. Resign yourself to the length and texture of your lashes – it is colour that makes the difference. Apply mascara in three very thin coats, wiping the wand with a tissue between each layer. Brush top lashes from above and below, and lower lashes from above, looking straight ahead. For a wide-eyed look, separate lashes with a dry mascara wand or small toothbrush, or if they are straight, curl them with an eyelash curler.

Lipstick is a very individual cosmetic. Some people use a special lipstick colour as an individual hallmark, and are never to be seen without their shocking pink or pillar-box red mouth. Too many people underestimate what a focus lips can be. However subtle or minimal the colour, the whole face will come alive if lips are defined. It is important to create a balance between lips and eyes; they should complement each other. If you put strong eye make-up and lipstick together, one detracts from the other. It is more effective to play up one area at a time. If you draw attention to your mouth it must be in great condition; rough, chapped lips, dark hairs on the upper lip, neglected or stained teeth are all accentuated by lipstick. Out-of-condition lips are best kept natural, just

Top models prove how cosmetic skill and expertise make all the difference to the final face

outlined with soft brown pencil and brushed with clear gloss.

Many people abandon the idea of lipstick because they eat it off so quickly, or leave it smeared across a glass. The secret of long-lasting, non-smudge lipstick is in the application. The best base is foundation lightly brushed with powder, then outline the lips with a lipbrush or soft pencil, fill in with a matching lipstick or the same pencil, blot firmly with a tissue to set the colour and repeat the fill-in stage. To add shine, brush a stroke of clear gloss in the middle of the lower lip. The brighter the colour, the more striking the lips become. Pale, frosted colours make thin lips look fuller, and dark, matt colours, especially plum and dark red shades, make full lips look thinner. The various ways of altering the natural line of the mouth do need to be expertly practised, and any changes must be fractional. For seductive, pouting lips add a touch of dark brown pencil just under the centre of the lower lip. For smiling lips, erase the corners of the mouth with foundation or a skin tone concealer stick. To counteract a square face, treat lips as a triangle, and to widen a long face, extend the natural line of the lips with a fine brush or pencil stroke.

FROM DAY TO NIGHT

However carefully you make up your face in the morning, it will require some fixing by lunchtime. You need a portable prop kit to deal with minor repairs, which should include a concealer stick for unexpected blemishes, a compact of compressed translucent powder to check shiny patches, cotton buds to remove specks of eye make-up, foundation to cover the smudges, a colour pencil to brighten under the eye, and lip equipment to repair your mouth.

At night faces can take more colour. Brighter, stronger make-up becomes a vital part of an evening look – an accessory that creates a definite sense of dressing up. A night make-up accentuates the glamour of party clothes, but changing the face is also a way of moving from day to night without changing your clothes. Stronger make-up means more intensity; deeper, brighter colours, some shine, gleam and sparkle. You decide how far to take it, but the application must be perfect, with every colour blended smoothly, and no hard lines anywhere. Eyes can be dramatized with bright flashes of colour. Try drawing violet or cobalt-blue pencil along the inner rim of the eye. (Warming the pencil tip near a flame softens the point and produces a deeper, more permanent colour.)

For party eyes, brush neutral shadow across the lids, winging softly out to the temples and under the eye, then add a touch of frosted, highlight shadow (gold, pale pink, or pearl) in the centre of the top lids. Use a subtle slick of golden highlighter on the brow bone, never stark white which is too obvious and changes your natural expression. Use the same shadow to highlight shoulders, cleavage and collarbone, brushing it where the light catches. Stroke frosted blusher on cheeks and temples, try a touch down the middle of the nose and chin, but always blend well. Set the shine with a light dusting of glimmer (or nonglimmer) translucent powder. Be daring with lip colours and experiment with bolder shades, especially if you wear natural lips during the day. But beware of overplaying the dazzle. There must be a balance between eyes, lips, cheeks and nails. Alternate the area you focus on; with iridescent lips, tone down your eye make-up and leave off the sparkle; with brilliant eyes, keep your mouth and cheeks in a soft matt colour. To add instant sparkle to everyday products, buy a pot of gold or silver glitter. Dip a glossed lipbrush into the glitter, or drop a tiny amount over your lashes as the mascara is drying, or stroke a few specks over eyelids, cheeks or freshly painted nails. An alternative for night nails is to paint a thin coat of frosted polish over your day colour.

HANDS AND FEET

Beautiful **hands and nails** are details that count as much as the rest of your appearance. To look good they need to be healthy, which means regular pampering. Constant care is more beneficial than an occasional manicure, however thorough. But if nails are in bad shape, a beauty salon manicure can restore them to a passable condition. It is pointless to let nails grow too long; besides looking ugly, they are more likely to split and are difficult to keep in a natural oval shape. Imperfect nails can be concealed with coloured polish which, if used with a base coat, is not harmful and can strengthen and protect the nails. if you wear polish, every nail must be immaculate, there are few things more ugly than chipped fingernails. For a professional finish, apply the polish in three thin coats, letting each one dry completely. Paint each nail with three vertical strokes – one down the middle, then one either side. If you prefer natural nails, use a clear polish, or pale shell pink, or forget about colour and shine your nails with a chamois buffer and line the tips with a white nail pencil.

The rule of matching lip and nail colour is not rigid, but it is a good idea to keep the two colours in the same range. As hands are nearer the body than the face, the nail colour needs to work with your clothes. The most versatile shades are a dusty coral pink, a pale nail pink, or the classic pillar-box red. If you have brown hands, nails look prettiest painted a frosted pale colour, which also helps to enhance brown skin. Black clothes, especially in the evening, look more striking with strong red or

To look their best, hands and feet need to be pampered all through the year

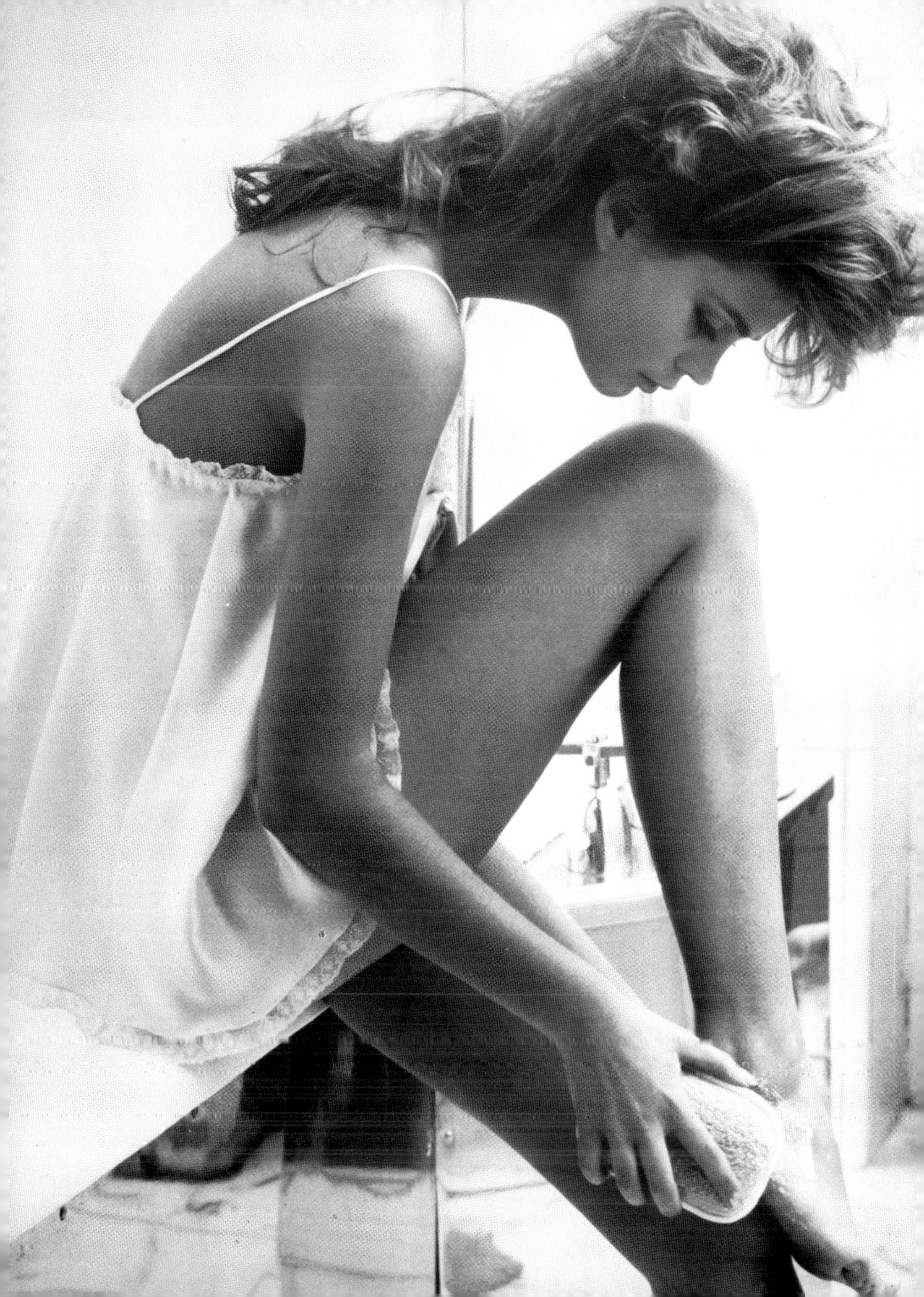

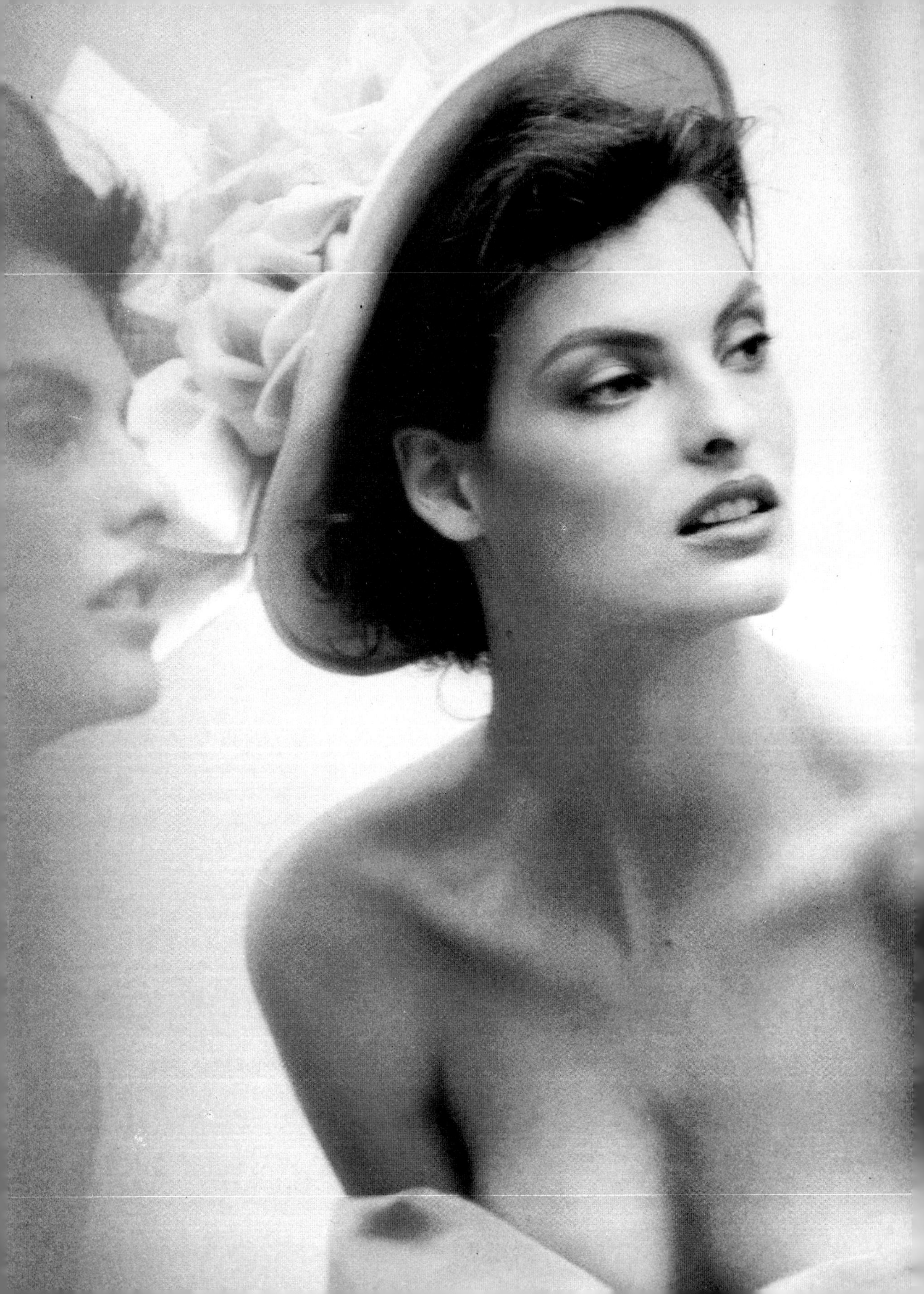

crimson-coloured nails.

When they are visible, toenails need the same care and attention. If feet emerge from winter hibernation in a shameful condition it is worthwhile investing in a professional pedicure and/or a chiropody treatment. Bright red toenails look good with most open sandals or peep toes, unless you can find an exact pink, purple or red colour to match your shoes.

ECONOMIZE WITH DOUBLE-DUTY PRODUCTS

The trouble with tips about make-up is the list of products essential to achieve the look. Obviously it is in the cosmetic manufacturer's interest to sell you a separate product for every make-up stage, but it makes economic sense to use cosmetics with a double or treble life. One soft brown pencil is a great basic for outlining lips, defining brows and shaping around the eye socket. A neutral tawny, peach or rose powder blusher doubles as eye shadow (but check for sensitivity), and a soft pencil blusher can colour eyes, cheeks and lips. The other option is to buy from noncosmetic counters. Baby powder costs far less than translucent powder and, if you apply it finely, does the same job. In emergencies it is a useful dry shampoo as well. Vaseline jelly is also multipurpose; it shines and conditions lips, adds a slick of gloss to straggly eyebrows, a subtle gleam to cheekbones, and some say it encourages eyelashes to grow.

Getting the maximum from cosmetics means using every ounce of each product. When a lipstick breaks in half, you can salvage it by softening the ends over a flame, joining them together and then leaving them in the fridge to set. A lipbrush is invaluable for rescuing the last of a lipstick. Dried up eye and lip pencils can be softened overnight by putting them point down in a jar containing an inch of baby oil. Mascara is past its best after six months, but can be improved by dipping the wand end of the case into very hot water for five minutes. Old nail varnish can be unclogged temporarily with the same hot-water treatment. Cakes of powder blusher or eye shadow that start to crumble can be ground into loose powder and decanted into small jars or glass salt shakers – a good way to create original colours.

The last word is for **scent** – a necessary luxury that makes you feel special. Discreet wafts of quality scent create an aura that is an elusive blend of glamour, femininity and style. Let it be a daily treat, not something to hoard for red-letter days. Buying scent is an extravagant luxury, so persuade other people to give you the one you love. Alternatively remember that Madame Chanel insisted, 'luxury is a necessity which starts where necessity ends'.

Indulge in your favourite scent – a necessary luxury

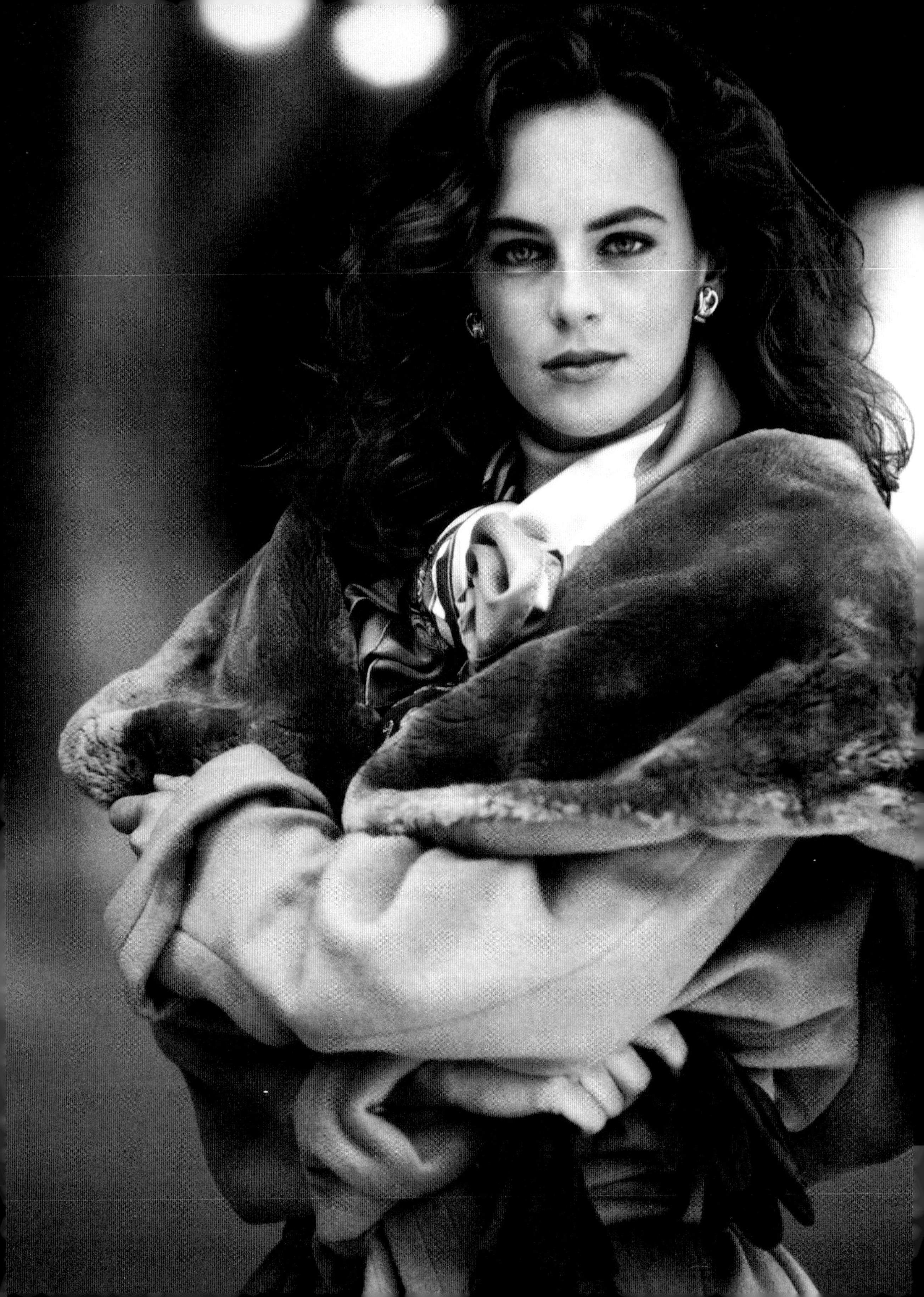

FASHION CHARACTERS

When it comes to individual style it is easy to put other people into categories, but where do you fit in? Do you identify with any of these fashion profiles, or recognize your style overlapping into several characters? It is not a definitive list, but a lighthearted checklist of individual looks that live through the volatile flights of fashion. If each character appears to own an extensive wardrobe, it is because she represents the archetype of a style.

THE CLASSIC

She has an organized, disciplined approach to clothes, investing in quality rather than quantity. She keeps a close eye on fashion but bypasses all shortlived trends, remaining faithful to understated classics that endure from year to year. It is a style of indisputable good taste, consistent yet individual. Sales are vital shopping times when she scoops up cashmeres, classic shoes, bags, belts and occasional extravagances from favourite sources Yves Saint Laurent, Chanel, Hermès and Calvin Klein, perhaps a cashmere coat, an immaculate suit, little black dress or fur lined raincoat.

She makes a point of dressing to suit the occasion. Outfits are planned in advance and time is set aside for her appearance, day and night. Clothes are carefully maintained, laundered or dry-cleaned before being stored away between seasons. She relies increasingly on a dressmaker – a treasure who runs up a silk cocktail dress or ballgown for a fraction of the cost of the designer label that inspires them. Colours are kept neutral: navy, burgundy, grey, camel, bottle green, lifted with white, cream and primrose yellow.

Day wear means classic trousers in gaberdine, flannel, linen or drill (never jeans); straight skirts in wool crepe, jersey, gaberdine, twill, or

The Classic collector: investing in quality, long-term clothes

long and full in viyella, tweed, suede or linen. On top go cotton, silk or linen shirts that wrap, button or tie; polo necks, long cardigans, gilt-buttoned golfers or crew necks worn with pearls or a silk scarf. Jackets make an alternative top layer to knitwear. Favourites are a smooth tweed classic, a Chanel cardigan style and black velvet smoking jacket – worn at night with a straight gros grain skirt or silk trousers. For smart affairs, there is a ballerina length taffeta skirt to wear with a cashmere wrap top or fichu collared lace blouse. Accessories qualify for a large share of the budget, adding colour and contemporary edge to the classics. Jewellery is important but kept simple; mostly Chanel-style pearls and gilt intensified with diamanté, rhinestones and jet at night. Favourite shoes are low-heeled pumps, some with a gros grain bow, flat loafers, neutral suede and leather courts. Plaited and stamped leather belts come in black, navy, white and tan. Large wool and silk scarves are essential in plain, polka-dotted and floral prints, as are fringed cashmere stoles and black kid gloves. She carries minimal clutter in a neat quilted leather bag on a gilt chain – the real thing from Hermès or Chanel, or a clever imitation from an Italian street market. At night she transfers to a small black velvet bag with an Art Deco clasp.

The immaculate image is emphasized by her hair, groomed into a low ponytail with a black velvet bow, or coiled into an elegant chignon. Her beauty approach is practical and consistent. Refusing to be lured by cosmetic hype or extravagance, she remains loyal to one make-up brand, one hairdresser, one beauty salon and her favourite scent, Chanel No 19.

THE YUPPIE

The yuppie personifies today's modern woman – metropolitan, career-minded, ambitious and energetic. It is a fast-moving lifestyle where appearances matter. Clothes are an essential priority and absorb a large share of her sizeable income, earned in the City, fashion, marketing or media world. She is highly clothes conscious, checking out all the glossy magazines for new directions from the fashion capitals. Her wardrobe has a brief lifespan, renewed each season by an updated version when the new collections appear in the shops. She prefers to buy in bulk, choosing clothes and accessories together to save on time and ensure maximum coordination. Favourite haunts are small, personal boutiques that know her style and present an edited selection from exclusive designer labels.

She prefers feminine allure to competitive power dressing and chooses sophisticated clothes, more glamorous than severely tailored. Suits with interchangeable double-breasted jackets and slim skirts are the main-

The Classic by night: a timeless mix of silk and cashmere

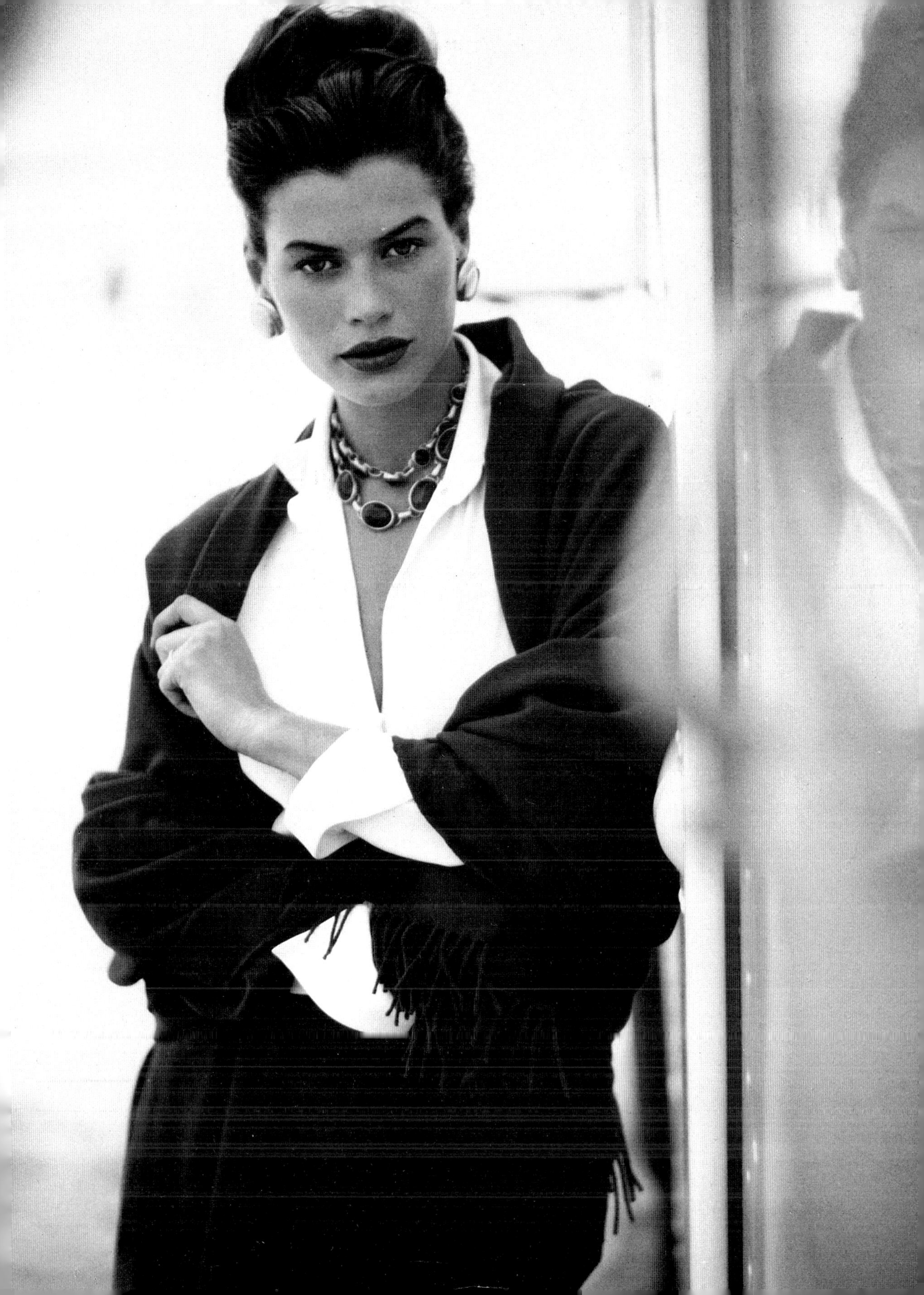

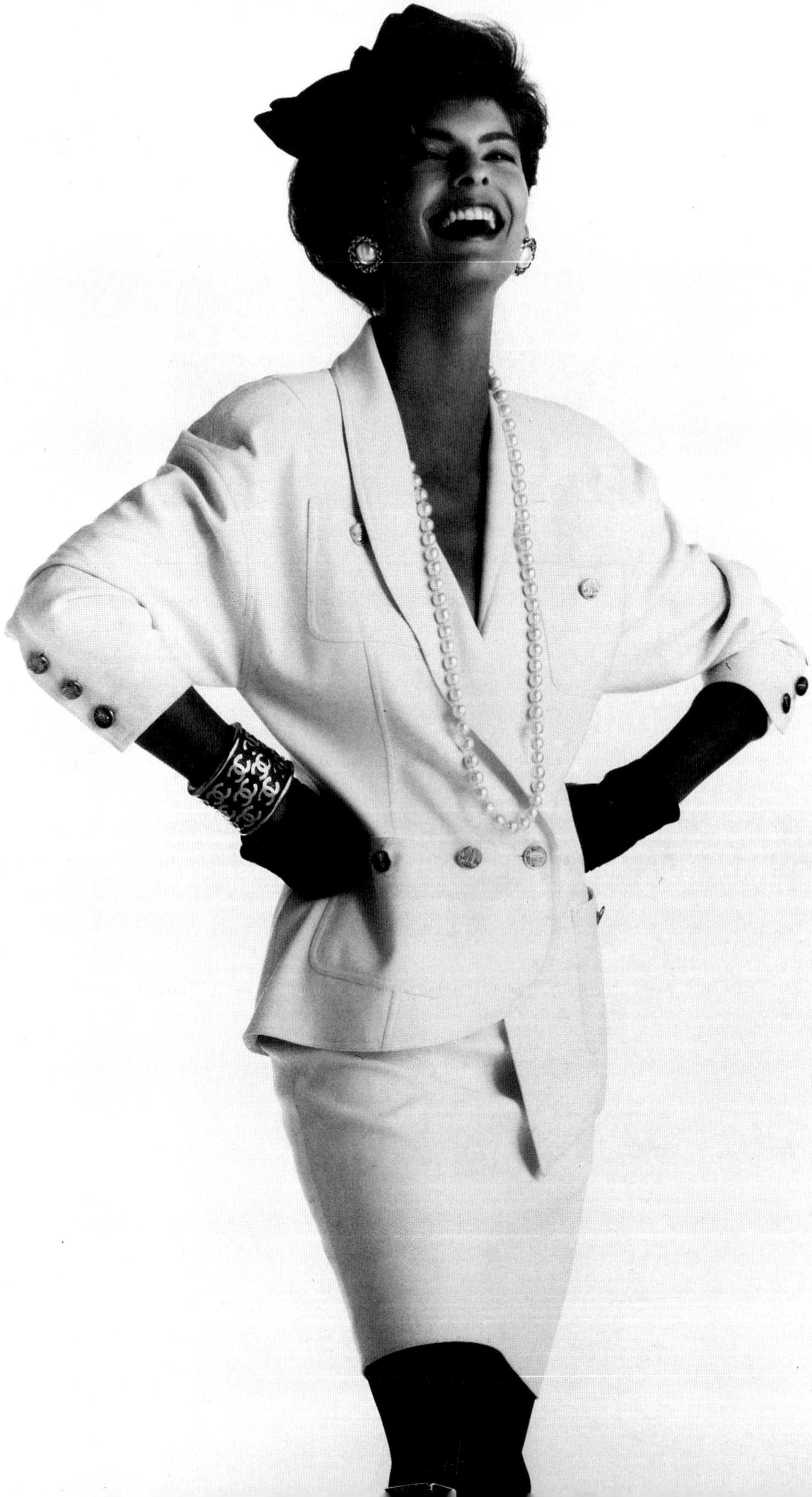

stay, worn with a wrap jersey top, a silk satin blouse or silk tee shirt. These alternate with a draped jersey dress or softly tailored coat dress, unbuttoned to a calculated degree.

Her colours are black, taupe, charcoal, cream, navy, with touches of peach, pale pink and white. She prefers plain or quietly checked fabrics to loud patterns, relying on texture and a striking cut that skims and wraps the body. Jackets have discreet shoulder pads for a feminine line. Waists are emphasized with a wide mock croc or patent belt. Legs are an important focus, in sheer seven-denier black or neutral stockings. Footwear is leather and suede courts or correspondent sling backs.

As the yuppie often goes straight out from the office, her clothes need to be dynamic enough for day and evening. After slotting in an exercise class, she changes into higher heels, bolder jewellery, switches her blouse (or removes it in favour of a bare décolletage), refreshes her make-up and sets off to a restaurant, dinner party or nightclub. For special occasions, there is time, somehow, to slip into a more outrageous designer dress of black sequins or stretch lace – something short, revealing and up-to-the-minute. As she travels frequently, day clothes come in seasonless fabrics – light wool jersey, gaberdine or crepe. Packing is tailored to a fine art; the minimal quantity expertly folded into designer hand luggage. She does have a weakness for luxurious silk lingerie and expensive swimsuits, but never bikinis.

Foreign climates provide a year-round tan, but her skin is well-protected by high factor lotions. When work allows, she takes long weekends abroad; skiing in Gstaad, a party in Manhattan, a health farm in Spain. Accessories are status conscious essentials – the Filofax, Vodaphone, leather briefcase, Ray-Bans and gold Rolex. Her hairdresser is another vital accessory, visited after work for a quick boost to her shoulder length bob, or to dress it up for a special night out. Conscious of health and skincare, she spends freely on new make-up and beauty products, stocking up at duty free shops with cosmetics and her favourite scents, Shalimar and Private Collection.

THE PREPPIE

With her relaxed, clean-cut style, she is the casual younger sister of the classic. It is an easy timeless look, identified by the bright colours and characteristic mix of Sloane with American campus style. The preppie image remains constant, ignoring most high fashion trends, although concessions might be made to a token pair of Ray-Bans, hoop earrings or shortened hemline.

Being a traditional girl at heart, the preppie favours familiar country-

The Yuppie: leading a fast, career-minded life, where appearances matter

orientated classics for town life, sharpened with an occasional urban accessory to suit her job, lifestyle and status. It is an informal, seldom scruffy style, put together from high street separates. Key pieces are well-cut jeans in denim, drill or corduroy, classic Oxford cotton shirts with button down collars, mansize knitwear and sweatshirts, college loafers and the ubiquitous Argyll sock in every colour. These correspond with her extensive collection of Shetland, lambswool and cotton knit classics. Thick ribbed cardigans and baggy Fair Isle sweaters replace jackets, although she has a large denim jacket, barbour or puffa for cold, wet weather. For smart occasions she owns a double breasted navy coat with velvet revers. In summer, once her legs are brown she wears a straight drill or denim mini. Pedal pushers are another option, often worn in the evening with a long tee shirt or jazzy sweatshirt. She does have a ballgown for dressed up affairs – a ballerina length taffeta with bustier bodice and bow at the back.

Accessories are crucial to the preppie wardrobe, often inspired by royal role models. Essentials are velvet or tortoiseshell hairbands, hair bows, shoe bows to smarten flat pumps and court shoes, a canvas fishing bag, Davy Crockett fur hat and black lace tights – the only glimpse of black in the wardrobe. Jewellery hallmarks are drop earrings, diamanté brooches (preferably animal or reptilian), a Swatch or Cartier watch.

Make-up is barely discernible during the day, just mascara, blusher and lipgloss, but the long hair is scrunched with mousse for a windblown effect. At night she plays up her eyes and lips, dresses her hair with extravagant bows, diamanté clips or silk rosettes, then adds a spray of Diorella to the final appearance.

THE ROMANTIC

She has an original, eclectic style, drawn from diverse inspirations. The key influence is her desire to look feminine without being predictable. She keeps a discerning eye on fashion, knowing instinctively what will suit and what will not. Regardless of her figure, she loathes any skirt to come near or above the knee. In fact, a long full skirt is characteristic of the look. Period nostalgia is a great inspiration, often sparked by a cult film, opera or ballet. *Annie Hall*, *Out of Africa* and *White Mischief* have all been catalysts.

Her wardrobe contains an unconventional mix of expensive designer labels (Ralph Lauren, Kenzo), old-fashioned classics, Victorian nightdresses, silk dressing gowns, beaded cardigans, lace camisoles and blouses, chiffon scarves, straw hats: and a scattering of ethnic buys from abroad – loden jackets, embroidered cardigans, waistcoats and slippers.

The Preppie in relaxed, campus style

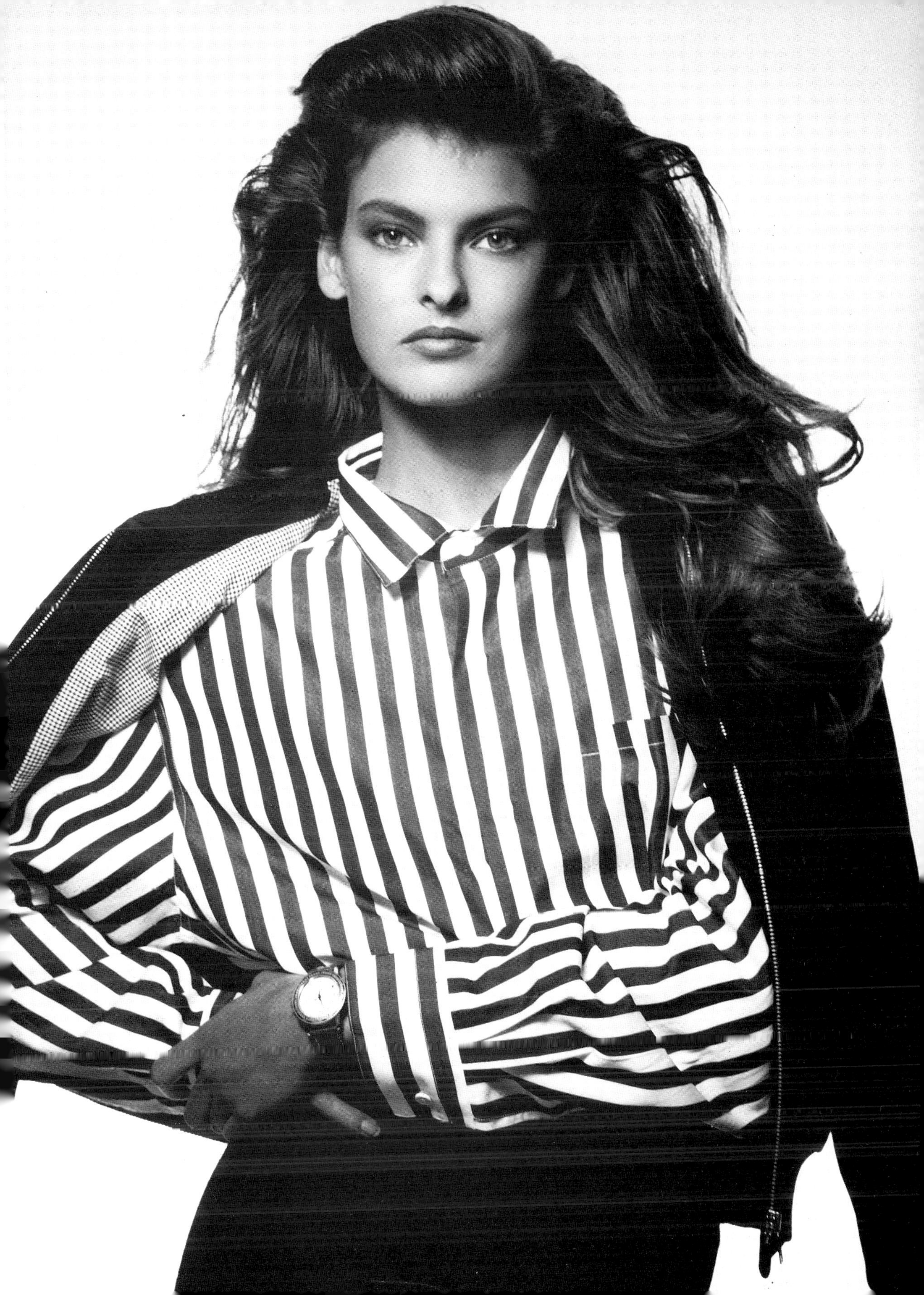

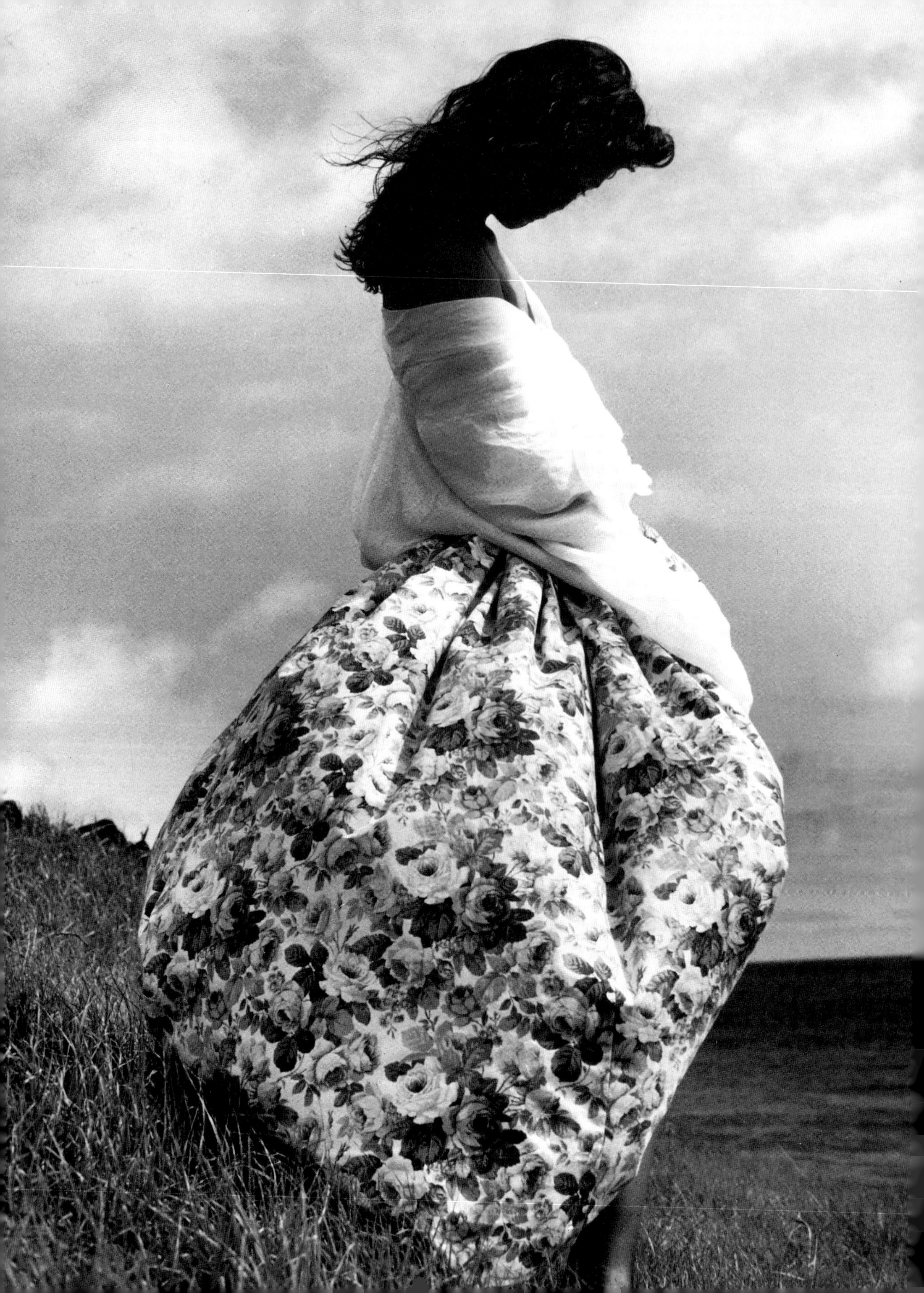

Clothes are chosen for their texture and pattern as much as their shape. Favourite fabrics are soft tweeds, suede, silk, velvet, chamois, chintz and starched white cottons. She has an affinity to anything floral and trawls furnishing fabric departments for cabbage rose and convolvulus chintzes, linen unions or toile de jouy to make into sweeping skirts and fitted summer dresses. The waist is a focal point, kept defined by a wide leather belt. Other skirts come in denim, suede, tweed, corduroy, linen and lawn. On top, whatever the season, she wears an antique white cotton blouse with a lace collar, or mansize chambray shirt below a chamois or embroidered cotton waistcoat. Knitwear tends to be neat and fitted; forties style Fair Isles or lambswool twinsets with pearl buttons. But more often she prefers a jacket – a perennial favourite is in cropped tweed with a short peplum, velvet collar and covered buttons. Her coat is a schoolgirl classic with a touch of dandy: full-skirted Harris tweed with a cape and velvet collar.

Accessories are vital to the look. Besides belts, other essentials are large floral and paisley shawls, spotted silk and chiffon scarves; an oversized chocolate brown trilby or straw panama. Footwear is cowboy boots with unobtrusive stitching, laced ankle boots, walking shoes, tasselled brogues, beaded slippers and a buckled suede pair with Louis heels from an antique market. Incapable of going anywhere without her current book, spare spectacles, scarf, sketchbook and bluebell scent, her handbag has to be a substantial tapestried duffel or battered Gladstone bag. Jewellery is limited to an Art Deco watch, tortoiseshell spectacles strung on a chain and gold hoop earrings – changed at night for pearl and marcasite drops.

In the evening she reinforces her original style in a crepe de Chine dressing gown cinched with a silver-buckled belt, or a fragile silk blouse and chiffon skirt with a dipping hemline. Black is taboo. She keeps to pastels, spiced with scarlet, sapphire or emerald. Make-up, low key by day, is intensified at night with shocking pink or crimson lips and striking eyes. Her long hair, contained by tartan ribbons, spotted bandannas and gypsy kerchiefs is released at night into a voluminous gloss of curls and decorated with fresh flowers.

THE VAMP

She is a fashion extrovert, using clothes, jewellery and make-up as a vital part of her seduction. Her appearance is calculated to attract attention in the most provocative and sexy manner possible. She is never caught out looking casual. Even the postman cannot be met without an outside face. Hers is a dressed-up style, inspired by Dynasty role models, relying on

The Romantic: loyal to her essentially feminine, floral mood

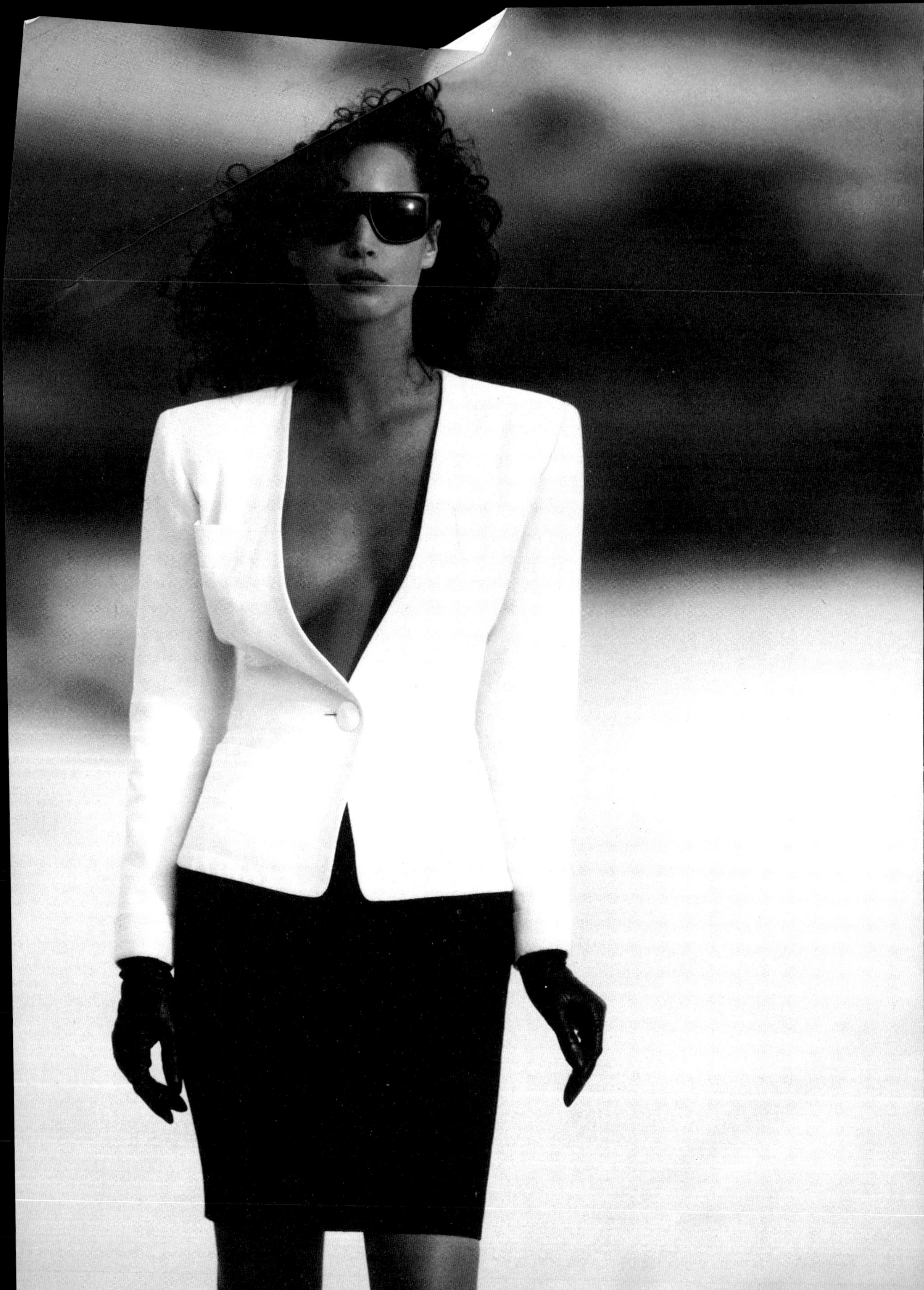

perfect make-up and immaculately accessorized outfits for full impact.

The vamp comes to life around midday, stimulated by black coffee and cigarettes, ready for a lunchtime appearance at a smart restaurant. She is unquestionably a night person, a fact emphasized by her preference for glamorous party clothes, day or night. She totters at all hours on impressively high heels, making no concession to comfort; chooses the tightest, briefest and barest clothes that reveal glimpses of ever bronzed skin, toned by her masseur rather than strenuous exercise.

When the budget allows, it aspires to Jean Paul Gaultier, Anthony Price and Rifat Ozbek. Although her sharp eye can pick out passable high street imitations at fractional prices, she does hanker for expensive labels and dreams of affording Christian Lacroix couture. The materials she chooses have a sensuous clinging quality that drape and stretch across her curve-conscious body. Silk jersey, lycra, velvet, satin, fur, lace and leather appear together, blending tough with smooth: a brief lace skirt goes with a heavy fringed leather jacket over a plunging lycra body or strapless bandeau. Favourite colours are white, cream, scarlet and black, with touches of shocking pink and purple. Lamé or sequinned silver and gold are the closest shade to neutral. Apart from leopard skin prints, she prefers plain rather than patterned fabrics. She feels her best in a striking suit with a short, tight skirt and bare décolletage beneath a fitted, shoulder-padded jacket, worn with matching leather or embroidered suede shoes, long kid gloves and perhaps a veiled hat or fur toque in winter. Jewellery is dramatic, whatever the hour; plenty of heavy gold bangles, watch and earrings, replaced at night by dazzling amounts of diamanté or colourful rocks that match her evening outfit – whether it is a sculpted sequin sheath, gold lamé cocktail dress or strapless lace number. Until she can afford, or better still is given, a mink, she goes without a coat, believing that anything too practical detracts from her appearance.

Underwear is appropriately glamorous in cream or peach satin. Black is a little too obvious, although she does always wear sheer black stockings. She has a Japanese silk kimono to slide over an exotic lace nightdress – her standard morning attire before dressing at midday – and for rare evenings at home catching up with the video. Out of town she dresses down in white or black denim jeans and cowboy boots, or tight capri pants with an equally tight tee shirt or blouse knotted at the midriff. But however informal, she feels uncomfortable without brilliant red nails and lips, a splash of Poison or Chloé scent and dark glasses close to hand. Her torrent of long blonde hair is streaked regularly both by the sun and hairdresser. She pampers herself at the beauty salon with manicures, pedicures, facials and aromatherapy sessions that restore her energy for the next party.

The Vamp: a fashion extrovert, dressed for attention at all hours

THE TOMBOY

Her style is drawn from the most coveted elements of a man's wardrobe – quiet classics with a nonchalant ease, underlined by their natural texture and subtle colour. It is a relaxed look that recalls the uncontrived glamour of Katherine Hepburn's khaki trousers and crisp white shirts – mannish but never butch. The tomboy likes tailored clothes, providing they are supple and unconstricting, worn on the large size for comfort. Angular lines are softened by the feminine essentials in her wardrobe, like a pastel cashmere cardigan or slipper satin blouse.

Colours are neutral, based on a spectrum of sand, cream, white, pale grey, khaki and tan, softened with shell pink, duck egg blue and eau de nil. Fabrics are typical of classic menswear: leather, suede, linen, flannel, tweed, corduroy and fine shirting. She chooses plains in preference to patterns, except for discreet polka dots, stripes or plaids. The tomboy is not strictly opposed to female clothes, but enjoys the cut and roominess of menswear, especially for shirts and knitwear.

Trousers are variations of the wide-legged, pleat top, turn-up shape, slotted with a plaited leather belt. On top she wears linen shirts with pyjama revers, button down poplin classics, polo shirts in wool or knitted cotton, white tee shirts, lambswool waistcoats, polo necks or long V-neck cardigans. Top layers are a mansize tweed or linen jacket, a Bogart-style trench or stone cotton mac that doubles as a summer coat.

She is seldom seen in skirts – except for a high waisted riding skirt – but does wear linen or khaki drill shorts for her colonial *Out of Africa* look, complete with lace-collared blouse, tan leather sandals and wide brimmed straw. For evening wear, she owns a classic black dinner suit that goes with a cream satin tee shirt or high-necked dandy shirt. As a trouser alternative she slips into a long burgundy velvet peignoir, worn with sheer black tights and monogrammed velvet slippers. For summer evenings there are Mao-style silk pyjamas or wide palazzo pants and cropped jacket.

She has a weakness for shoes. Favourites are bespoke tapestry slippers made by a traditional cobbler. Being more practical, she also owns tasselled loafers and lace-ups from both male and female shoe shops. For casual days there are navy docksides and white plimsolls. Her bag is a roomy leather holdall, carried in all seasons. Belts are leather and suede classics, plaited and stamped. Jewellery is underplayed. Besides cufflinks and an antique Rolex, she occasionally wears silver disc earrings and a cuffed bangle. Make-up and scent are treated as daily essentials – muted colours used day and night, with a restrained splash of Calèche. Her hair is uncomplicated; worn long and smoothed into a low ponytail or cropped into a soft boyish cut.

The Tomboy: enjoying the uncontrived ease of menswear

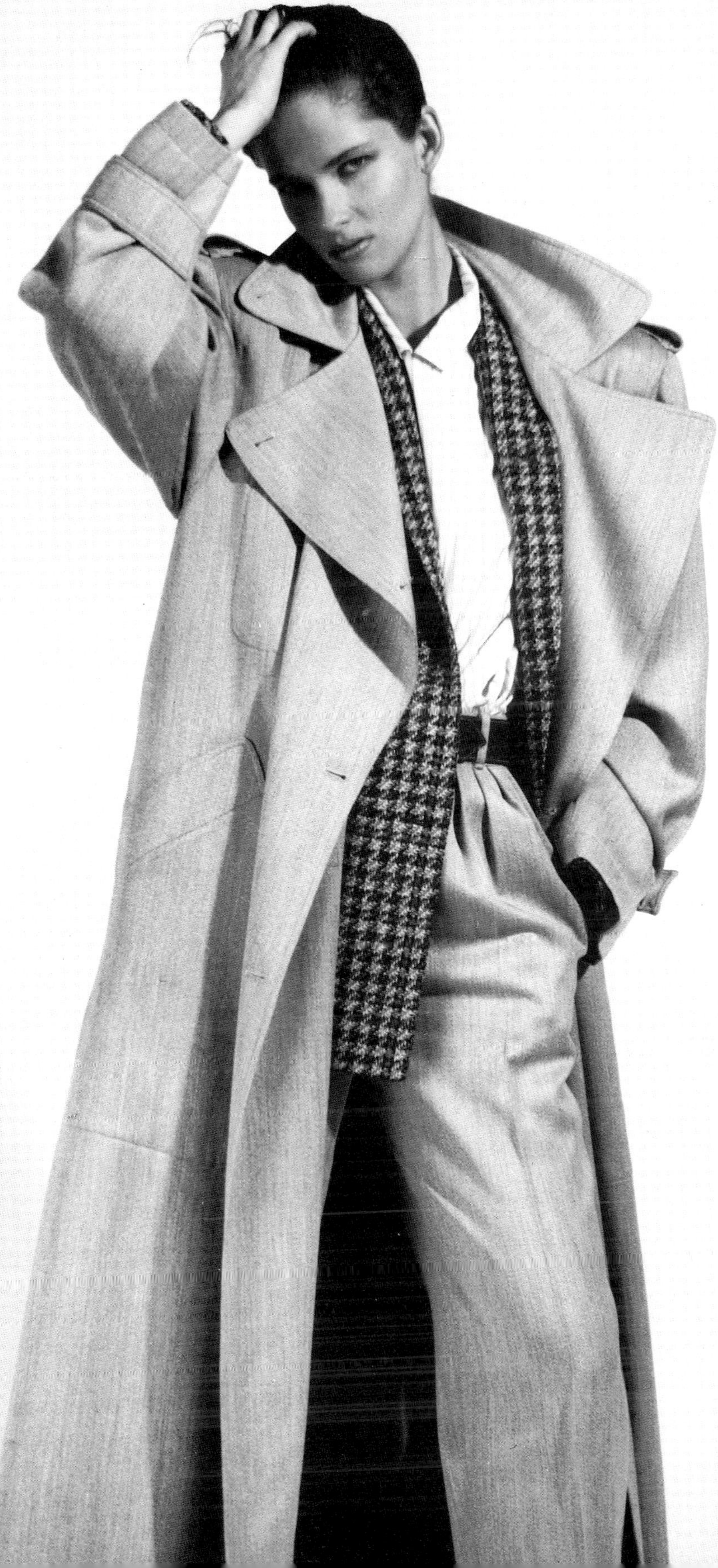

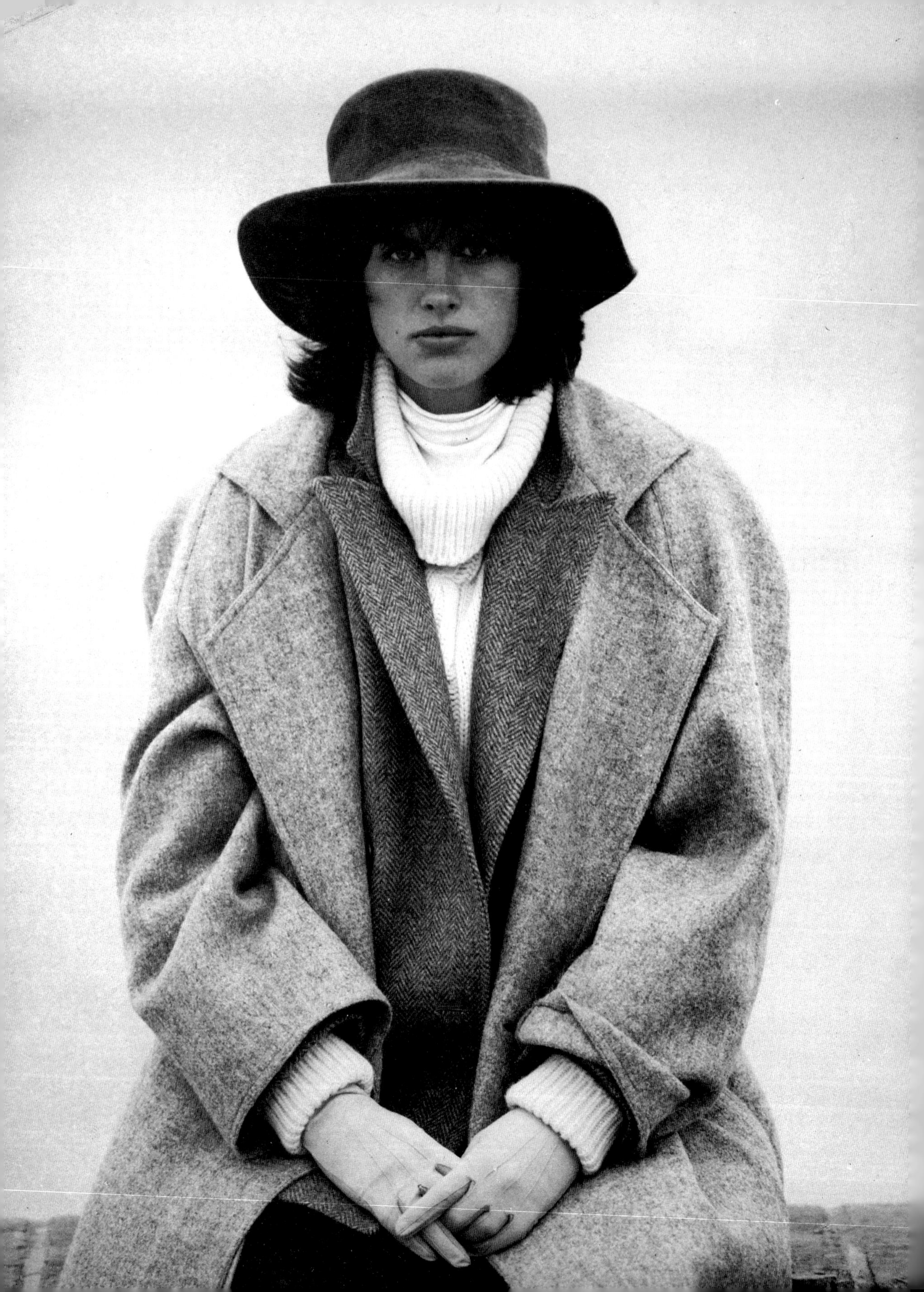

THE COUNTRY GIRL

This wardrobe has to meet the demands of a country lifestyle. It needs comfortable, practical clothes to suit the surroundings and stand up to the elements. Her style has a timeless charm that ignores the whims of fashion. Loyal to country classics, she chooses tweeds, sheepskin, Shetlands and thick cottons in soft colours that echo the landscape.

But she does have clothes for all occasions: for grand country evenings and garden parties as well as gardening and muddy hikes. Much of the time is spent in trousers and gumboots, although the country girl never looks rugged from head to toe. There are always feminine touches – a lace collar peeping from a thick sweater, a bright floral scarf, pastel Argyll socks. In winter she dresses in layers. First comes a thermal vest, pretty enough to wear as a summer singlet. Shirts come next, in checked or sprigged viyella, chambray or white piqué. Alternatives are cotton polo necks, tee shirts or lambswool sweaters muffled with a scarf. Her jersey collection is expansive. Besides Shetland and lambswool classics, there are vegetable-dyed Fair Isles, thick Arans, skiing knits patterned with snowflakes, and embroidered folkloric cardigans. They come in all different sizes to layer into original twinsets. Trousers are jeans, baggy corduroys or moleskins (from the local farm stores). Skirts in viyella, corduroy, tweed or denim are full and trailing, worn with thick tights, long Argyll socks, brogues or riding boots. For a traditional look she puts her classic kilt with a white lace shirt and long Shetland cardigan. (Shorter skirts are easier to wear at night when she feels more adventurous.) Jackets range from tidy to battered. Favourites are a well-worn tweed classic that goes with jeans or skirts; a tartan-lined barbour for country pursuits and conker brown sheepskin for midwinter. Coats have no trace of fashion detail: a mansize Harris tweed and canvas riding mac, large enough to pile several layers beneath.

Evening wear depends on the occasion. For informal dinners she might wear velvet jodhpurs with a gilt-buttoned cardigan, or a tartan taffeta skirt and lambswool sweater. In summer it could be a crepe de Chine or cotton lawn dress with a deep lace collar, or a rose-strewn chiffon ballgown for smarter parties.

Summer days inspire a more pastoral look in floral cotton frocks, gathered skirts with printed blouses and cotton knit cardigans, loose cotton shorts and check trousers with tee shirts and lacey cotton scarves. Except for a large leather cartridge bag and assorted wicker baskets, accessories rotate with the seasons. Winter essentials are furlined boots, woollen gloves, an old felt trilby, lambswool mufflers and floral shawls. Summer calls for a wide-brimmed straw, espadrilles, gardening gloves and sunscreen.

The Country Girl: dressed for the elements in natural colour and texture

The Country Girl at large: well equipped with waxed cotton waterproof, walking shoes and picnic hampers

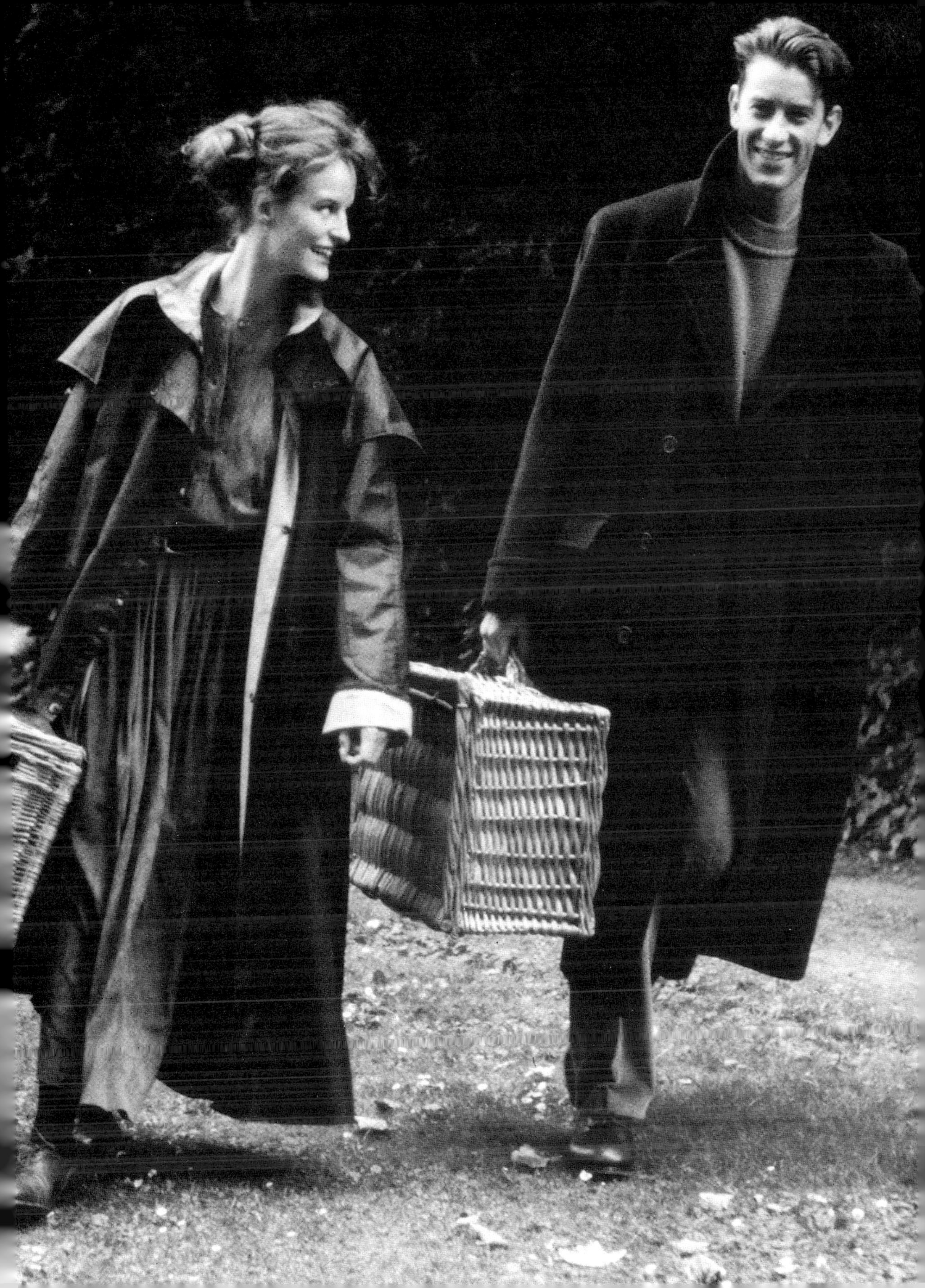

THE DANCE GIRL

The dance girl lives under the spell of health and fitness. It is a way of life that shapes her supple body as well as her wardrobe. She flaunts her energy with second-skin clothes, intended both for exercise and well-exercised figures. Hers is well-toned by daily workouts and a high fibre, vegetarian diet, packed with energy boosting vitamins and minerals – free from junk food or alcohol.

After a dance class, gym or yoga session, she changes from workout leotard, sweats and leggings into an almost identical set of clothes to wear through the day and occasionally into the night. The dance girl shops mostly in health clubs, dance bars and genuine ballet outfitters, but keeps a close watch on the innovations of Romeo Gigli, Alaia and Norma Kamali, following their ideas of colour and texture. She loves the ease and comfort of cotton jersey with lycra for its flattering stretch and contour. By day she keeps to understated colours: grey, taupe, black, navy, cream, mushroom pink, replaced at night with acid-bright lime, lemon, tangerine or turquoise, when matt textures give way to a lycra biased sheen. Make-up is minimal: tinted moisturiser, natural lip colour and eye pencil around dyed black lashes. At night she adds mascara, blusher and dusty pink lipstick.

Her wardrobe consists of a few versatile pieces that can all be layered together and peeled on or off to suit the season or occasion. Leotards are essential in every shape and plain colour (never patterned), sleeveless, cap sleeved, cross-over and all-in-one unitards. With these she wears leggings, cropped vests, tee shirts or sweatshirts and a brief stretch or ruched jersey mini, straight or skating style. For cold days, or early morning jogs, she slips on a perfectly plain cotton track suit in grey or navy, with legwarmers, a cotton polo neck and well-sprung track shoes. In a more balletic mood, she wears a long jersey wrap skirt, with a cross over cardigan or leotard. An evening version comes in filmy chiffon, worn with a sleeveless bodysuit and satin ballet shoes. For romantic summer nights she has a sheer silk chiffon dance dress, reminiscent of Isadora Duncan, with a low boat neckline and dipping handkerchief hem. In winter she may turn theatrical with a principal boy velvet doublet, black leggings and suede thigh boots.

Dance girl accessories tend to be functional as well as decorative. In place of jewellery she has wrist bands, headbands, chenille hairnets for a chignon and wide, elasticated belts to cinch the waist and elongate the legs. Footwear is fitness-orientated: either white jazz shoes, plimsolls, ballet pumps or Reeboks. Spares are carried in a capacious parachute silk duffel bag, along with skin and haircare essentials, and high energy snacks.

The Dance Girl: ready for workout in simple stretchwear

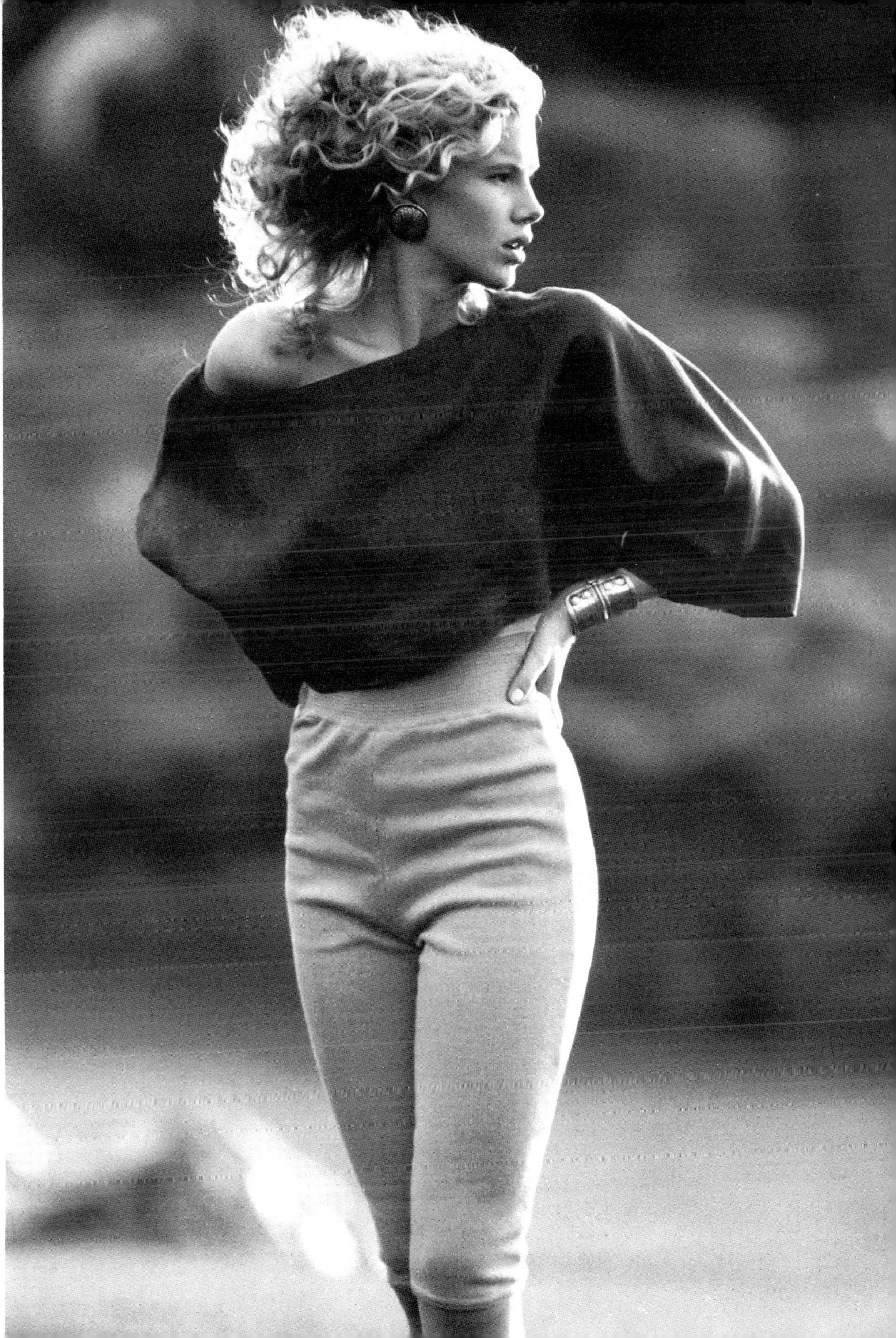

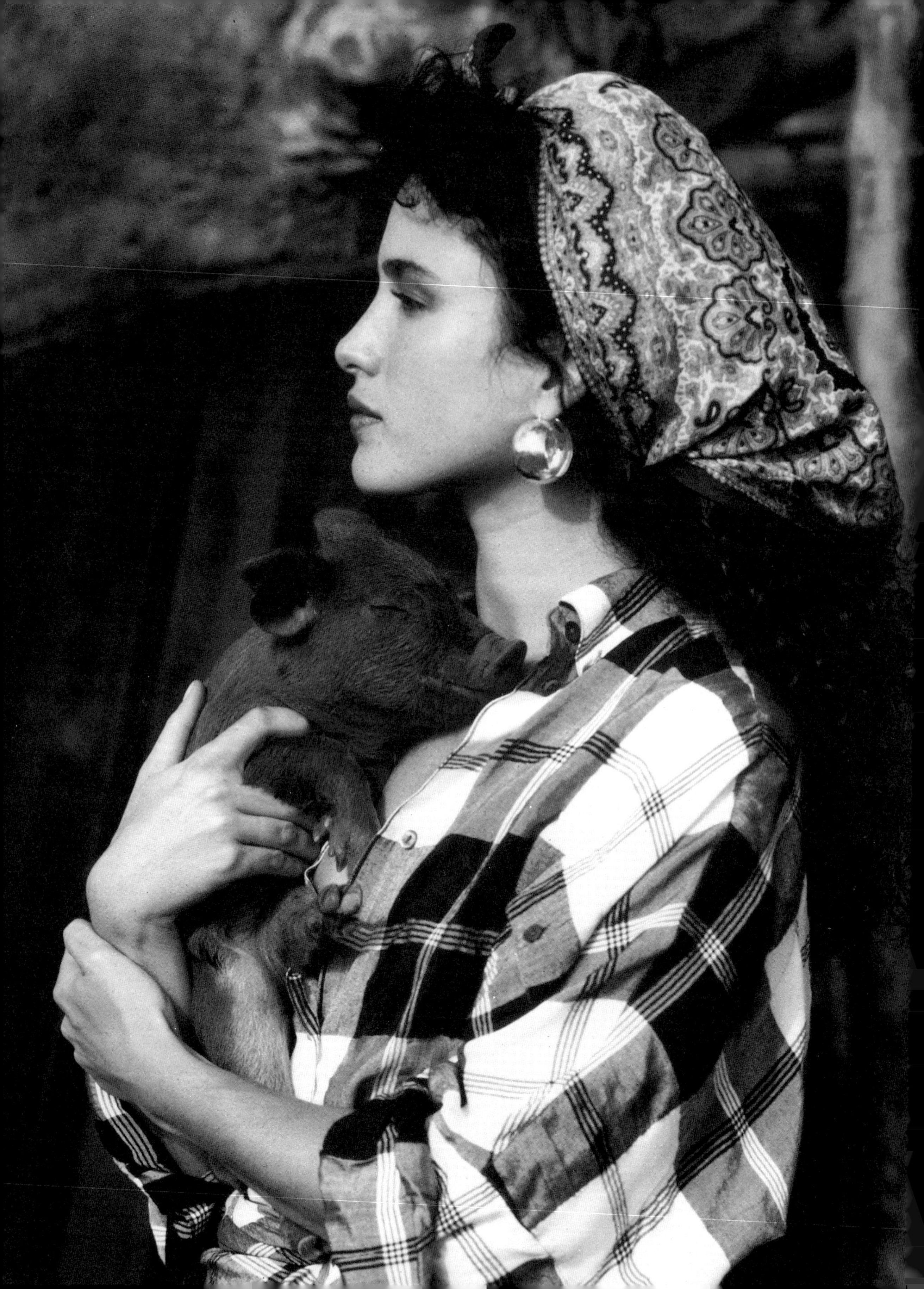

THE NOUVEAU HIPPY

She is a connoisseur of ethnic fashion, tracking down the genuine article from out of the way sources. Market stalls and specialist shops in unfashionable corners of town arouse far more interest than any high street ethnics. Each garment in the hippy wardrobe is prized for its true origins, its rarity value of being worn in by an Afghan tribesman or Turkish peasant. In spite of ethnic principles, the hippy girl delights in assembling her own national costumes from the most appealing textures, patterns, colours and embroideries. She mixes countries together, combining an Indian drawstring skirt, Peruvian sweater and Russian shawl. Whenever travelling to a good hunting ground, preferably eastbound, she takes or buys an extra carpet bag for new finds — ethnic fabrics, embroidered slippers, beaded belts, antique silver, turquoise and coral jewellery – tracked down in back-street markets away from the tourists.

What helps such original style is an ability to sew or adapt her own clothes: transforming lengths of ikat, batik and embroideries into smocks, zouave trousers or drawstring skirts. She follows the tradition of ethnic costume, cutting out simple designs based on flat, rectangular shapes. She tends to dress in layers; partly because her clothes come in fine cotton, crushed velvet or woven silks, and partly because it is the best method to show off her finery. This seasonless style is characterized by embroidered muslin skirts, smocked tunics (prized from the Indus Valley in Pakistan), sheepskin, felt or tapestry weave waistcoats, Nehru jackets and frail drawstring blouses. Skirts have assorted nationalities created from Indian muslin or saris, an African sarong, or length of Thai batik. Trousers are zouaves or cropped harem pants, wrapped at the waist with a long silk scarf or beaded belt. She has a choice of outer layers. The finest Afghan Ikat has a warm lining adapted from an old fur coat. Ethnic blankets and shawls also alternate as impromptu cloaks or wall hangings. Her most treasured bags are a Moroccan leather duffel and Kenyan straw basket. Like her clothes, shoes are not exclusively ethnic. She changes between tan leather sandals, espadrilles, embroidered slippers, cuffed suede or cowboy boots. For dressing up, she chooses low-heeled pointed court shoes in bright leather or gros grain.

Jewellery is essential to the hippy look. She loves antique silver cuffs, bangles and charm bracelets. Fingers are crowded with stone-encrusted rings. Ears dangle with gold gipsy hoops, coins and filigreed silver. Necklaces strung with bells, chunks of amber, turquoise, coral and carved wooden beads are piled on together. Her beauty routine is based on herbal skincare and aromatic oils, but make-up is unpredictable, switching from a fresh-faced look to a seventies revival of kohl eyeliner,

The Nouveau Hippy: following the trail of ethnic treasures

plum lip gloss and wafts of patchouli oil.

THE CLUB GIRL

Her appearance may seem unconventional but she conforms to her own set of fashion rules. The club girl – young, city-based and partying – wears the cult uniform of the day: an eclectic street style influenced by new wave designers, retrospective cult films, pop music and the media. In spite of subtle shifts in emphasis, depending on career and location, the look has a simple, casual identity, easily recognized by its tendency towards anything black and androgynous. It is never smart. The same clothes work day and night, carrying on from college, studio or office to bar, club or party.

Club girl shopping reflects their budget. Some can afford their coveted streetwise designers Katharine Hamnett, Vivienne Westwood, or occasionally Azzedine Alaia. Others make do with cheaper high street or market stall versions. With an eye for a bargain and originality, their leather jackets come from authentic biking sources, or ready distressed from second-hand shops, along with well-worn fly button Levis. Club girl uniform is highly label conscious. She has to have exactly the right style of Doc Marten boots; jeans have to be black denim or loose fitting 501s, some pairs with strategic designer rips. If the cropped leather biking jacket cannot be a true Jean Paul Gaultier, it must have an appropriate complement of zips and buckles. Denim is the alternative to leather; a bomber style, cropped to the midriff. Under the jacket goes a white crew neck tee shirt, a buttoned up white or pale denim shirt with a tough leather belt slung on the hips. Below go the jeans, black leggings, lycra biking shorts, tight drill or denim mini, or full skirted mini-crini, Westwood style.

As the club girl works all day and parties all night, pallor is part of the image. Legs are always covered in black opaque tights, some with graffitied patterns. Between cropped jeans and lace-ups there might be a flash of day-glo socks to sharpen the monochrome outfit. Black canvas plimsolls are a summer alternative to Doc Martens. High heels are worn very occasionally at night with a short, tight skirt. She carries a small metallic silver briefcase and blocks out traffic noise with a Sony Walkman playing the song of the day. Her complexion is kept pale, accentuated by matt red lips and black rimmed eyes, often masked by impenetrably dark glasses. Her hair is cropped short like a boy, or cut to a chin length bob, sleeked with gel or tied with a polka dot handkerchief. Jewellery is minimal: just silver hoop earrings and an occasional funky brooch pinned to her jacket.

The Club Girl: right in step with street fashion

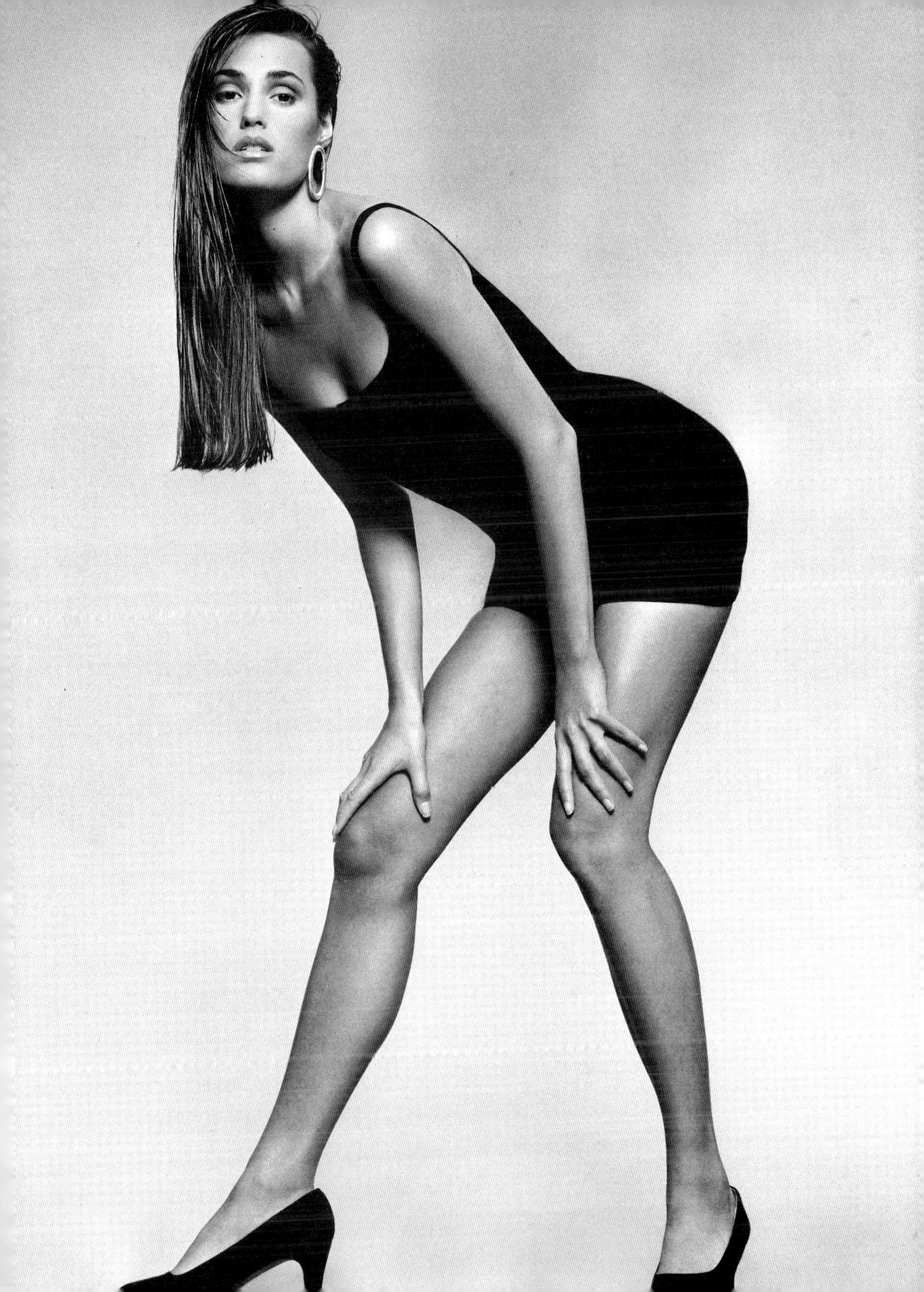

The Nouveau Hippy (left) *covered in an antique paisley shawl*

The Dance Girl (right) *in balletic, evening mood*

The Club Girl (overleaf) *playing it cool in Marlon Brando peaked cap*

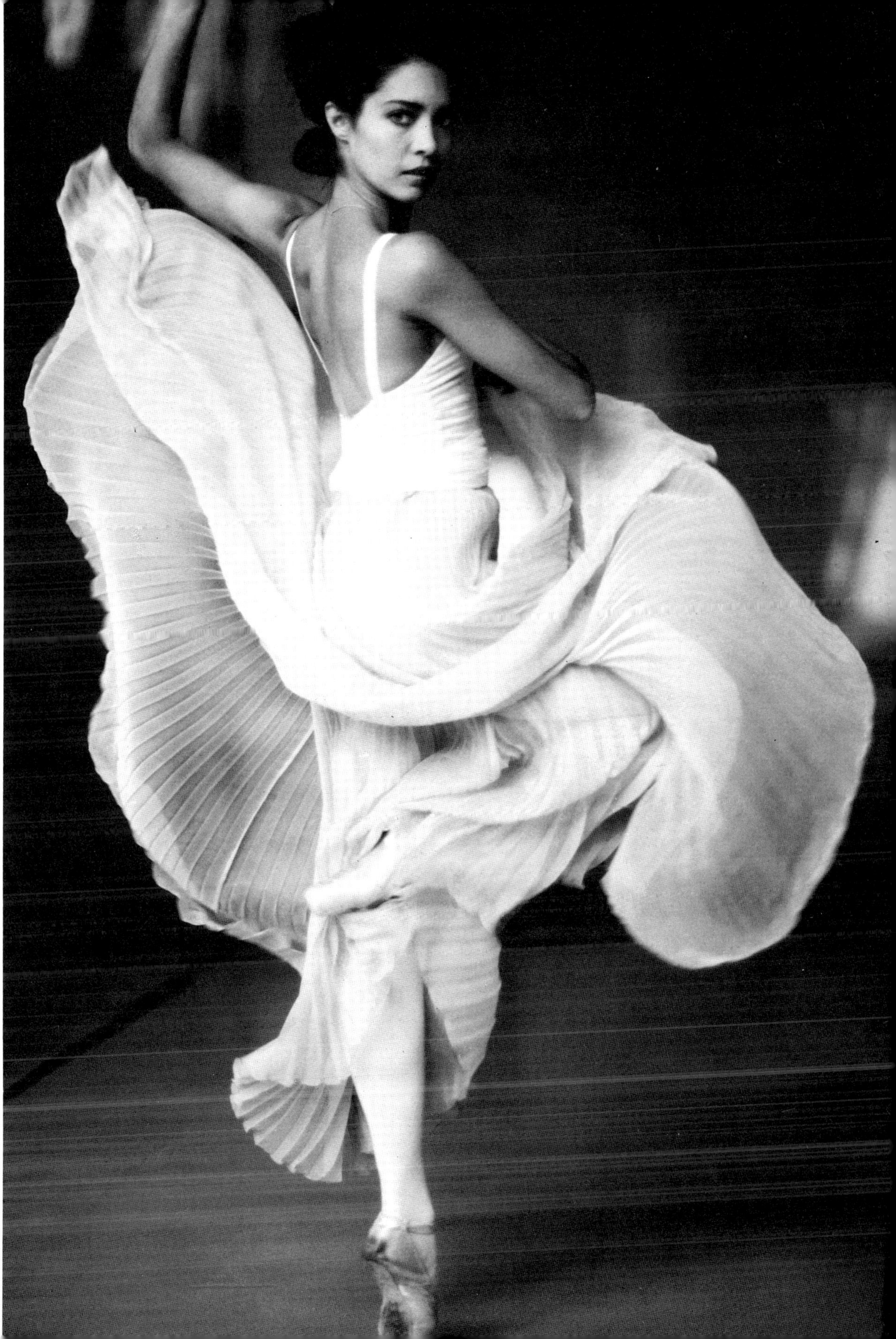

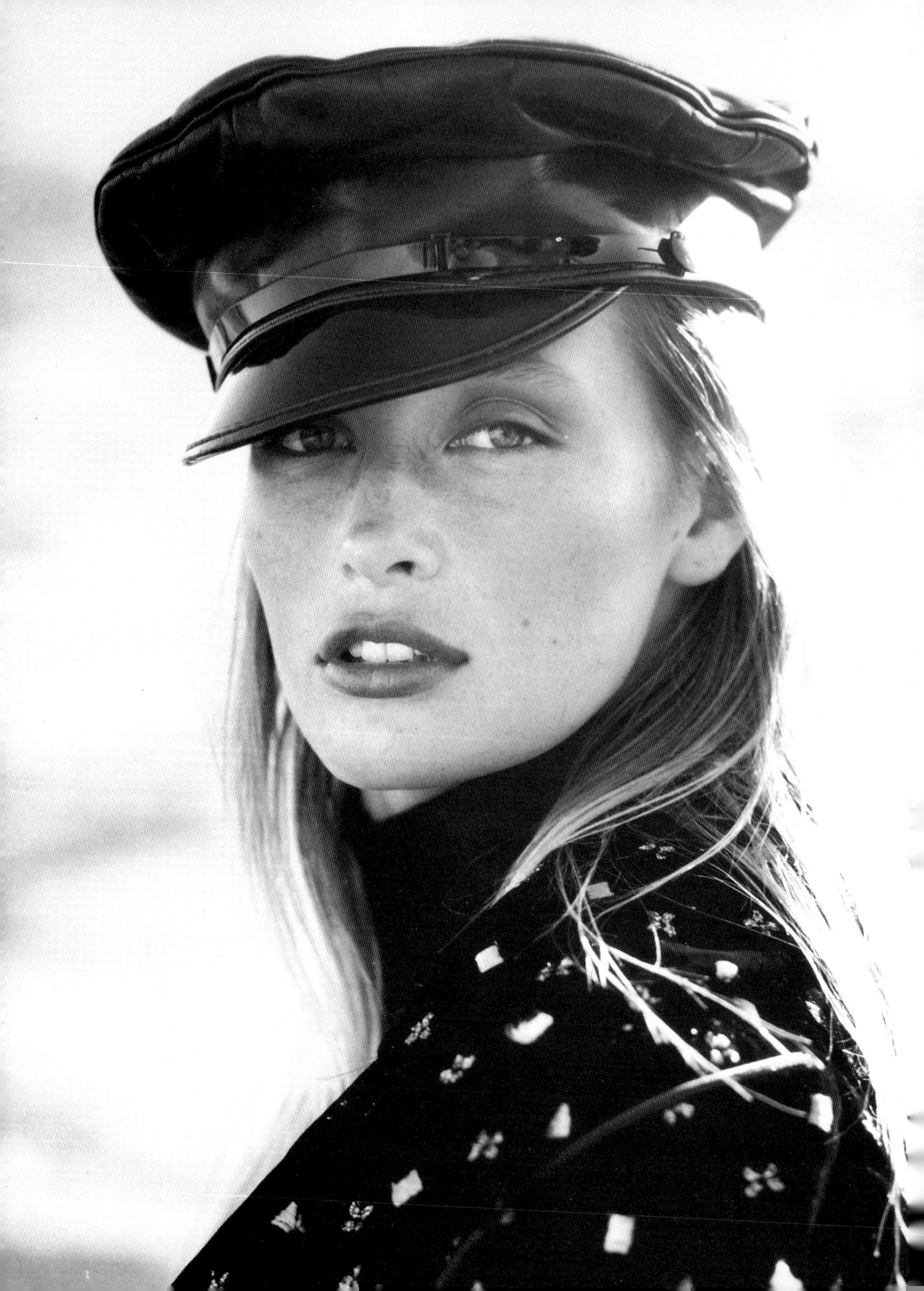

ACKNOWLEDGEMENTS

I would like to thank everyone at *Vogue* who helped me with ideas and inspiration for the original version of this book – especially fashion editors past and present, Sheila Wetton, Anna Harvey and Antonia Kirwan-Taylor.

Updated thanks go to Liz Tilberis, Georgina Boosey and Alex Kroll for their enthusiasm and support for *Even More Dash Than Cash*. Finally a special thank you to Camilla Milton and Anna Hogg for their invaluable advice and information.

LIST OF PHOTOGRAPHERS

2/3	Bruno Juminer	44	*Left* Robin Saidman	84	Paul Lange	126	*Left and right* David Bailey
6/7	Peter Lindbergh		*Right* Patrick Demarchelier	86	Bruce Weber	127	*Top* Eammon J. McCabe
10	Peter Lindbergh	48	David Bailey	88	Alex Chatelain		*Bottom left* Louis Salvatore
14	Alex Chatelain	50	*Left* Brian Duffy	91	Mike Reinhardt		*Bottom right* David Bailey
15	Mike Reinhardt		*Top right* Arthur Elgort	94	Albert Watson	128	Michel Arnaud
16	Michel Arnaud		*Bottom right* David Bailey	95	Albert Watson	129	*Left and right* Michel Arnaud
17	*Left* Steven Meisel	53	Eammon J. McCabe	96	Patrick Demarchelier	130	Arthur Elgort
	Right Patrick Demarchelier	54/5	Mike Reinhardt	98	Eammon J. McCabe	132	Alex Chatelain
18	Arthur Elgort	56	*Left* Hans Feurer	99	Arthur Elgort	135	Alex Chatelain
19	Alex Chatelain		*Right* Robert Erdmann	100	Oliviero Toscani	136	Albert Watson
20	Michel Arnaud	57	Marc Hispard	101	Terence Donovan	138	Eammon J. McCabe
21	Michel Arnaud	58	Neil Kirk	102	Bruce Weber	140	Neil Kirk
22	Wayne Stambler	60	*Top* Eammon J. McCabe	103	George Barkentin	143	Arthur Elgort
23	Eddy Kohli		*Bottom* Eric Boman	104	Arthur Elgort	144	Bruce Weber
24	Patrick Demarchelier	61	Steven Meisel			147	Patrick Demarchelier
26	*Right* Neil Kirk	62	*Top* Jean Pierre-Masclet	*Colour Section*		148	Neil Kirk
	Top left Patrick Demarchelier		*Bottom* Robert Erdmann	A	Bruce Weber	149	Patrick Demarchelier
	Bottom left Mike Reinhardt	63	Patrick Demarchelier	B	Bruce Weber	150	Bruce Weber
27	Eric Boman	65	Pamela Hanson	C	Bruce Weber		
28	Robert Erdmann	66	Michel Arnaud	D	Albert Watson	*Colour Section*	
29	Hans Feurer	68	Martin Brading			A	John Bishop
30	*Right* Arthur Elgort	71	*Top left* Uncredited	105	Alex Chatelain	B/C	Albert Watson
	Top left Hans Feurer		*Top right* Georges Hurrell	107	Terence Donovan	D	Albert Watson
	Bottom left Arthur Elgort		*Centre left* John Koball	108	Peter Lindbergh		
31	Eddy Kohli		Collections	109	*Left* Bruno Juminer	154	Albert Watson
32/3	Patrick Demarchelier		*Centre right* Uncredited		*Right* Arthur Elgort	156	Michel Arnaud
34	Mike Reinhardt		*Bottom left* Herb Ritts	110	Eric Boman	159	Marc Hispard
35	*Left* Zatecky		*Bottom right* Tim Graham	111	Arthur Elgort	160	Peter Lindbergh
	Centre George Barkentin	72	Eammon J. McCabe	115	*Top left* Patrick Demarchelier	162	Neil Kirk
	Right Patrick Demarchelier	73	Andrew McPherson		*Top right and bottom left* David	165	Arthur Elgort
36	Bruce Weber	75	Alex Chatelain		Bailey	166	Neil Kirk
37	*Top left* Michel Arnaud	76	David Bailey		*Bottom right* Patrick	169	Robert Erdmann
	Top right Michel Arnaud	77	Michel Arnaud		Demarchelier	170	Hans Feurer
	Bottom left Michel Arnaud	78	Michel Arnaud	116	Alex Chatelain	172	Patrick Demarchelier
	Bottom centre Michel Arnaud	79	Eddy Kohli	119	Patrick Demarchelier	175	Lothar Schmidt
	Bottom right Michel Arnaud	80	Mike Reinhardt	120	*Top left* Michel Arnaud	176	Terence Donovan
39	Patrick Demarchelier				*Top right* Eammon J. McCabe	178/9	Arthur Elgort
		Colour Section			*Bottom left* Michel Arnaud	180	Paul Lange
Colour Section		A	Bruce Weber		*Bottom centre* David Bailey	182	Patrick Demarchelier
A	Eammon J. McCabe	B	Norman Parkinson		*Bottom right* Michel Arnaud	183	Arthur Elgort
B/C	Arthur Elgort	C	Eddy Kohli	122	*Left* Eammon J. McCabe	185	Hans Feurer
D	Peter Lindbergh	D	Alex Chatelain		*Right* David Bailey	186	Patrick Demarchelier
				123	*Left and right* Michel Arnaud	187	Andrew McPherson
42	Barry Lategan	81	Mike Reinhardt	124/5	Neil Kirk	188	Herb Ritts
		83	Mike Reinhardt